Sport and Modern Social Theorists

Also by Richard Giulianotti

FOOTBALL: A Sociology of the Global Game

FOOTBALL IN AFRICA (*co-editor with G. Armstrong*)

FEAR AND LOATHING IN WORLD FOOTBALL (*co-editor with G. Armstrong*)

Sport and Modern Social Theorists

Edited by

Richard Giulianotti

First published 2004 by
PALGRAVE MACMILLAN
Houndmills, Basingstoke, Hampshire RG21 6XS and
175 Fifth Avenue, New York, N.Y. 10010
Companies and representatives throughout the world

PALGRAVE MACMILLAN is the global academic imprint of the Palgrave
Macmillan division of St. Martin's Press, LLC and of Palgrave Macmillan Ltd.
Macmillan® is a registered trademark in the United States, United Kingdom
and other countries. Palgrave is a registered trademark in the European
Union and other countries.

ISBN 0–333–80078–8 hardback
ISBN 0–333–80079–6 paperback

This book is printed on paper suitable for recycling and made from fully
managed and sustained forest sources.

A catalogue record for this book is available from the British Library.

Library of Congress Cataloging-in-Publication Data
Sport and modern social theorists / edited by Richard Giulianotti.
        p. cm.
    Includes bibliographical references and index.
    ISBN 0–333–80078–8 (cloth) — ISBN 0–333–80079–6 (pbk.)
    1. Sports—Sociological aspects. I. Giulianotti, Richard, 1966–

    GV706.5.S69424 2004
    306.4'83—dc22
                                                    2004050021

10   9   8   7   6   5   4   3   2   1
13   12   11   10   09   08   07   06   05   04

Printed and bound in Great Britain by
Antony Rowe Ltd, Chippenham and Eastbourne

Contents

Acknowledgements   vii

Notes on Contributors   viii

Introduction: Sport and Social Theorists – A Plurality
of Perspectives   1
Richard Giulianotti

1   The Sportification Process: A Biographical Analysis
Framed by the Work of Marx, Weber, Durkheim and Freud   11
Alan G. Ingham

2   Social Structure and Social Theory: The Intellectual Insights
of Robert K. Merton   33
John Loy and Douglas Booth

3   Reclaiming Goffman: Erving Goffman's Influence
on the Sociology of Sport   49
Susan Birrell and Peter Donnelly

4   Consciousness, Craft, Commitment: The Sociological
Imagination of C. Wright Mills   65
John Loy and Douglas Booth

5   Theodor Adorno on Sport: The Jeu D'Esprit of Despair   81
David Inglis

6   Antonio Gramsci: Sport, Hegemony and the
National-Popular   97
David Rowe

7   Sport, Colonialism and Struggle: C.L.R. James and Cricket   111
Brian Stoddart

8   Anthony Giddens: Structuration Theory, and Sport
and Leisure   129
John Horne and David Jary

9   Civilizing Games: Norbert Elias and the Sociology of Sport   145
Richard Giulianotti

10 Pierre Bourdieu and the Sociological Study of Sport:
   Habitus, Capital and Field   161
   Alan Tomlinson

11 Habermas on Sports: Social Theory from a Moral Perspective   173
   William J. Morgan

12 Querying Sport Feminism: Personal or Political?   187
   Jennifer Hargreaves

13 Michel Foucault: Studies of Power and Sport   207
   C.L. Cole, Michael D. Giardina and David L. Andrews

14 The Fate of Hyperreality: Jean Baudrillard and the
   Sociology of Sport   225
   Richard Giulianotti

Index   241

Acknowledgements

The production of this book has been a long-running affair, lasting several years. I am immensely grateful to the book's contributors and to the publishers, Palgrave (originally named, Macmillan), for displaying remarkable patience while the papers for the final text were gradually accumulated.

In the process of working on the book, I benefited particularly from the various suggestions, advice and guidance of Gary Armstrong, Margaret Duncan, Eric Dunning, Gerry Finn, Michael Gerrard, Richard Gruneau, Mary Holmes, John Hughson, Jim McKay, Megan O'Neill, Geneviève Rail, Betsy Wearing and Nikki Wedgwood. I have also appreciated the comments and good humour of students at the University of Aberdeen who have been exposed to many arguments within this book, in particular the fourth-year undergraduates taking my course on 'Sport and Leisure' and the third-years taking the 'Modern Social Theory' course that is coordinated by Chris Wright.

Notes on Contributors

David L. Andrews is an Associate Professor in the Sport Commerce and Culture programme, Department of Kinesiology, at the University of Maryland-College Park. His research focuses on the critical examination of contemporary sport culture. An assistant editor of the *Journal of Sport and Social Issues*, he also serves on the editorial boards of the *Sociology of Sport Journal* and *Leisure Studies*.

Susan Birrell is Professor and Chair of the Department of Health and Sport Studies at the University of Iowa, and holds joint appointments in the Department of Women's Studies and the Department of American Studies. She is the co-editor of three books, including *women, Sport and Culture* (1984) with Cheryl Cole and *Reading Sport: Critical Essays on Power and Representation* (2000) with Mary McDonald, which won a Choice Award from the American Library Association. Her current research project is an analysis of the cultural meanings of mountaineering entitled 'Reading Mt. Everest: Narrative, History, Power'.

Douglas Booth is a Professor of Sport and Leisure Studies at the University of Waikato, New Zealand. His primary research interests cover the study of sport as a form of popular culture with a particular emphasis on political relationships and processes. Specific areas of investigation have included racism in South African sport, the olympic movement, and the beach. He is an executive member of the Australian Society for Sport History and on the editorial boards of several journals including, *Journal of Sport History* and the *International Journal of the History of Sport*.

C.L. Cole is an Associate Professor of Gender & Women's Studies, Kinesiology, Criticism and Interpretive Theory, Afro-American Studies, and Sociology at the University of Illinois at Urbana-Champaign. Cole is the editor of the *Journal of Sport and Social Issues* and co-editor of the SUNY book series, *Sport, Culture & Social Relations*. Currently, she is completing a book length project on post-war American identity, sport, and deviance.

Peter Donnelly is Director of the Centre for Sport Policy Studies, and a Professor in the Faculty of Physical Education and Health, at the University of Toronto. Recent books include *Taking Sport Seriously: Social Issues in Canadian Sport* (1997; 2nd edition, 2000), *Inside Sports*, and the first

Canadian edition of *Sports in Society: Issues and Controversies* (both with Jay Coakley, 1999, 2004). He is a former editor of the *Sociology of Sport Journal* (1990–94), current editor of the *International Review for the Sociology of Sport* (2004–2006), and a past President of the North American Society for the Sociology of Sport (2001).

Michael D. Giardina is a doctoral candidate in the Department of Kinesiology and The Program for Cultural Studies & Interpretive Research at the University of Illinois, Urbana-Champaign. He has published on a variety of topics related to flexible citizenship, stylish hybridity, and the politics of culture, as well as numerous performative pedagogical texts that engage with the popular cultural response to/in post-9/11 America. He is currently completing a book for Peter Lang on critical pedagogy, performative cultural studies, and sport.

Richard Giulianotti is a Senior Lecturer in the Department of Sociology at the University of Aberdeen. He is the author of *Football: A Sociology of the Global Game* (1999) and *Sport: A Critical Sociology* (2004), as well as various journal and book articles on sport. He is joint editor of several books, most recently (with Gary Armstrong) *Football in Africa* (2004) and *Fear and Loathing in World Football* (2001). He is currently working on an ESRC-funded research project concerning Scottish football and globalization.

Jennifer Hargreaves is Professor of Sport Sociology (Research) in the Department of Sport Sciences at Brunel University, London. She is an early pioneer of sport sociology specializing in gender issues; the politics of sport; and the social construction of the sporting body. Among her publications are the watershed-edited text, *Sport, Culture and Ideology; Sporting Females: Critical Issues in the History and Sociology of Women's Sports* (best sports sociology book of the year awarded by the North American Society of Sports Sociology); and *Heroines of Sport: The Politics of Difference and Identity*. She is joint editor of a new series: *Routledge Critical Studies in Sport*.

John Horne lectures in the sociology of sport at the University of Edinburgh. With Alan Tomlinson and Garry Whannel he is the co-author of *Understanding Sport* and with Wolfram Manzenreiter the co-editor of *Japan, Korea and the 2002 World Cup*, and *Football Goes East*. His substantive research interests are the social significance of sports in East Asian Societies (focusing on Japan, and more recently China and Japan), sport and globalization (with particular reference to sporting mega-events) and sport in consumer culture.

Alan G. Ingham was born in Manchester, England. He is currently a Senior Professor of Sport Studies and Assistant Chair in the Department of Physical Education, Health & Sport Studies at Miami University, Ohio. From 1984 to 1987, he was President of the International Sociology of Sport Association. He has served on the editorial boards of *Exercise & Sport Science Reviews*, the *Journal of Sport History*, the *International Review for the Sociology of Sport*, and the *Sociology of Sport Journal*.

David Inglis is a lecturer in sociology at the University of Aberdeen. He holds degrees from the University of Cambridge and the University of York. He writes in the areas of the sociology of culture, and social and cultural theory. His most recent book is *Confronting Culture: Sociological Vistas* (with John Hughson, 2003). He is currently writing with Roland Robertson *Globalization and Social Theory: Redefining Social Science.*

David Jary is Visiting Professor at the Learning and Teaching Support Network Subject Centre for Sociology, Anthropology and Politics (C-SAP) at the University of Birmingham and Emeritus Professor at Staffordshire University. He has written widely on social theory, sport and leisure, and social issues. Recent books include: *The Contemporary Giddens: Social Theory in a Globalizing Age* (with C. Bryant), *The New HE: Issues and Directions for the Post-Dearing University* (with M. Parker) and *Benchmarking and Quality Management: The Debate in UK Higher Education*. He is co-editor (with Julia Jary) of the *Collins Dictionary of Sociology*.

John Loy retired as Dean of the School of Physical Education at the University of Otago in 2000 and now serves as Adjunct Professor in the Department of Sociology and Anthropology at the University of Rhode Island. The University of Jyvaskyla awarded him an honorary doctorate in 2000 for his scholarly contributions to the sociology of sport. More recently, the North American Society for the Sociology of Sport gave him its Distinguished Service Award.

William J. Morgan is a Professor in the Cultural and Sport Studies sections, Ohio State University. He is interested in the ethics of popular culture, and especially in the ethics of sport, as well as social and critical theory in sport. He has published extensively on these topics and is the author of *Leftist Theories of Sport: A Critique and Reconstruction*. He is presently working on a book tentatively entitled *Why Sports Morally Still Matter*.

David Rowe teaches in the School of Social Sciences and is Director of the Cultural Industries and Practices Research Centre (CIPS) at the

University of Newcastle, Australia. His books include *Popular Cultures: Rock Music, Sport and the Politics of Pleasure; Globalization and Sport: Playing the World; Sport, Culture and the Media: The Unruly Trinity* (Second edition) and the edited *Critical Readings: Sport, Culture and the Media*.

Brian Stoddart is Deputy Vice-Chancellor at Victoria University in Melbourne, Australia. Educated first in New Zealand, he has lived and worked in Australia, India, Canada, Malaysia and the Caribbean. An Australian pioneer in sports history and culture, he is an international authority on sport in the British Empire and Commonwealth, especially on Australia/New Zealand and on the Caribbean cricket. His *Saturday Afternoon Fever: Sport in the Australian Culture* is one of the defining works in the field, as are his numerous writings on West Indies. Professor Stoddart has also written extensively on golf history and sociology, as well as on other sports, and is well known as a media commentator.

Alan Tomlinson is Professor of Sport and Leisure Studies and leads the Sport and Leisure Cultures Area at the University of Brighton's Chelsea School. He is also Head of the Chelsea School Research Centre, and Course Leader of the university's postgraduate Diploma in Research Methodology. He has published many books and articles on sport and popular culture, and his book *Sport and Leisure Cultures: Global, National and Local Dimensions* will be published by the University of Minnesota Press in 2004. He edited the *International Review for the Sociology of Sport* from March 2000 to March 2004. He is currently working on a social historical and socio-cultural study of the place of spectacle in popular culture.

Introduction: Sport and Social Theorists – A Plurality of Perspectives

Richard Giulianotti

In 1997 Alan Ingham and Peter Donnelly published a long and challenging article detailing the history of the sociology of sport in North America. In conclusion, they posed the twin questions: 'Is any position hegemonic in our current stage of development?' and 'Should any position be hegemonic in the future?' While answering firmly in the negative on both counts, Ingham and Donnelly lamented the lack of constructive dialogue within sport sociology across the spectrum of theoretical standpoints, rather than *within* those standpoints. Despite their North American focus, Ingham and Donnelly's observations have a striking resonance within other English-speaking settings where no single theoretical perspective prevails in sport studies while the climate is often fractious between rival schools. From Australia and New Zealand, we may cite the conflicts between traditionally powerful 'narrative history' analysts of sports and those more inclined towards sociological or cultural studies perspectives (Rowe *et al.*, 1997). In the UK, rancorous exchanges have decorated relations between scholars from different disciplinary backgrounds.

This book seeks to encourage the abandonment of sectional division and to embrace theoretical diversity among communities of sport scholars within the social sciences. To that end, this book does not concentrate on the theoretical 'schools' themselves that have emerged to evolve particularized senses of collective identity, and which can feed senses of rivalry towards other schools. Rather, the chapters return us to the arguments of specific social theorists themselves, to the originators or decisive interventionists within these specific theoretical traditions. Each theorist is evaluated according to theoretical coherence, plausibility of ideas, and contribution (potential or realized) to the social understanding of sport. By considering individual social theorists, we arrive at a fuller understanding of how a specific theory comes to be advanced in the first place. One exceptional chapter is on feminism, covering a range of arguments from feminist scholars that highlight both the absence of a dominant feminist theoretician and a 'postmodern' commitment to engaging with other theoretical traditions.

The chapters reflect the major theoretical turns and tribulations in the modern social scientific reading of sport. The fourteen chapters discuss the:

- classical theorists – Marx, Weber, Durkheim and Freud
- Marxist and critical theory strands via Adorno, Gramsci and Habermas
- distinctive modern North American contributions from Merton, Mills and Goffman
- differences of 'race' and gender through James and feminist theory
- contemporary, post-dualist theories of Giddens, Elias and Bourdieu
- post-structuralist and postmodern positions via Foucault and Baudrillard.

As this suggests, the social theorization of sport has had a relatively autonomous relationship towards developments within mainstream social theory. Key theoretical periods – such as the rise of structural-functionalism or the birth of Gramscian cultural studies – have been faithfully shadowed within sport studies. Conversely, while some highly influential social theorists (such as Giddens and Habermas) have seen their work relatively ignored within Anglophone sport studies, others (like Elias) have enjoyed arguably more status in the sport and leisure domain than in mainstream theory.

For reasons of brevity, the book is primarily concerned with the contributions of historians and sociologists to our theoretical understanding of sport. These two disciplines have generated by far the largest and most complex discursive formations within sports studies since its foundation in the 1960s. That point is illustrated by the kinds of sports studies courses and well-found journals that have developed, particularly in North America, Australasia and Western Europe. Other disciplines have made notable and interrelated, long-term contributions to the conceptual understanding of sport. For example, a similar book on the contribution of specific philosophers (such as Nozick, Rawls, Walzer and MacIntyre) for our understanding of sport would be an invaluable resource for scholars and students within sport studies. In some contrast, the more positivist and 'applied' disciplines of economics and management studies have generated sport-centred journals and bodies of literature, although their interface with sociological and historical research has been relatively limited.

Nevertheless, in representing the theoretical depth and plurality within the social scientific study of sport, 'team selection' has been difficult. Globally renowned theorists like Merton, Habermas, Giddens, Bourdieu and Foucault pick themselves. Others like Gramsci and Elias are arguably less prominent within the world league of modern social theory, but clearly exercise strong conceptual influence within the social scientific study of sport, leisure and culture. A similar point might be made for apparent non-theorists like Goffman and C.L.R. James, whose distinctive perspectives have served to found theoretical traditions in interactionist studies and post-colonial social theory respectively. Inevitably, cases may be made for the inclusion of other theorists not considered here – Parsons, Althusser, Garfinkel and Said spring to mind. Their omission should not be read as an intellectual dismissal, but merely a reflection of this book's organization to capture the theoretical diversity and locations of conceptual influence inside sport studies, with due deference to the exigencies of publishing space.

Collectively, the chapter authors have biographical and intellectual backgrounds that extend beyond the Anglo-American realm. All of the chapter authors have written previously and with critical reflection on the specific theorists under question. The aim of the chapters is to examine critically the value of each theorist for our understanding of sports practices. To that end, the theorists undergo a critical sociological examination, as their respective biographies, intellectual influences and cultural milieux are considered.

This collection will hopefully demonstrate that an intellectual reciprocity exists between sport studies and social theory. Most obviously, sport studies can afford social theorists a lively and increasingly germane empirical field within which to develop and test conceptual claims. More subtly, there are domains within sport studies where particular theories might be most fruitfully generated, moulded and tested, before being extended back into the wider public domain. A future goal might be to use researches within sport studies to prise open and to subject to more rigorous analysis those theories that prefer, in Althusserian terms, 'closed problematics' wherein the conceptual answers and empirical findings are already decided before research begins. Logically, serious dialogue across disciplines and across theoretical traditions is only viable if it occurs in an open manner and accepts the possibility of unexpected outcomes. Indeed one appeal of developing social theory, like that of sports engagement, lies in the chance of a surprise result.

Book contents

The book carries fourteen chapters. We begin with an analysis of the 'founding fathers' of modern social theory: Karl Marx, Max Weber, Emile Durkheim and, to a lesser but noteworthy extent, Sigmund Freud. As Alan Ingham explains, each theorist provided discipline-founding answers to the questions that we pose ourselves as to why we do and believe certain things. Ingham synthesizes these theorists' works to show how their respective concepts of valorization, rationalization, collective representation and repression serve to explain much of our social and psychological engagement within sporting practices. He achieves this through a relatively unusual technique of illustration that examines the individual rather than societal consequences of these processes. Reflecting the importance of a political economic reading of sport, Ingham concludes that Marx offers the most plausible perspective, and so favours the reading of sport socially through a historical materialist lens.

We then turn to consider three of the most influential North American sociologists: Robert K. Merton, Erving Goffman and C. Wright Mills. As John Loy and Douglas Booth demonstrate, Merton argued that modest 'middle-range' theories should try to explain social patterns within specific areas of social life. In particular, they may focus on the intended and unintended consequences (manifest and latent functions) that surround social actions, and how these relate to the maintenance of social structure (such as social class differentiation) (Merton, 1967). Loy and Booth illustrate Merton's utility to the study of sport by referring to the problem of 'stacking' – the unintended placing of athletes in team positions according to racial typologies. Stacking thus reproduces the racist structure of Western societies through sport.

As Susan Birrell and Peter Donnelly note, Goffman announced himself professionally through his earliest book, *The Presentation of Self in Everyday Life*. Although Goffman is typically associated with action-orientated perspectives (such as symbolic interactionism), much of his work was intended to modernize the Durkheimian focus on social order (Goffman, 1967, p. 47). Goffman noted that in modern societies, the individual's personality had become the most sacred of objects, hence social order is to be maintained through interaction rituals between people in situations of co-presence. Perhaps understandably given his (unjust) reputation for quirky work and use of diverse methods, Birrell and Donnelly observe that Goffman's influence within the sociology of sport has become less obvious but more implicit. They reject the common charges laid against him, particularly that his studies may only explain the tense ambiguities of Western middle-class propriety.

By some contrast, radical intellect and professional values characterize Mills's implicit contribution to the social understanding of sport. Mills lived a short and combative life, but his conception of the 'sociological imagination', as a kind of consciousness that is publicly aware, has become a defining notion of sociology. Mills did not accord much explicit significance to sport, locating the rising symbolic importance of sports celebrities within his broad analysis of the 'power elite' (Mills, 1956, p. 74). However, as John Loy and Douglas Booth submit, a 'corporeal sensibility' may be discerned in his writings, alongside historical, cultural, structural and critical sensibilities. The works of two sport studies scholars – John Hargreaves (providing a Marxist history of sport) and Susan Brownell (providing an anthropology of the body, China and sport) – are illustrative of Mills's sociological principles, reflecting his cross-disciplinary purchase.

The critical component within social analysis is given fuller assessment when we turn to look at the imaginative Marxist contributions of Theodor Adorno, Antonio Gramsci and C.L.R. James. As David Inglis notes, Adorno, like the rest of the famous 'Frankfurt School' of critical theory, is popularly associated with a cerebral contempt for the mindlessness of popular cultural pastimes. Evading his impending persecution in Nazi Germany, Adorno arrived in the United States only to witness the masses' rationalized enslavement to the 'Culture Industries'. Modern sports, he argued, 'train men all the more inexorably to serve the machine. Hence sports belong to the realm of unfreedom, no matter where they are organized' (Adorno, 1981, p. 56). However, this is not the whole story. Employing suitably vivid language, Inglis argues that Adorno's colourful if depressing prose has been read too literally by exponents and critics alike. Like Morgan (1988), Inglis forwards a sympathetic reconstruction of Adorno's reading of sport: that modern play is currently over-rationalized and controlled, but potentially positive when freed from domination.

Compared to Adorno, the Italian Marxist Antonio Gramsci adopted a more willful optimism in desperate circumstances. A leading Communist during the rise of Fascism, Gramsci spent ten years in Mussolini's prisons, pondering the nature of contemporary capitalism (e.g. the Ford motor company) and its relationship to economic, political and intellectual domination. While Gramsci had little to say on sport generally, he did contend critically that 'Football is a model of individualistic society. It demands initiative, competition and conflict, but it is regulated by the unwritten rule of fair play.' As David Rowe demonstrates, Gramsci (1971) moved Marxist intellectual work away from a reductive economism, to confront how 'hegemonies' of power and domination are built within the political, cultural and social realms. Gramsci thus provided the philosophical base for the rise of 'cultural studies' within social science, through the late 1960s onwards, with its major analytical binary of domination and resistance. Sports researchers have drawn heavily, and at times routinely, on Gramsci to explain social conflicts and strategies of ideological control within sport, but more enterprising reinterpretation of his ideas may be needed to sustain his conceptual value within the contemporary era.

Of all the social thinkers here, the West Indian historian and social critic, C.L.R. James, has written most extensively and with the greatest public influence on sporting matters, specifically on cricket. As Brian Stoddart demonstrates, James recognized and negated the dilemma of squaring his Marxist philosophy of history with his passion for the most ideologically charged of English colonial sports. James's seminal text *Beyond a Boundary* provides not only a keen understanding of the aesthetics and historical peculiarities of cricket, but more importantly a reading of how the game became a venue of struggle for West Indians against structural inequalities and for the expression of their cultural identity and difference. Though he was most alive to the empirical complexities of specific historical moments, James was, according to the indebted Said (1995, p. 351), a 'distinguished thinker of the post-colonial', and his legacy reverberates far beyond Caribbean commentaries on cricket.

Our next three social theorists – Giddens, Elias and Bourdieu – are noteworthy for their respective attempts to transcend the classic socio-logical binary of action versus structure, or subjectivism versus objectivism. Giddens has written little on sport, and in partial consequence has barely registered within sport studies. Yet in the late 1990s he became arguably the most influential theorist within the English-speaking world, not least through his advisory role to the Labour Prime Minister Tony Blair. As John Horne and David Jary explain, Giddens's 'structuration theory' sets out a 'duality of structure' in which social structures are seen as emerging out of (rather than controlling) the actions of individuals. Latterly, Giddens has brought the principles of structuration theory to his 'third way' political philosophy, while weighing late modern issues of lifestyle and self-identity. Horne and Jary consider Giddens's cultural themes and social theory to have high potential within the sociology of sport and leisure, but we await the development of a fulsome research programme rooted in structuration theory.

In some contrast, Giddens's former colleague Norbert Elias has had a major impact within the social analysis of sport and in cultural theory generally. From the 1960s onwards, Elias built up a school of close and often partisan followers among some younger lecturers and students at the University of Leicester and latterly in Holland. Sport figured prominently in Elias's work, later in socio-historical work with Eric Dunning, and also to help illuminate his 'figurational' theory of human life as a social process. As I demonstrate in my chapter on Elias here, his major sociological contribution has been his 'theory of the civilizing process' which has been highly controversial within the social sciences generally and sport studies in particular.

The late Pierre Bourdieu established himself as a leading sociologist within the Francophone world, and his work holds a profound global influence across the social sciences. Bourdieu's early anthropological work in Algeria was heavily structuralist in orientation, and that emphasis has remained in later works that sought to dissolve the opposition between objectivist and subjectivist theoretical perspectives. Unusually, Bourdieu argues that social theory must be orientated towards empirical research into the practices of social actors. Alan Tomlinson shows that Bourdieu's seminal text, *Distinction*, is a meticulous dissection of French society, and in particular the divisions (mainly class ones) that are realized through differences in economic, educational, cultural and social resources and practices. Thus sport figures prominently in Bourdieu's work, demonstrating a distinctive relationship to the reflexive reproduction of social differences. Bourdieu's (1998) later critical reading of sport has been to the fore, arguing against American individualism in favour of French 'solidarism', and thus setting out a 'utopian' series of state-directed social policies to bolster sport's moral and socially integrative dimensions.

Like Bourdieu, the German social theorist Jürgen Habermas has been a hugely influential academic within his native country and a committed critic within the public sphere. For Habermas, there is explicit need to re-establish the normative principles of modernity, to promote an open, tolerant, democratic community. As William J. Morgan shows, Habermas was acutely concerned that Western bourgeois society has become preoccupied with 'instrumental rationality', thus ignoring the dialogical and critical aspects of reason. Hence in sports, the social and moral aspects of play atrophy, and the instrumental (often violent) elements of competition are prioritized. Habermas's solution is to found a moral discourse with universal purchase, and within sports that means examining issues according to the common good rather than sectional interest or competitive efficacy. Morgan is highly sympathetic but asks us to consider if Habermas's universalist stance would be overly abstract if it were applied in the 'practice communities' of specific sports.

We begin our consideration of postmodern social theory through examining its influence within feminist theory. The latter, as Jennifer Hargreaves notes, has been notable for not producing a single dominant theorist, but rather a diversity of feminist theoretical standpoints. Postmodernist theorizing has had ambiguous effects on feminist thinking: while understandings of difference and marginalization have been enhanced, postmodernism's lack of concern with praxis has blunted much of the practical and political edge of feminism. Nevertheless, Hargreaves argues that it remains possible to restore a critical normative dimension to feminist thinking that is attuned to contemporary cultural changes and forms of social oppression.

The book concludes with two chapters on social theorists closely associated with the postmodernist and post-structuralist intellectual turns. The French social theorist Michel Foucault argued that power and knowledge are interdependent rather than mutually exclusive resources. Cole, Andrews and Giardina trace Foucault's 'analytics of power' with particular reference to embodiment and the socio-political construction of selves. Thus, we pass through the role of systems of surveillance in making docile, passive bodies, to the facility of contemporary social policies in 'conducting the conduct' of active bodies. In sport, this means a respective focus on the social control of spectators within stadiums and on the connections of charitable athletic events to consumerist, neo-liberal discourses. The authors draw additional attention to Foucault's (often forgotten) concern with the relationship of bodily 'knowledge' to forms of racialization.

The French social theorist Jean Baudrillard provides a logical conclusion to the book, as he is often regarded as the most extreme 'postmodern' theorist, and one who claims that the social itself has been abolished. In my chapter on Baudrillard, I note that while his theoretical statements are characteristically fragmentary, he does refer regularly to sporting practices. Through main themes such as simulation, seduction, hyper-reality and the end of the social, Baudrillard offers us a diverse set of ideas through which to read changes within sports culture. In particular, he points to the greater significance of consumption and the impact of the electronic mediation of sports upon the events themselves, while suggesting that more 'tribal' aspects of sports culture, notably inter-club rivalries, will not be dissolved.

References

Adorno, T. (1981) *Prisms*, Cambridge, Mass.: Harvard University Press.
Bourdieu, P. (1998) 'The State, Economics and Sport', *Culture Sport Society*, 1(2): 15–21.
Goffman, E. (1967) *Interaction Ritual*, Harmondsworth: Penguin.
Gramsci, A. (1971) *Selections from the Prison Notebook*, New York: International Press.
Ingham, A.G. & P. Donnelly (1997) 'A Sociology of North American Sociology of Sport: Disunity in Unity, 1965 to 1996', *Sociology of Sport Journal*, 14(4): 362–418.
Merton, R.K. (1967) 'Manifest and Latent Functions', *On Theoretical Sociology*, Glencoe: Free Press.
Mills, C.W. (1956) *The Power Elite*, Oxford: Oxford University Press.
Morgan, W.J. (1988) 'Adorno on Sport: the case of the fractured dialectic', *Theory and Society*, 17: 813–838.
Rowe, D., J. McKay & G. Lawrence (1997) 'Out of the Shadows: the critical sociology of sport in Australia, 1986 to 1996', *Sociology of Sport Journal*, 14(4): 340–361.
Said, E. (1995) *Orientalism*, Harmondsworth: Penguin.

1

The Sportification Process: A Biographical Analysis Framed by the Work of Marx, Weber, Durkheim and Freud

Alan G. Ingham

Marx, Weber, Durkheim, and Freud were giants of the sociological/psychological imagination. They live with us whenever we theorize sport's relationship to long-term social development. They thought holistically, providing a form of consciousness with which to read our personal, positional (status interests), and class locations in society. Moreover, the classical theorists challenged us to ask, 'Why do we do what we do and why do we believe in what we believe?'

Here, I engage in a synthetic exercise. I use one key theme from each theorist – Marx's concept of *valorization*, Weber's concept of *rationalization*, Durkheim's concept of *collective representation*, and Freud's concept of *repression*. These concepts enable an explanation of the sportification of play and agonal games as they intersect with our biographies. They help us to understand social relations in the contemporary institution of sport. Most of us have engaged in play, games and sport or have been engaged by them. Sometimes this engagement *appears* to have been voluntary; other times it has felt coerced. For those who move from play to higher (elite) levels of sport, often the distinction between wanting to and having to becomes blurred. Sport is little different from any other social institution – wanting to learn versus having to learn in a certain way (education), wanting to be productive and having to be productive (the political economy of work), wanting to play a piano and having to do so in a specific way (music), and so on. Whenever considering the 'wanting to'/'having to' relationship, we address the dialectic of personal freedom and structured authority (Gruneau, 1983, pp. 19–51). We are both incorporated into the rules of the game and critical of them. Asking ourselves 'What we want to do, can do, and may do?' reveals our selves in their internal contradictions. Institutions such as sport offer particular resolutions to the contradictory relations between our selves and the broader social order.

Institutionalization seems intrinsic to human beings as social beings. To grasp the process of institutionalization, we should be concerned with which groups of people hold power and how this power is maintained through the articulation of the dominant institutions. Moreover, we should ask upon what bases do some groups exercise power over others. To ignore these questions is to pass over an understanding of how the structures of institutions foster domination in a given society. In any institution, some people feel empowered while others feel disempowered. Often these feelings are anchored in our ability to choose between doing this or that thing, living this way or that way, being able or not being able to, having or being denied opportunity.

Institutionalization as a process sets limits on personal practices and self-interests. If we agree that we cannot just do as we please, some repression of needs and desires is necessary for us to live with others. I shall call this positive institutionalization. But how much repression is necessary and who decides? Do our institutional arrangements regarding repression favour some while denying others? When we question our 'life chances' (Dahrendorf, 1979), we tend to focus on systems rather than people or groups. We are engaged in reification if we think in such terms, forgetting that all institutions have histories that are authored by people. More importantly, we forget that some people historically have had more power to shape institutionalized life. This power – social domination – constitutes negative institutionalization or surplus repression (Marcuse, 1966, p. 35). I argue that the processes of valorization, rationalization, and bourgeois civilization (the processes associated with modernity) constitute the modern forms and relations through which class domination has been made institutionally effective.

Institutions can achieve only a partial incorporation of individuals. Working within and outside of institutions are conscious formations that are loyal or critical towards the epistemic meanings, values, and learning experiences intrinsic to the formal institutions. Importantly, while institutions set limits on actions, these limits are contested and are, therefore, variably effective. This contestation places the old concept of socialization (functionally defined) in jeopardy. The complexity of our lived experiences and the turmoil of our inner psyches suggest that socialization is only partially effective in determining how a society reproduces itself across generations (Wrong, 1961). Yet, we know that the articulation between dominant institutions is powerful ideologically and influences the ways in which we live our lives. We also know that the failure to live our lives according to the dominant precepts makes us expendable, even criminal. Failure to conform has consequences.

Marx [Engels] and the sportification process: valorization

How might we view play, games, and sport from a Marxian perspective? One way is historical: examining how the capitalist mode of production transforms use-values into exchange-values, and into surplus-values over time – a transmutational process called valorization. Another way is biographical: examining how valorization embraces our move from childhood play, through games, to professional and Olympic sport. Here, I focus on the latter.

Capitalism is an economic system: production is oriented to the real-ization of surplus-value (profit) that generally accrues to privately held capital. It presupposes a market for buying and selling commodities via monetary exchange (Mandel, 1970, pp. 9–10). Most people are wage labourers and work under conditions they cannot control. Their only commodity is labour power which, treated as a thing, is sold to those who own the means of production or control its administration – capitalists, managers of capital (CEOs), or state agencies. Surplus-values accrue when someone buys a commodity at a price above its production costs. The capitalist's buying of labour power is a key relation of production. It is rooted in exploitation since workers work beyond what is necessary for their own needs and beyond what is needed to supply a return on a capitalist's investment costs. However, labour contests being pushed to its absolute limits, to its absolute surplus value. This engenders class struggle. To extract more surplus value from labour power where class struggle had produced an eight-hour day or shift, changes were made in both the forces and relations of production. The forces of production initially were industrialized – machines assisted labour to produce more commodities than labour could itself achieve. The relations of production were also rationalized (Taylorized). Through assembly line production the division of labour was made more efficient, engendering the production of relative surplus-value. While working hours are not increased, work itself becomes repetitive and boring. Assembly line production requires less on-line skill, so the lesser skilled worker can replace the highly skilled craftsman, creating divisions within the working class. This overall process, combining valorization, rationalization, and the co-option of labour (through higher wages and benefits) has been called 'Fordism' (Gramsci, 1971, pp. 279–318).

As machines become more productively efficient, less labour is needed. This creates a 'reserve army of labour' (the underemployed and unemployed) that also puts disciplinary and monetary pressures on those working. Thus, the higher the unemployment, the lower the wage paid to those employed, and vice-versa. Unemployment becomes a permanent feature of capitalism. Valorization plus the rationalization of the mode of production make for conditions of expendability within the producer (labour) categories (Marx, 1867/1967, Vol. 1, pp. 628–648).

Capitalists always seek areas of use-value which can be transmuted into exchange values with a view to realizing profit (surplus-value). In sport, valorization depended upon a market of consumers being created. Sport historians and sociologists have argued the 'urban-industrial society thesis' in this regard. But this falls short of the explanatory mark (Gruneau, 1983, pp. 85–88). What should be emphasized is how the capitalist mode of production became so naturalized that it influenced production in other spheres (such as sport) and became hegemonic. Thus, in a capitalist society, the valorization of sport would have occurred when conditions were ripe. Urban-industrialism merely accelerated the process (Ingham, 1978; Ingham & Beamish, 1993).

In this chapter, I treat play as a form of human practice in which the sensory and limbic, the motoric and the practical consciousness combine. Play is a sensori-motor schema involving our emotions and thoughts, the raw material from which systematic game forms emerge. Children play with the medium to build transitional forms. In early childhood, we do not play at ourselves, we play with ourselves in various self-centric practices or autocosmic play (Erikson, 1963). The playing with/ playing at distinction is important because later (social) play involves a split between the 'I' and the 'Me' – I the subject and me the object (Mead, 1934). An infant makes no such distinction. S/he has no concept of social role. The 'I' is pure 'I'. Play is a narcissistic self-indulgence that all children need to develop healthily. It requires a high level of 'empathic resonance' (Kohut, 1977) from the care-giver – the adequate tuning into or mirroring of the child's needs. Since such play is all interiorization, the taking into the self, we can regard it as the preparatory work for higher forms of self-expression or externalization.

For a child in play, the more a practice provides pleasure or avoids pain, the more it is repeated. The sensori-motor schemas involved in such play are relatively discrete. The connecting of these discrete schemas comes later in childhood. But repetition is the basis of habit formation – good or bad. It provides us with the basics upon which the 'I/Me' integration can proceed. With habituation come self-imposed rules so that, from 'primitive' sensori-motor schemas, play forms can emerge. For the child, because the pleasure principle has not been repressed by the reality principle (Freud, 1960, p. 19), play is not work that is in the form of alienated labour. Thus, it only produces a use-value (pleasure) for the player, which is consumed immediately in the act of production.

Forms of play, as against play activities, emerge both from the acquisition of technical habits and the capacity for synthesis. For children, play is often co-actional – separate but in conjunction with others. Their fledgling subjectivities are still self-centered. Playing with others requires 'reciprocal typification' (Berger & Luckmann, 1966, pp. 31–34) – putting one's self in the other's shoes. Play is less random; complementary roles are assumed. Rules are less subjectival and more mutual. Behaviours become more predictable – a precondition for tradition. With predictability, individuals can attribute meanings and intentions to the behaviour they observe. Once the means-ends relation is understood, practices become taken-for-granted; knowing the goal, the means to its attainment become expected, even morally evaluated. Thus, constitutive rules are developed, ordering and guiding social interaction. Habituation and reciprocal typification are necessary for play to become games.

Rules do not necessarily take games away from the pleasure principle or the realm of use-value production. Here, I am talking about those directly involved in the game. Certainly, many games require equipment; depending upon social class, this may be home-made or bought. Thus, while game-players may be producing use-values, the equipment may provide exchange- and surplus-values for others (the manufacturers). Game-playing requires that the more civilized 'me' takes control over the instinctual 'I'. Games provide for pleasure, but also require the renunciation and/or deflection of instincts to minimize conflicts with the reality principle that the engagement with others produces (Freud, 1961, p. 52). This is what I referred to as repression in the form of positive institutionalization.

Games are far more social democratic than either play or sport. Play is too self-centered; sport is too objectified (reified) for democratic processes to work. In gaming, we know that we create rules to recognize the needs of others, the time and space in which we play, and the number of people present in the game. Games originally were not watered down sports. Only over time and with external determinations, including the imposition of a new discourse on old forms, did games become sports and childhood games become watered down sports. If we, adults, did not impose our will on children, then maybe they would game before they sport. But we adults do not let ontogeny repeat phylogeny. We have socially constructed expectations and our children become miniature 'sportsters' while, in terms of development, they should be 'gamesters' (Ingham & Chase, 1999).

I focus only on agonal games – competitive games, involving skill and strategy, two or more sides (even if one side is Nature), with rules that produce winners and losers. This is the stuff out of which sport is made. For any cultural form to persist, there has to be (e)valuation. Should we commit ourselves to 'it' relative to other things we might do? There have been many games in history and few of these are gamed today. Persistence requires commitment, some degree of power, and a community of like-minded competitors – a *formation*. Persistence of a cultural form requires a moral judgement that if something is good it should be shared, but even this cannot sustain many game forms. Exogenous factors – for example, how civilized a game is relative to our conceptions of civilization; how profitable a game is in a capitalist system; how rural a game might be relative to industrialization, and so on – influence a game's sustainability.

A game's viability may depend on the pleasurable, controllable, and creative tension generated (Elias & Dunning, 1966). Following Simmel (1950, p. 47), we may consider the game's level of sociability. An individual's satisfaction and pleasure in being sociable is closely bound to the pleasure and sociability of those with whom s/he interacts. If one side always wins, there is little pleasurable tension or pleasurable sociability. If the rules favour offense over defense, there is no pleasure in defending. If rules favour the tall over the short, the heavy over the light, then there is little pleasure in being either short or light.

Games are democratic. They require inter-subjective negotiation to constitute rules that give us pleasurable satisfactions even if we get some bumps and lumps in the process. No participant wants to be told that his or her rules do not count. For an expressive configuration of positive affect to hold, the instrumental concerns and ego-demands of participants must be minimized, equalized, or ruled as irrelevant (Ingham & Loy, 1973). To remain sociable, intrinsic outcomes must be available to all; extrinsic gains should be seen to be shared. Games, unlike sports, must pay their way in immediate and potential long-term pleasure.

Since a game provides for pleasure, it can be sold for such. Gregory Stone (1971) recognized this paradox when he talked about play and display. To use Marxian concepts, play as productive work is undertaken for its use-value. Neither the child nor the child's labour has been socialized economically. Although I have used the term value, there are really no external or abstract standards by which to judge the child's labour either quantitatively or qualitatively, much as we adults might try. Games are undertaken for their [simple] social exchange-value. In giving of oneself, one expects to receive in equal measure. Given that game participants are not equally skilled, each producer gives in different measure both qualitatively and quantitatively. Some will produce efficiently, others inefficiently. Where this affects the stability of social interactions, stratification may occur – the more efficient may seek those of similar ability and the same goes for the less efficient. Such stratification does not eliminate weaker producers. Where the social interaction commitment is to be maintained, adjustments accommodate the quantitatively and qualitatively different. In simple social exchange games, meta-narratives of fairness, and justice prevail. Even when some games become more established as customs or traditions, our involvement cannot be absolutely coerced. We retain some control over our private labour. For those of us who wish to retain all such control, then the heteronomous systems of organized sport may not be for us.

Sports are undertaken in an exchange- and surplus-value creating relation. While play had a use-value for players, sport has a use-value for the owner of the athletes' labour power who realizes its exchange-value through the consumer. An athlete's labour is appropriated to create surplus value. Games sold as sports require that some people (athletes) produce other people's (spectators) pleasure, and other people's (the owners of the athletes' labour power) profits, be they egocentric – an exchange-value as a prestige-value – or economic. In sport's feeder system, athletes give up control over private labour but at the early stages they can still walk away. The more we commit ourselves to the athletic role/identity, the more our labour becomes qualitatively determined by skills and quantitatively determined by efficiency. To advance in the feeder system, we do not produce to exchange socially as we do in a game. We have to exchange in market-value terms on the nebulous basis of our 'potential'.

By showing potential in a specific sport, we can begin to exchange that potential for the means of production. Potential *buys* new, higher quality means of production. Eventually, we may exchange the products of our labour for a wage. Those who supply the means of production (sponsors, owners, organizations, associations, etc.) buy our potentials as labour power. They expect a return on investment. They sell us higher quality means of production (better facilities, uniforms, travel, etc.) only if our talents warrant it and only if the wages (and their investments in the means of production) are lower than the overall exchange-value. The cheapest payments are honorific (cups, medals, and other trophies). The more expensive are professional player contracts. But, the entire feeder system, from bottom to top, is overdetermined by the exchange-value creating capacities of labour – anticipated and real.[1] Our commitment to produce at the Prolympic (the confluence of Olympic and Professional elite athletic systems[2]) level renders us complicitous in our own and our parents' exploitation.

All of us do play. All of us can game pleasurably. Few can display for a wage. Sport provides for both moral and material rewards, so many give it a try; but very few achieve a Prolympic identity. For sport to exist as a valorized industry, structures have to be developed which insure its continued reproduction through the production of athletic labour power with high levels of skill.

Like many other institutionalized systems and structures in liberal democratic societies, the feeder system of sport is, at its base, relatively inclusive. At its apex, it is quite exclusive. From the base to the apex, most of us will be made expendable. We may enter it for the fun of using our talents. Later, we realize the feeder system is one of allocation (Kerckhoff, 1976). As we advance, progressively fewer positions are available, until only a tiny fraction of athletes remain.[3] What once was playful and fun-filled has now become damned hard work. In joining the sport feeder system, we begin learning to labour (Cantelon, 1981). This *toil* separates sport from games and play, yielding exchange- and surplus-values for those who control the mode of sporting production. Sport becomes part of a larger system of domination and exploitation, illustrating Marcuse's surplus repression or 'negative institutionalization'.

The sports feeder system is instrumentally rational (Weber, 1978). Fun and pleasure – the libidinal, use-values of play – yield to career-survivalist strategies anchored in performance *and* perfection principles (in the form of ego-ideals). Interest gives way to competence where one's best is never good enough – there is always someone waiting to take your place or record – there is, to use Marx's (1867/1967, Vol. 1, pp. 628–648) concept, a reserve army of Prolympian labour. We also need a gate value beyond performance value. We can earn good wages based on performance value, but gate value (a display persona attractive to sport merchandisers) adds to these through endorsements even after a playing career is over (e.g. Michael Jordan whose annual income is $37 million).

In sum, as we move from play through games to sport, our physical practices become commodified. Valorization subsumes our practices and bodies. We are evaluated on our capacities and potentials to do rather than to be. We move from private to socially productive labour. This is a process of *alienation*. This concept is complex: it can refer to humankind's alienation from nature. If play is a natural component of 'man's' species being, then sport deflects the natural into acts of production over which the producer has little control. If play has some intrinsic satisfaction, then sport is more concerned with exchange-values – the satisfaction of others. The primary libidinal, use-value satisfaction gives way to securing employment and the selling of potentials to sports capitalists. The products of labour become alien to the workers/athletes and yet have power over them. Consider the 'what have you done for me lately?' attitudes of owners and coaches. We are only as good as our last performance! Few positions are available; hence potential Prolympic athletes are prone to being estranged or alienated from each other. Our humanness is debased through capitalistic processes, encouraging us to objectify the competitive Other. The objectified Other can be a target of our violence – after all, in a market economy it is a 'Me' versus the Other world. The market economy may encourage the aggressive as well as the pleasure components of the instinctual drives. Pleasure in achieving gratification runs together with an 'in your face' attitude towards your opponent. To summarize the theoretical positions of Freud/Marcuse and Marx, one can discern two conceptual trilogies that help in the analysis of the sportification process:

	Marx	Freud/Marcuse
Play	Use-value	Instincts/eros/pleasure principle
Games	Exchange-value	Repression/reality principle
Sport	Surplus-value	Surplus repression/performance principle

Max Weber: rationalization and sportification

For Weber, estrangement (alienation) is not purely determined by the political economy of capitalism, but by the hegemony of instrumental rationality and the rationalization of social relations. Capitalism was not the enemy and socialism the friend. For Weber, socialism's central-ization of power in the bureaucratized State could only curtail individual freedom and responsibility for personal choices.

Rationalization is one of several concepts linked to Weber's more generic use of the concept of rationality, especially instrumental rationality. Instrumental rationality in 'higher capitalism' involves action in relation to a goal which is deliberately selected by the actor from the plurality of goals that are available, *none of which is absolute*. Instrumental rationality is cold, calculative, and conditional, and from a more Marxian reading implies that human beings, as well as physical objects, can be considered as means to another individual's end. For Weber, instrumentally rational action characterizes social action in the material structures of advanced capitalism. Instrumental rationality is the hegemonic orientation to social action in the institutionalization and modernization of the industrial capitalist way of life and thought. It subsumes other forms of social action almost bending them to its will. Less legitimacy is granted to action anchored in tradition,[4] emotion, and absolute values.

Rationalization is not so much an orientation as *a process*, one of systematization and standardization, increasing the number of cases to which the explicit, abstract, impersonal rules, and procedures are applied (Wrong, 1970, p. 26). Bureaucracy is Weber's ideal type of the combination of instrumental rationality and rationalization. Rationalization facilitates the trend from particularism to universalism, but it does so at the price of depersonalization and, often, oppressive routine. There is an elective affinity between rationalization and valorization with the latter perhaps providing the impetus for the former.

My immediate problem is to link valorization to instrumental rationality and rationalization. Valorization and rationalization are not independent processes. They articulate (partially connect, maybe congeal) *in a class* and its domination over other classes (Giddens, 1973, p. 140). To over-simplify Weber: the expansionist dynamic of capitalism resulted in the rationalization of technique and the rationalization of the labour process (see Hobsbawm, 1968), the latter being possible because workers had been expropriated from the ownership of the means of production. Thus presented, Weber's position does not significantly differ from Marx. However, Weber also used the idea of expropriation to include the loss of control over the means of administration (the bureaucratic State, the managerialized workplace). Thus, both Marx and Weber attempted a kind of philosophical sociology of modern 'man', but what Marx called the alienation of the workers from the means of production, Weber broadened into the more inclusive category of the rationalization of modern life (Hughes, 1958, p. 317).

Valorization and rationalization are closely linked processes, but in sport the initial impact of their joint form was accidental. After some time and as a result of class struggle, rationalized capitalism produced mass publics with some discretionary income and time. Technological innovations (in transportation, communications, and electrification) inadvertently increased consumers of live events and through the sport pages and telegraphed reports (see Betts, 1953; Loy, 1968). Such innovations allowed the public to reclaim an interest in sport even though it was initially at the level of consumerism. A sustainable industry, however, requires a quality product to realize exchange- and surplus-values. With the valorization of sport, the rationalization of its means and relations of production would follow. Science/technology and bureaucratic/ managerial forms of administration would intentionally be applied to sporting production.

Bureaucrats might appear 'disinterested', operating 'without regard for persons' (Weber, 1978, p. 975). However, bureaucracies always serve interests and the heads of bureaucracies are appointed by those who hold those interests. Such imperatively coordinated groups may fall prey to interest groups that attempt to influence the decision-making process. It thus becomes a question not necessarily of who is making decisions but why they make the decisions that they do. As Weber (1946, p. 280) observed, not ideas, but material and ideal interests, directly govern men's conduct. It is easy to point to the lobbying characteristics of modern representational politics, but major sport 'Committees' and associations are as likely to fall prey to such practices. Jenkins (Simson & Jennings, 1992; Jennings, 1996) details the impact of material interest groups upon the 'ideal' interests of International Olympic Committee (IOC) members. In the transition from Brundage (the millionaire who could afford to be an 'amateur' sportsman and an ideologue of Olympism) to Samaranch (the former Franco-ite), the Olympics have been professionalized, McDonaldized, Snickerized, and so on. The material has subjugated the ideal, as we should expect from my analysis of the valorization process even though the Olympic ideology is proclaimed from on high and reinforced in the Olympic 'ceremonials'.

A force for rationalization resides in the expansion of the corporate group over which imperative control is to be exercised. Athletes, after all, were not members of the IOC until the instrumental and devious proclamations of the 2000 Sydney Games, but they must adhere to its rules and regulations to compete. In sport, the distinction between voluntary association and compulsory organization is often blurred for athletes. Regardless of our level in the feeder system of sport, we lose our autonomy in the decision-making process and find ourselves confronted by a heteronomous and abstract power which, either through the market or through its rational-legal authority, can exercise a far-reaching even despotic hegemony (Weber, 1978, p. 945). As we move from play through games to sport, we encounter what Weber

(1958, p. 181) called an 'iron cage' of rationality policed by 'specialists without spirit, sensualists without heart' (p. 182). It induces passivity among those non-unionized amateurs and child-youth athletes (also their parents) engaged in organized, representational sports. Such passivity involves the subjugation of substantive rationality – personal choice, awareness of responsibility, action, commitment, and faith – by a formal or functional rationality whose structures operate without regard for persons and which become 'the walls of our imprisonment in history' (Berger, 1963, p. 92). Weber's iron cage of estrangement thus bears certain resemblance to the Marxian concept of alienation.

There is a dark side to *Citius, Altius, Fortius* – the Olympic sub-motto (see Hoberman, 1992; Voy, 1993). To go faster, higher, and become stronger requires excess: in training, in how we manipulate our bodies. To earn sport's extrinsic rewards, we turn into freaks – 350 lb football linemen, steroid, andro, and creatine monophosphate aided muscularities, youthful freaks aided by growth hormones, and so on. We allow our lives to be organized by a cadre of experts and administrators both on and off the field. This 'scientization', 'technicization', and managerial/bureaucratic organization of our athletic labour is part of Weber's rationalization process. Through rationalization, the nature of our work and the relation we have with our bodies, our selves, and others at work is significantly altered.

To avoid becoming expendable, we might seek some competitive advantage, an edge – the extra credential, attending a management workshop or a coaching school, for example. In the rationalization of our athletic selves, we tinker with the contents (our bodies, techniques, technological props) and forms (tactics and rules) of sport. But rarely do we tinker with the relations of social relations for this would take a commitment to usurp the power of the powerful.[5] Tinkering with the contents and forms are acts of novel production, but they are not acts of relational transformation. Tinkering with the contents and forms does not constitute a high level of political agency. It may even reaffirm the legitimacy of the prevailing institutions – we have 'fixed' this or that problem. Tinkering with and fixing things are quite predominant practices in instrumentally rational, social systems.

If we consider rationalization in the ludic domain, two biographical perspectives should be considered: the first involves the instrumental use of the body; the second involves the shift from relative autonomy to relative heteronomy as we progress from play to sport. Many men see their bodies in instrumental terms – as things to be developed and used in work and sport. This is especially true of the working classes: manual labour involves the body as both an instrument and force of production.

Physical play, agonal games, and sport primarily involve manual labour and an instrumentally rational orientation to the actions of the body.

In play, the body is not seen instrumentally, but as part of an expressive totality (the emerging human being) in the pursuit of the pleasure principle. There may be some painful moments as the child explores the body's limits. But, the object of play is not to incur pain, nor to repeat practices to the point of boredom. And, unless we have an over-bearing parent present, children will make up their own rules of conduct. They are not expropriated from the means of administration and regulation. Much of what they do is constituting rather than constituted. In play, pleasure is the use-value and relative autonomy seems to be tolerated even by those in 'authority' for a while.

In games, due to positive institutionalization (repression), rules are less subjectival and more mutual, and therefore behaviors become more predictable. Rules become constitutive and constituting. We know that we have to create and follow rules that take into account the needs of others, the time, places, and spaces in which we game, and the number of people present in the gaming situation. Rules are a means to an end; they are not ends in and of themselves. In games, we stand somewhere between the autonomy/heteronomy dualism. In games this dualism is really a duality – a negotiated compromise between extremes. In sport, however, athletes are rarely involved in the rule-making process. They are not represented on administrative bodies or central regulatory agencies. Heteronomously governed, an athlete's choice is limited. To be successful, one has to 'play' by the rules constituted by those with imperative power in compulsory organizations (mistitled clubs and associations).

In the modern period, then, there is no 'natural athlete'. We do not participate just as we are. We perform within boundaries set by others and by selected traditions. If there is a new god it is that created by scientific, technological, and administrative rationality as significations of progress. In combination, they seem like an anonymous and diffuse force superior to individuals – Durkheim's definition of religion. United as an abstract and diffuse force, they render us complicit in our own exploitation.

	Marx	Freud/Marcuse	Weber
Play	Use-value	Instincts/pleasure principle	'Irrational' social action (affectual/traditional)
Games	Exchange-value	Repression/reality principle	Substantive rationality
Sport	Surplus-value	Surplus repression/ performance	Formal rationality/ efficiency

Why do we do what we do? Because sometimes our very identities are dependent on doing the socially acceptable if we are to be validated, be seen as functional and, hopefully, indispensable. Of course, the positive and negative valencies that we apply to incorporative, accommodative, and resistant identities are meaningful only in terms of the moral limits set by our culture. That is, they represent to varying degrees how our 'civilized' education/enculturation seeks to deny us the opportunities to satisfy, or require us to substitute for, our more primal desires. But sometimes, despite cultural pressures, we do what we do because we want to do it – the repressed child shakes free its civilized (adult) chains. As Horkheimer and Adorno (1972, p. 105) stated: 'Pleasure is, so to speak, nature's vengeance. In pleasure men disavow thought and escape civilization'.

Durkheim: the legitimizing function of rituals

I have spent too little time on ideology and hegemony. How do those in positions of dominance secure the consent of those in subordinate classes/ranks? Perhaps the subordinate classes suffer from 'false consciousness', believing in a system that does not promote their interests. Most Marxians have abandoned this concept because it assumes that class subordination implies intellectual subordination. So why do subordinate groups fall prey to 'bourgeosification'? All institutions do have doctrinaire agendas and are involved in an indoctrination/socialization process. Perhaps, it is through our institutions that the dominant sense becomes sedimented into the common sense. Is this enough? Do ideas, as ideologies, need a closer connection to our lived experiences and, if so, how is this to be achieved?

Some people seem compelled to make sense of the world for us. They are the legitimation and delegitimation specialists, the dominant and oppositional ideologues. Dominant ideologues have more power, legitimating institutions in which they become organically institutionalized. Oppositional or critical ideologues offer alternative explanations, pointing to how existing social arrangements favour the interests of some but not others. Their agenda is to offer hope to the disempowered. But, typically, when we hear the two or more sides arguing, their discourse is foreign to us and, unless reduced to sloganeering (e.g. election campaigns) does not penetrate our common sense. Faced with their technical jargon, we might become 'naturally' conservative.

The idea that everyone else is doing 'it' or believes in 'it' raises ideology to a new plane: It is that of hegemony. Hegemony, as used by Gramsci, means that the ruled give consent to their being ruled. As Raymond

Williams (1977, pp. 109–110) noted, such consent depends upon ideas *being detached* from specific ideologies that can be shown to be representative of a particular class or political party. Hegemonic ideas saturate the whole process of living so that we take them for granted. Yet, some individuals and groups question this legitimacy. It is in this questioning that we realize the fragility of hegemony. It is at such times that we may realize that the sedimented is indeed the dominant and ideological in the narrow definition of being the expression of a particular class or political-economic interest.

It may seem strange to come to Durkheim from this Marxist perspective, but this is the way I want to situate his work and his ideas concerning collective representations, collective conscience, and collective consciousness. Of all of the theorists, Durkheim is most alien from my own perspective. His penchant for reifying 'society' and his deification of this reification has always troubled me. But I have to take serious note of Durkheim's ideas concerning the force of religion in everyday life. Marx may have said that religion is the opiate of the masses and Brohm (1978) may have said that sport is the opiate of the masses. But these arguments just return us to the false consciousness position. I argue that sport has become mobilized in a really instrumental and secularized sense to serve the interests of social domination, and that there are divisions in subordinate groups between those who do buy and those who do not buy into the dominant's interpretations of reality.

For Durkheim, groups move from relatively homogeneous, mechanically bonded units where there is little if any division of labour to organically bonded or functionally differentiated societies in which all are dependent on all. With the increased division of labor, the length of the chains of interdependency is increased. In religion, groups move from highly rigid forms of totemic control into more abstract and secularized forms of collective consciousness. Regardless of how advanced the division of labour and the forms of religious thought are, for Durkheim, society itself is, in a *transfigured* state, the 'sacred' power, the overarching authority – it provides the moral glue that binds all together and, fundamentally, is the object of worship. Because Durkheim's analysis of religion is an attempt to show how the totemically primitive undergirds religious faith regardless of a society's 'level' of development, in *The Elementary Forms* he does not distinguish between 'society' and the 'state'. From a Marxian interpretation, I would have to see the 'Church' of society as residing in the moral authority given to the State to act as an arbitrator of the social order. It represents the sacred – society's moral and ethical guardian, and the highest court of appeal. At both the

State and sub-state levels, it provides the rituals and 'totemic' symbolism that reaffirm the faith. The profane lies in the workings of everyday life or what Marx would call, 'civil society'. The ritual element or the rite is still needed even in advanced societies and its symbolism remains now, as in the past, as a collective representation of a collective conscience and consciousness. The societal *is* (the rational-legal in Weberian terms), through transfiguration, becomes also the moral (the value-rational in Weberian terms) *ought*! As Durkheim (1995, p. 208) asked, is god and the society not one and the same?

For Durkheim, the ritual preceded the belief. The latter grew out of the former and for a system of belief to be sustained, the ritual had to be repeated. Durkheim assumes that as long as the ritual is repeated the belief is sustained. My argument is that, in contemporary societies, secular rituals only sustain the belief for as long as the reality is suspended – Durkheim's notion of collective effervescence and Victor Turner's (1969, 1974) notion of spontaneous 'communitas'. After the ceremony, people go home to the lived experiences of their immediate environments. They realize the properties of illusion and delusion. They also realize that a version of the sacred is only that – a version. I think we are very aware that rites and rituals are forms of 'moral toning' (Durkheim, 1995, p. 213). In secular rituals (e.g. Mardi Gras) I am not sure what we think the sacred and the profane are – the two collapse into each other in modern rituals as simulacra, where the real is confused with the ideal model (Baudrillard, 1983, p. 4). Similarly, in post-Fordist societies, the line between the State and civil society is increasingly and intentionally blurred. In ceremonies and festivals, the public (the state) and the private (civil society) or the sacred and profane work together to mutually reinforce the liberal democratic ideology of capitalism. Regardless of epoch and episteme, what is called the sacred is what those in power deem the sacred to be. Thus, to twist Durkheim's logic, we can argue that at some time, some one or some group had to decide what was sacred and what was profane and that the group could not, except in the most primitive case (the clan), be the society as a whole. In the modern period, the 'entrepreneurs in the public interest' (urban officials, see Hill, 1983, p. 116) and those in the private interest conflate the social and political economic with the moral and ethical. The *civic* is the new domain which blurs the distinction between the public and the private, the State and civil society, and self-interested ideologies with the 'common good' or the 'commonwealth'.

Given these ideas, modern Prolympic sports serve as rites and representations that reproduce liberal democratic society in hegemonic terms. They also provide *serialized civic rituals* (Ingham *et al.*, 1987) that mask the differences between dominant and subordinate groups in both class and community terms. They are part of the renewal, recreational, defensive, and modificational processes through which *the* hegemony fends off its challengers. I argue, then, that the organic intellectuals of the capitalist classes (the public relations, media relations, advertising and marketing specialists) are spin merchants who dream up euphoric rites/rituals to reaffirm the moral authority of liberal democratic societies as the capitalist classes and the functionaries of the State have envisioned it on their terms.

To return to institutionalization and the biographical form of analysis, I could argue from a Durkheimian perspective that serialized civic rituals such as sport are the equivalent of Durkheim's positive rites. In this guise, they support hegemonic viewpoints about what our urban/suburban existence is *ideally* like. In its use to preserve the hegemonic, I am not saying that sport itself is a picture of harmony. There have been far too many instances of nasty capital/labour disputes, racial and sexual discrimination (in the USA), blackmail attempts on the part of franchises to have new stadia built with taxpayer monies, and so on, for any such claim to be sustained. What I would say, if I were a Durkheimian, is that at a match *per se*, the profane is suspended and we are transformed from consumers to celebrants of a serious ritual. Or as Bill Shankly has been credited with saying, 'Some people think football is a matter of life and death, I assure them that it is much more serious than that.' Yes, winning and losing are important in the emotional experiences, but what is far more important is that, regardless of whether *our* team is winning or losing, the faithful seem compelled by an abstract force, larger than themselves, to go and worship at the shrine. We buy symbols of our devotion even though we know symbols such as 'away' shirts are changed frequently as a money-making ploy (the English Premier League). We listen to the 'liturgies' and sing the 'hymns'. We buy souvenirs to keep the sacred alive after our pilgrimages (see Slowikowski & Loy, 1993).

We take our children with us and transport them into realm of the sacred. Little wonder that when Piaget (1965) asked his child subjects about the rules of the game, they responded in ways that showed that they harboured an almost mystical respect for the rules, that they saw these rules as eternal so that they were forbidden to change them. Of course, our moral consciousness develops and we come to realize that we do have a part in the construction of rules. But the distinction of the sacred and the profane we take with us. Biographically speaking, we generalize the game rules into rules of the social order. Game rules become metaphors for the metanarratives of life. Playing by the rules for some is so obligatory that it constitutes a neurosis. Some children will develop into hyperconformists and attempt to achieve at higher levels than their abilities permit – the ideal subjugates the real and is often a cause of burnout. Most of us will just try to get things right because getting things right is a virtue. Of course, what is deemed to be right will depend upon our reference group and being right is still related to the hegemonic order of things.

Athletes, like it or not, are for many children role models. They are a significant reference group, totems of the sacred. Their gifts are like 'manna'. Not surprisingly we think, 'There, but for the grace of god, go I'. Unfortunately, some go one step farther and say, 'God did not grace me, but grace will come to me through my sons and daughters'. Lacking in perfection ourselves, we impose the perfection principle on our off-spring. We engage them in the rites of affirmation making them feel that they are indispensable to its reproduction. We put them, especially our male offspring, through various *rites de passage* in which the boys are turned into men. And then they fail as we must all inevitably fail in sport because of the 'what have you and your body done for me lately' aspect of the profane. Sooner or later, we join the ranks of the expendable (Ingham *et al.*, 1999). But we have watched the ideal and learned the important messages of how the ideal became the ideal. We know from these experiences how our subjectivities become evaluated by an abstract force beyond our control. In trying to be perfect, we may not succeed necessarily in the profane world, but surely in the world of the sacred. To refuse to try condemns us in both the sacred and the profane. Biographically, then, sport delivers powerful messages through which the profane and the sacred can be distinguished.

The political economy of capitalism no longer has an elective affinity for a particular religion as Weber described in his *Protestant Ethic and the Spirit of Capitalism*. But capitalism must not be understood as a purely instrumentally rational endeavour. The fundamental values of capitalism are value rational – they are absolute and non-negotiable. Durkheim knew that any society could invent the new in the sacred. What Durkheim could not see was how late capitalism could make the sacred out of the profane and how it could profane the sacred.

Conclusion

I have sought to demonstrate that the sociological/psychological classics represent unsurpassed theories of social development. Marx provides the only plausible theory of historical development and its determinations. No contemporary theorist can ignore Marx even if only to reject his ideas. At the heart is the labour theory of value. As an heir to Marx, Weber's theory of rationalization partially fits with Marx on relative surplus-value production. Marcuse could not have developed his Marxian/

Capitalist Structuration

PLAY

Use-value production
Affect-laden, sensori-motor activites
Eros/life instincts
Self as human *being*
habitualization
Synthesis of content – syncretism

PLAY RITUALS/FORMS

Reciprocal typification
Constitutive codification

Autonomy   Embodied
Reification Tendency --- --- --- ---GAMES--- --- --- --- --- --- ---
Heteronomy   Estranged

Simple exchange-value production
Substantial rationality
Socially necessary repression
Constitutive rules – determination of outcome
Winning and losing
Skill and strategy development
Self as human *being* & human *doing*

AGONAL GAMES

Zero-sum competition
Constituted rules
Appropriation
Valorization/expropriation/extraction
Rationalization
Ideological legitimation

SPORT

Exchange- and surplus-value production
Surplus repression
Formal/functional rationality
Alienation/estrangement
Self as human *doing*

Figure 1.1

Freudian theory without contesting Weberian conceptions of instrumental rationality and technobureaucratic domination as residing outside of conditions of capitalist exploitation. Like Weber, he asked 'and this you call reason?' Regarding Durkheim, to read many postmodernist thinkers, it seems he never existed. Yet he talked about the politics of epistemes, symbols as representations, and rituals as simulacrum long before Foucault and Baudrillard. For those of us trained in classical theory, there is much old wine in new, postmodernist bottles. Freud fell outside of the classical sociological theorists' historical purview. But he could have informed their work much as he can inform ours. As Parsons, Elias, Marcuse and, more recently, Ian Craib have shown, no sociologist should refuse to read Freud.

Serious students of sport should not be satisfied with secondary sources (including mine), or later theoretical interpretations of the classics. All of us interpret the classics through particular lenses. But as an application of the sociological imagination, in response to the questions 'Why do we do what we do?' and 'Why do we believe what we believe?', the insights of Marx, Weber, Durkheim, and Freud are critical and crucial.

It is said that a picture is worth a thousand words. My words are encapsulated in Figure 1.1.

Notes

This chapter builds upon the work of Ingham and Loy (1973). We focused upon the institutionalization process using Berger and Luckmann (1966) as our template. But Marx would have considered this as an exercise in philosophical anthropology, lacking in historical specificity. Thus, the present contribution is an attempt to outline what is historically specific about the modern in modern sport as contoured by the maturation of industrial capitalism. I dedicate this chapter to Ian Taylor (1944–2001) who boosted my self-confidence and nurtured my intellectual capacities over the past 27 years.

1. I am grateful to John Weeks (1981) for clarifying my thoughts on the law of value.
2. I have borrowed this concept from Donnelly (1996).
3. See Leonard (1996) for critical statistics from the United States.
4. While Weber regarded traditional rationality as a form of cultural reflex, traditions can be manipulated through the use of instrumental rationality. They can be selectively recalled to serve the interests of social domination and, as Hobsbawm and Ranger (1983, p. 1) assert, can be invented in an attempt to establish continuity with a suitable historic past.
5. There have been counter-hegemony movements. Few have changed the sport form, but have attempted or are attempting to change the relations of social relations in sport. We can think of socialist inspired workers' games, gay games, Special Olympics, and the 'sports for all' movements. We can also

think about the institution of bills of rights for children and child-labour laws. The latter have been applied more to child actors than child athletes and have been more European in their enforcement. Moreover, the last few decades have seen the increased influence of player associations and unions in the collective bargaining process.

References

Baudrillard, J. (1983) *Simulations*, New York: Semiotext(e).

Berger, P. (1963) *Invitation to Sociology*, Garden City, NY: Anchor Books.

Berger, P. & Luckmann, T. (1966) *The Social Construction of Reality*, Garden City, NY: Anchor.

Betts, J. (1953) 'The Technological Revolution and the Rise of Sport, 1850–1900', *Mississippi Valley Historical Review*, XL: 231–256.

Brohm, J.-M. (1978) *Sport: a prison of measured time*, London: Ink Links.

Cantelon, H. (1981) 'High Performance Sport and the Child Athlete', in A. Ingham & E. Broom (eds) *Career Patterns and Career Contingencies in Sport*, Proceedings of the 1st Regional Symposium, International Committee for the Sociology of Sport, Vancouver, Canada.

Dahrendorf, R. (1979) *Life Chances*, Chicago: University of Chicago Press.

Donnelly, P. (1996) 'Prolympism', *Quest*, 48: 25–42.

Durkheim, E. (1995) *The Elementary Forms of Religious Life*, New York: Free Press.

Elias, N. & Dunning, E. (1966) 'Dynamics of Sport Groups with Special Reference to Football', *British Journal of Sociology*, 17: 388–401.

Erikson, E. (1963) *Childhood and Society*, New York: W.W. Norton.

Freud, S. (1960) *The Ego and the Id*, New York: W.W. Norton.

Freud, S. (1961) *Civilization and its Discontents*, New York: W.W. Norton.

Giddens, A. (1973) *The Class Structure of Advanced Societies*, New York: Harper & Row.

Gramsci, A. (1971) *Selections from the Prison Notebooks*, New York: International Publishers.

Gruneau, R. (1983) *Class, Sports, and Social Development*, Amherst, MA: University of Massachusetts Press.

Hill, R. (1983) 'Crisis in the Motor City', in S. Fainstein, N. Fainstein, R. Hill, D. Judd & M. Smith (eds) *Restructuring the City*, New York: Longman.

Hoberman, J. (1992) *Mortal Engines*, New York: Free Press.

Hobsbawm, E. (1968) *Industry and Empire*, Baltimore, MD: Penguin Books.

Hobsbawm, E. & Ranger, T. (eds) (1983) *The Invention of Tradition*, Cambridge: Cambridge University Press.

Horkheimer, M. & Adorno, T. (1972) *Dialectic of Enlightenment*, New York: The Seabury Press.

Hughes, H. (1958) *Consciousness and Society*, New York: Random House.

Ingham, A. (1978) *American Sport in Transition*, unpublished doctoral dissertation, University of Massachusetts.

Ingham, A. & Beamish, R. (1993) 'The Industrialization of the United States and the "Bourgeoisification" of Sport', in E. Dunning, J. Maguire & R. Pearton (eds) *The Sports Process*, Champaign, IL: Human Kinetics.

Ingham, A. & Loy, J. (1973) 'The Social System of Sport: a humanistic perspective', *Quest*, 19: 3–23.

Ingham, A., Blissmer, B. & Davidson, K. (1999) 'The Expendable Prolympic Self', *Sociology of Sport Journal*, 16: 236–268.
Ingham, A., Howell, J. & Schilperoort, T. (1987) 'Professional Sports and Community', *Exercise and Sport Sciences Reviews*, 15: 427–465.
Ingham, A., Chase, M. & Butt, J. (2002) 'From the Performance Principle to the Developmental Principle: Every Kid a Winner?', *Quest*, 54: 308–331.
Jennings, A. (1996) *The New Lords of the Rings*, London: Pocket Books.
Kerckhoff, A. (1976) 'The Status Attainment Process', *Social Forces*, 55: 365–381.
Kohut, H. (1977) *The Restoration of the Self*, Madison, WI: International Universities.
Leonard, W. (1996) 'The Odds of Transiting from One Level of Sports Participation to Another', *Sociology of Sport Journal*, 13: 288–299.
Loy, J. (1968) 'The Nature of Sport: a definitional effort', *Quest*, 10: 1–15.
Mandel, E. (1970) *An Introduction to Marxist Economic Theory*, New York: Pathfinder Press.
Marcuse, H. (1966) *Eros and Civilization*, Boston: Beacon Press.
Marx, K. (1967) *Capital* (Vol. 1), New York: International Publishers.
Masculinity', in M. Messner & D. Sabo (eds) *Sport, Men, and the Gender Order*, Champaign, IL: Human Kinetics.
Mead, G. (1934) *Mind, Self, and Society*, Chicago: University of Chicago Press.
Piaget, J. (1965) *The Moral Judgement of the Child*, New York: Free Press.
Sabo, D. & Panepinto, J. (1990) 'Football Ritual and the Social Reproduction of Masculinity', in M. Messner and D. Sabo (eds) *Sport, Men, and the Gender Order*, Champaign, ILL: Human Kinetics.
Simmel, G. (1950) *The Sociology of Georg Simmel*, New York: Free Press.
Simson, V. & Jennings, A. (1992) *The Lords of the Rings*, New York: Simon & Schuster.
Slowikowski, C. & Loy J. (1993) 'Ancient Athletic Motifs and the Modern Olympic Games', in A. Ingham & J. Loy (eds) *Sport in Social Development*, Champaign, IL: Human Kinetics.
Stone, G. (1971) 'American Sports: play and display', in E. Dunning (ed.) *The Sociology of Sport*, London: Frank Cass.
Turner, V. (1969) *The Ritual Process*, Chicago: Aldine.
Turner, V. (1974) *Dramas, Fields, and Metaphors*, Ithaca, NY: Cornell University Press.
Voy, R. (1993) *Drugs, Sport, and Politics*, Champaign, IL: Leisure Press.
Weber, M. (1946) 'Bureaucracy', in H. Gerth & C. Mills (eds) *From Max Weber*, New York: Oxford University Press.
Weber, M. (1958) *The Protestant Ethic and the Spirit of Capitalism*, New York: Charles Scribner's Sons.
Weber, M. (1978) *Economy & Society*, Berkeley, CA: University of Berkeley Press.
Weeks, J. (1981) *Capital and Exploitation*, Princeton: Princeton University Press.
Williams, R. (1977) *Marxism and Literature*, New York: Oxford University Press.
Wrong, D. (1961) 'The Oversocialized Conception of Man in Modern Sociology', *American Sociological Review*, 16: 183–193.
Wrong, D. (ed.) (1970) *Max Weber*, Englewood Cliffs, NJ: Prentice-Hall.

2

Social Structure and Social Theory: The Intellectual Insights of Robert K. Merton

John Loy and Douglas Booth

Many sociologists argue that "structural-functionalism" was the dominant theoretical perspective in sociology between the late 1930s and the early 1960s, especially in North America. From the perspective of sport sociology, Jarvie and Maguire contend that structural-functionalism "played a key part in the early development of the sociology of sport in North America and on both sides of what was then the European 'iron curtain'" (1994, p. 5). Although the degree of dominance of structural-functionalism in general sociology and sport sociology is a moot matter (see Loy & Booth, 2000a), there is no doubt that Robert K. Merton and Talcott Parsons were the twin theoretical towers of structural-functionalism.

However, it is also evident that structural-functionalism in general, and Merton's form in particular, had little impact on general sociology or sport sociology during the last quarter of the twentieth century. A cursory glance of articles published in the last two decades in the *Sociology of Sport Journal* and the *International Review for the Sociology of Sport* reveals few residuals of the functionalist tradition still in existence.

Yet, if the present generation of sociologists consider Merton's approach unfashionable, we maintain that key aspects of his theoretical perspectives remain relevant for the sociological analysis of sport. In this chapter we trace the development of Merton's career, including his two main theoretical orientations, and attempt to illustrate the import of his intellectual insights for the study of sport.

Intellectual biography[1]

The second of two children of Eastern European immigrants, Robert Merton was born on 5 July 1910 and raised in a South Philadelphia slum. As a young boy he developed an obsessive hunger for learning; by age eight Merton was a regular visitor to his neighbourhood public library. Graduating from South Philadelphia High School in 1927, he won a scholarship to Temple University to pursue a Bachelor of Arts degree. He intended majoring in philosophy but transferred to sociology in his sophomore year after completing an introductory course taught by George E. Simpson. Describing his conversion, Merton attributed it to "the joy of discovering that it is possible to examine human behavior objectively and without using loaded moral preconceptions" (Hunt, 1961, p. 55).

In 1931 Merton received a graduate fellowship at Harvard. His major intellectual influences there were Pitirim Sorokin, Talcott Parsons, George Sarton and L.J. Henderson. As a graduate student, he published in several scholarly journals including the *Quarterly Journal of Economics*, *American Journal of Sociology*, *American Sociological Review*, *Isis* and *Osiris*. After completing his dissertation in 1935 on science, technology and society in seventeenth-century England (1938a), Merton continued to work as an instructor at Harvard. But it was his essay "Social Structure and Anomie" (1938b), a systematic formalization of Durkheim's theory of *anomie* (the breakdown of social standards leading to a lack of cohesion and solidarity within a society), published in the *American Sociological Review* in 1938, that catapulted Merton's career.

From 1939 to 1941 Merton taught at Tulane University. He was appointed to the rank of Associate Professor and then promoted to Professor, and served as chairman of the Department of Sociology. In 1941 he accepted an appointment as Assistant Professor in the Department of Sociology at Columbia University. Although he took a great reduction in academic rank in moving to Columbia University, his promotion was rapid: Merton became an Associate Professor in 1944 and a Full Professor in 1947. He was made head of department in 1961 and appointed Franklin Henry Giddings Professor of Sociology in 1963. In 1974 Columbia University bestowed on him the distinguished title of University Professor, a title shared by only three other faculty members at Columbia University at the time (Clark *et al.*, 1990, p. 447).[2] Robert King Merton died on 23 February 2003. He served as President of the American Sociological Association in 1957 and was awarded the National Medal of Science by the President of the United States in 1994. There is little doubt that he was one of the truly influential social scientists of the twentieth century. For example, "at the time of his death, Merton's own writings had been cited in more than 17,500 published pieces" (Brickley, 2003).

Merton made substantive theoretical and empirical contributions to a variety of areas, including the sociology of knowledge, sociology of science, reference group theory, organizational sociology, the sociology of deviant behaviour and the sociology of time. Perhaps most significantly, Merton's careful and considered scholarship and involvement in the development of sociology as a discipline places him on equal footing with leading social theorists past and present. Stinchcombe, for example, ranks Merton with Durkheim, Marx, and Trotsky as a classical writer (1968, p. vii). He also believes that "of all [the] contemporary theorists of social structure, Merton has had the greatest impact on empirical research" (1975, p. 11).

Merton's two main theoretical perspectives

Throughout his career Merton studied social structure. Initially he approached it from the viewpoint of functional analysis but in the latter stages of his career he adopted structural analysis. In this section we highlight the main features of his two perspectives of social structure.

Functional analysis

Merton's form of functionalism grew from his attempt to codify the many existing varieties of functional analysis. He believed that functionalism had "developed on [too] many intellectual fronts" and "grown in shreds and patches rather than in depth" (1957, p. 19). Merton commenced the task of codification by dissecting the prevailing postulates of functional analysis developed in anthropology by Emile Durkheim (Loy & Booth, 2000b), A.R. Radcliffe-Brown (1952) and Bronislaw Malinowski (1945). According to Merton, anthropological forms of functionalism rested on three erroneous postulates: "first, that standardized social activities or cultural items are functional for the *entire* social or cultural system; second, that *all* such social and cultural items fulfil sociological functions; and third, that these items are consequently *indispensable*" (1957, p. 25). Further, Merton (1957, p. 36) noted that the three postulates, individually and collectively, contain the source of "the common charge that functional analysis inevitably involves certain ideological commitments".

In rejecting these postulates, however, Merton did not "throw the baby out with the bathwater". Rather, he developed a paradigm for what he viewed as tenable functional analyses. A crucial, and enduring, element of Merton's paradigm was his distinction between "manifest" and "latent" functions and his subsequent discussion of the heuristic purposes of the latter. Merton (1957, p. 63) defines manifest functions as "those objective consequences for a specified unit (person, subgroup, social or cultural system) which contribute to its adjustment or adaptation and were so intended", and latent functions as the "unintended and unrecognized consequences of the same order". The distinction Merton (1957, pp. 60–61) maintains is essential "to preclude the inadvertent confusion often found in the sociological literature, between conscious *motivations* for social behavior and its *objective consequences*".[3]

Merton developed his functionalist paradigm over three decades (Merton, 1949, 1957, 1968). But "at some point between 1968...and 1975, Merton shed his 'functional analyst' label to become a 'structural analyst'" (Crothers, 1987, pp. 76–77).[4]

Structural analysis

Merton's first published use of the term "structural analysis" appears in a 1972 paper titled "Insiders vs. Outsiders: A Chapter in the Sociology of Knowledge". But his major explication of this theoretical perspective is contained in his 1975 essay "Structural Analysis in Sociology". In this publication he outlines the main features of his position by way of 14 stipulations. Within this set of tenets he notes the confluence of elements of Durkheim and Marx, and recognizes the need to span the micro and macro levels of analysis. He also points out that social structures generate social conflict, that they generate differing rates of deviant behaviour, and that they generate "both change within the structure and change of the structure" (p. 35).[5] Unfortunately, notwithstanding these specific stipulations, "Merton devotes little space to detailing this approach and gives no examples – in very considerable contrast to the vigour of his earlier essay on functional analysis" (Crothers, 1987, p. 78). Indeed, Giddens (1990, p. 100) notes that "it has been left to Merton's interpreters and followers to provide a more thoroughgoing explication of structural analysis than Merton himself has given".[6] In turn, his interpreters continue to debate the presence of a latent general theory of social structure in Merton's writings.

Middle range theory vs general theory

Merton is famous for fostering the idea of "theories of the middle range". These are theories which "are close enough to observed data to be incorporated in propositions that permit empirical testing" and which "deal with delimited aspects of social phenomena, as is indicated by their labels". So, for example, "one speaks of a theory of reference groups, of social mobility, or role-conflict and of the formation of norms just as one speaks of a theory of prices, a germ theory of disease, or a kinetic theory of gases" (Merton, 1968, p. 39). Merton's emphasis on theories of the middle range presaged C. Wright Mills' (1959) criticism of the twin evils of sociology: grand abstract theory and raw empiricism associated with microscopic or survey research.

Notwithstanding its corrective emphasis, some have questioned the logic of Merton's conception of the middle range. Willer (1967) takes Merton to task for implying that sociologists should strive for a "middling level of generality". While applauding Merton's emphasis on empirically testable theories, Willer contends that high levels of generality are perfectly consistent with theories of the middle range. Similarly, Stinchcombe (1975) points to what he calls the confusion between "generality" and "woolliness". "In taking the correct position on wool-liness", Merton has, he says, "tricked himself into taking up the incorrect position on general theory. The situation is precisely the opposite" (pp. 26–27). Boudon (1977) agrees with Stinchcombe, arguing that "there is more systematic and general theory in Merton's work than he himself has ever confessed" (p. 1356).

Stinchcombe (1975, 1990), Sztompka (1986, 1990) and Crothers (1987) all identify key components and dimensions of Merton's general theory of social structure. While spatial limitations preclude a full synopsis or synthesis of these elaborations on Merton's systematic theorizing, here we briefly highlight the main features of Merton's latent theory of social structure as described by these three interpreters.

Merton's latent general theory of social structure

Sztompka (1990, p. 56) identifies "four determining criteria" in Merton's variant of structural analysis: (1) a "focus on relations linking various components of society"; (2) an "emphasis on the patterned, regular, repetitive character of relations"; (3) the idea of "deep, hidden underlying" structural characteristics of social systems; and (4) "the idea of constraining or facilitating influences exerted by social structure on actual social phenomena (behaviours, beliefs, attitudes, motivations, etc.)". Crothers (1987, p. 101) divides Merton's conceptions of social structure into two levels: "the larger social structure (for example, the class or political structure of a society); and the social milieu (the patterns of interpersonal relations in which individuals are directly involved)". Lastly, Stinchcombe (1990, p. 81) recognizes a core process in Merton's theory of social structure, namely, "the choice between socially structured alternatives".

"The core variable to be explained", according to Stinchcombe, "is different rates of choice by people differently located in the social order".

In his interpretation of the core process and core variable in Merton's theory of social structure, Stinchcombe (1975) constructs a two-way causal chain. On the one hand, individual choice of structurally patterned alternatives is affected by general parameters of social structure. Specifically, Stinchcombe suggests that institutional structures influence individual rates of choice through structurally induced motives, structural governance of information, and structural patterns of sanctioning power. On the other hand, general parameters of social structure are affected by the frequency of choices by individuals in particular social positions.

We believe that Merton's theory of social structure has significant potential for the sociology of sport. To illustrate this potential, we apply the main features of Merton's theory as sketched above by Sztompka, Crothers and Stinchcombe to an examination of the socio-historical patterns of racial integration in North American sports, especially professional team sports during the last half of the twentieth century.

Merton's theory of social structure applied to sport

In brief, we show on the one hand how institutional patterns of social structure govern the choices minority group members make with respect to sport participation; and on the other hand we show how their choices affect the transformation of institutional patterns of social structure, especially the occupational structures of professional team sports.

Structural determinants of variations in patterns of choice

Sociology of sport research shows that for any given historical period, both the degree and rate of racial integration varies by type of sport, level of competition within a given sport, and specific playing and leadership positions within particular sports. Moreover, the degree and rate of racial integration is a function of the frequency of choices between socially structured alternatives.

Blalock's (1962) set of thirteen theoretical propositions concerning occupational discrimination offers an excellent summary of how the career choices of minority athletes in professional sports are socially structured. For example, Blalock hypotheses that low degrees of occupational discrimination are a function of: (a) "the greater the importance of high individual performance to the productivity of the work group";

(b) "the greater the competition among employers for persons with high performance levels"; and (c) "easier it is accurately to evaluate an individual's performance level" (pp. 245–246). We believe that Blalock's total set of propositions provides a substantive structural analysis and a convincing sociological explanation for: first, the over-representation of blacks in professional sport relative to other occupations; secondly, for the over-representation of blacks in specific sports and playing positions; and, thirdly, their under-representation in other sports and playing positions.[7]

Proportional representation of blacks in North American sports

African-American athletes have dominated many weight classes in amateur and professional boxing since the turn of the twentieth century, the sprinting and jumping events in track and field since the 1930s, and all ranks and levels of basketball since the 1970s. Significantly, in terms of Blalock's propositions eight and eleven, these sports emphasize the "importance of high individual performance" and, in addition, they are sports where it is relatively difficult for officials "to prevent minority members from acquiring the necessary skills for high performance". For example, innate abilities, rather than carefully nurtured skills, largely determine one's ability to fight, run, jump or throw a ball through a hoop; and individuals with these skills do not necessarily need access to top class coaches and expensive facilities.

Of course, there are many sports, both amateur and professional wherein African-American athletes are very much in the minority, as for example, golf, gymnastics, skiing, swimming and tennis. Significantly, these sports require prolonged and expensive training. But equally importantly, they involve a high degree of social interaction, both across genders and with individuals who possess large amounts of social and cultural capital (see propositions twelve and thirteen). Their class positions typically deny most black athletes the opportunity for such interaction.

In a national context, given that African-Americans comprise only 13 per cent of the American population, it is significant that in 1998 more than 80 per cent of the players in the National Basketball Association (NBA) and 68 per cent of the players in the National Football League (NFL) were African-Americans. It is also noteworthy that in the inaugural season of the two women's professional basketball leagues (American Basketball League, 1996 and Women's National Basketball Association, 1997) more than 75 per cent of the players were African-American (Sage, 1998, p. 91). Although African-Americans made up only 17 per cent of major league baseball players in 1997, they have been "a dispro-portionate offensive force, winning 41 per cent of Most Valuable Player awards" (Early, 1998, p. 14). In short, it is difficult to think of any other occupational sector so dominated by African-Americans. While all of Blalock's theoretical propositions concerning occupational discrim-ination offer convincing "structural reasons" to explain this conspicuous over-representation and achievement, here we single out propositions three and four: professional sports are highly competitive situations wherein individual performance can be readily evaluated and where high individual performance works to the advantage of all group members.

Over-representation of blacks in particular playing positions

Ever since the initial breakdown of racial barriers in American team sports in the late 1940s and early 1950s, African-American athletes have been over-represented at certain playing positions and under-represented at others. Sport sociologists call this phenomenon of positional segregation "stacking". Loy and McElvogue (1970) conducted the first empirical study of "stacking" some thirty years ago. Drawing upon Blalock's propositions they hypothesized that racial segregation in professional team sports is positively related to centrality. They found that in 1968 only 6 per cent of African-American athletes occupied central positions in professional football, on either offensive teams (centres, guards and tacklers) or defensive teams (linebackers); they also discovered that in 1967, African-American athletes occupied 65 per cent of the noncentral positions (i.e. outfield positions) in professional baseball. Dozens of research studies since 1970 have confirmed the "stacking" phenomenon in professional team sports (see Eitzen, 1989; Schneider & Eitzen, 1989; Snyder & Spreitzer, 1989). Although a number of alternative theoretical explanations have been proposed to explain "stacking" (see McPherson *et al.*, 1989, pp. 201–204), it remains true that, in terms of social structure *per se*, non-central positions are typically those that can be most readily and objectively evaluated, demand the lowest degree of task and social interaction, and involve the least leadership behaviour – and thus do not result in the player exerting power over other team members (see propositions six to ten).

In summary, racial integration in North American professional sports and Blalock's thirteen theoretical propositions about occupational discrimination illustrate the core process in Merton's theory of social structure, namely, the rates of choice that social agents make between socially structured alternatives.

Structural consequences of patterns of choice

Here we highlight how individuals' choices have intended and unintended consequences for the maintenance and transformation of institutional structures.

Manifest functions and intended consequences

When major league professional baseball teams banned African-American players in the late nineteenth century, little did they suspect that black baseball players would organize their own highly successful teams and leagues (Petersen, 1992). In the aftermath of the Second World War, major league professional baseball reconsidered its policy towards the recruitment of African-American players. In short, the recruitment of black athletes in the late 1940s and early 1950s was a conscious strategy on the part of team owners in major league professional baseball to capitalize on the talent of black players and to entice the growing numbers of black spectators away from the existent successful black leagues (Blalock, 1962, p. 242).

The competition for high-calibre players was fierce in this climate. Moreover, both leagues expanded to the West Coast following the war. The adding of California teams was significant because blacks were starring in college football there, especially at University of California, Los Angeles (UCLA).

Later, with the merger and/or expansion of professional leagues in baseball, basketball and football in the late 1950s and early 1960s, the demand for skilled athletic talent was such that it outstripped the talent pool of white athletes and forced professional franchises to hire black athletes. Another "positive advantage" for black athletes, to adopt Blalock's (1962) terminology, was the fact that they were typically willing to work for lower wages than white athletes (as, for example, signing non-bonus contracts).

Thus history shows that the manifest and intended strategy of recruiting and employing African-American athletes in professional team sports led to highly successful sport franchises in professional baseball, basketball and football. But the latent functions, or unintended consequences, of the rates of structurally patterned choices among African-American athletes are equally interesting.

Unintended consequences

First and foremost, there is little doubt that the over-representation of African-American athletes in professional team sports, especially basketball and football, is an unintended consequence. Historically, most sport franchises were less than keen to recruit minority athletes and likely preferred to employ only a small token minority. For example, Early (1998, p. 14) claims that Branch Rickey, the general manager of the Brooklyn Dodgers, who hired Jackie Robinson as the first black player in major league baseball in 1947 did so precisely because he knew that Robinson had become familiar with the world of white athletes while competing in football and baseball at UCLA.

Upon the initial lowering of the racial barrier in professional team sports, most sport franchises effectively embraced a "quota system" with teams employing only a small token minority labor force. However, for a variety of structural reasons, outlined by Blalock (1962), within a couple of decades African-American athletes have come to dominate professional basketball and football and have had enormous impact in professional baseball at the player level. An unintended consequence of racial integration reaching the saturation point is increased demands on the part of minority athletes for equal pay for equal ability, comparable bonus and endorsement contracts, and increased pressure for minority team members to be employed in leadership positions such as coaches and managers.

When team officials first employed blacks they did not anticipate that African-Americans would make such demands and in-roads (now including team ownership in the case of professional basketball). The degree to which these demands have been met varies markedly among professional baseball, basketball and football franchises. For example, in 1998 only three head coaches in the NFL were African-Americans, and only one general manager in major league baseball was black. Professional basketball has fared better, with as many as seven African-American head coaches at one time; but this is in a league where more than 80 per cent of players are African-American (Sage, 1998, p. 95).

Dysfunctional consequences

Although the majority of unintended consequences have been favourable with respect to reducing racial discrimination and enhancing the financial status of sport franchises, there are at least two negative or dysfunctional unintended consequences with respect to what Stinchcombe calls "structural patterns of individual risk" (1975, pp. 25–26). First, outstanding African-American athletes in professional team sports inadvertently serve as role models and as such they raise unrealistic expectations among black youth in terms of future careers as highly paid professional athletes. Leonard (1996, p. 296) demonstrates just how unrealistic these expectations are. He calculates the odds of African-American males attaining professional status in football as .0001, baseball .00002, and basketball .00005.

Lastly, we refer to anecdotal evidence that suggests that the dominance of African-Americans in selected sports at all levels, and especially basketball, has convinced at least some potential white athletes that they are unlikely to succeed against their black peers. Thus they opt for alternative pursuits. We cite this as a case of Merton's concept of a 'self-fulfilling prophecy' (1957).

Conclusion

Suffice to say we believe that Merton's variant of structural analysis is worthy of consideration. As Stinchcombe (1975, p. 11) has remarked, the "logical and substantive character of Merton's theories distinguishes him from almost all other contemporary currents of social theory". From our perspective the strength of Merton's form of structural analysis is twofold. First, he draws upon the classical work of Durkheim and Marx from the late-nineteenth century; secondly, he points to the key dimensions of sociological analysis that must be incorporated into substantive theories of the twenty-first century.

His blend of intellectual insights from Durkheim and Marx goes far to resolve the consensus–conflict debate among social theorists (see Bernard, 1983).[8] And his theoretical perspective in varying degrees incorporates the positional, dispositional and interactive-situational dimensions that Mouzelis (1995) contends are required for fully adequate social theories. In his reference to the nature of social games, Mouzelis (1995, p. 136) provides a good summary of the differences among these three dimensions:

> The first pertains to norms or rules as a set of potentialities or possibilities of rule-governed conduct; the second refers to the instantiation and realization of such rules in actual, situationally specific actions and interactions. Finally, as Bourdieu points out, human beings are able to play games because they carry within them a set of dispositions, a set of generative schemata of action, perception and evaluation.

In short, "the three dimensions (positional, dispositional and interactive-situational) are mutually complementary, but each has its own relatively autonomous logic and dynamic" (Mouzelis, 1995, p. 137).

Although Merton is not as explicit as Mouzelis, pertinent examples of each of these key dimensions of social games can be found throughout his writings. Given Merton's focus on social structure, it is not surprising that he assigns the *positional dimension* greatest priority in his social analyses. This is most evident in Merton's contributions to reference group theory (1957, pp. 225–386) wherein he develops his concepts of status-sets, role-sets, and status-sequences.

The *dispositional dimension* appears in Merton's discussions of socially patterned character development, as for example, in his analyses of "bureaucratic structure and personality" (1957, pp. 195–206) and "local and cosmopolitan influentials" (1957, pp. 387–420). As Stinchcombe (1975, p. 26) notes, it is not simply that an individual responds to the normal role expectations of a position, rather the individual brings a set of dispositions to that position and, moreover, acquires more dispositions through repetitive adaptations to their situation.

Last but not least, as Stinchcombe (1975, p. 14) points out: "the core process of structured alternatives owes a great deal (explicitly acknowledged) to the W.I. Thomas–G.H. Mead analysis of definitions of situations and self-conceptions". This is clearly seen in Merton's treatment of the W.I. Thomas Theorem in relation to "the self-fulfilling prophecy" (1957, pp. 421–436). As Merton ironically observes, "the self-fulfilling prophecy is, in the beginning, a *false* definition of the situation evoking a new behavior which makes the originally false conception come *true*" (1957, p. 423).

In summary, Merton's writings reveal and reflect the key three dimensions identified by Mouzelis (1995). Indeed, Mouzelis himself locates Merton at the centre of the contemporary sociological project, contending that "in addition to the strategic, grand theorizing of Parsons and Giddens, we are urgently in need today of more tactical, modest theorizing such as developed by Merton, Gouldner and Lockwood" (1995, p. 152). By "modest" Mouzelis does not mean "middle range", but "the elaboration of interrelated concepts which, rather than offering a global map, are useful for reducing distorted communication and asking interesting empirical questions on specific problem areas" (1995, p. 152).

Notes

1. For further details see, Clark *et al.* (1990), Coser (1975), Crothers (1987), Hunt (1961), Sztompka (1986).
2. Few honours escaped Merton. At least twenty universities granted him honorary degrees, including Yale, Chicago, Harvard and Oxford and scholarly organizations awarded him a variety of prestigious prizes, including the American

Academy of Arts and Sciences (Talcott Parsons Prize for Social Science), the American Sociological Association (Commonwealth Award and Distinguished Career Scholarship), and the MacArthur Foundation (MacArthur Prize). In 1995 he received the National Medal of Science, the highest scientific honour awarded in the United States. Merton was the first sociologist to win the award.

3. Giddens (1990, p. 12) believes that Merton "provides perhaps the classical discussion...of the unintended consequences of intentional conduct." A good example of Merton's concept of latent function is found in his theory of *anomie*. For examples of the application of anomie to involvement in sport, and drug abuse in sport, see Loy (1969) and Lüschen (1984) respectively.

4. Sztompka (1990) argues that the distinction between a functional and a structural analyst is overstated in Merton's case and that his two approaches are simply opposite sides of the same coin.

5. Merton shared his ongoing concern with structural analysis with his former colleague from Columbia University, Peter Blau in Blau & Merton (1981).

6. Neither Merton nor his interpreters attempt to distinguish his special form of structural analysis from other forms of structuralism. Admittedly, however, one confronts a minefield in trying to sort out the similarities and differences of the various forms of structural analysis and/or structuralism within the sociological tradition. Wallace (1969) distinguishes among functional structuralism, exchange structuralism, and conflict structuralism; others speak of Marxist structuralism (Heydebrand, 1981) or structuralist Marxism (Gimenez, 1982); Alexander (1984) compares instrumental and normative forms of structural theory; still others discuss the structural sources of French structuralism (Sturrock, 1979; Clark & Clark, 1982); not to mention the special forms of structuralism found in the works of Jean Piaget and Noam Chomsky. And to compound matters further, there is much current sociological debate surrounding the topics of 'the duality of social structures, structuration, and the intentionality of human action' (Smith, 1983; Giddens, 1984; Archer, 1988; Mouzelis, 1989, 1995).

7. Later Blalock (1967) included these propositions in a formal theory of minority-group relationships. Interestingly, although not surprisingly given his interest in theory construction, Blalock (1990) also has a chapter in Clark *et al.*'s (1990) seminal text on Robert Merton wherein he highlights one of Merton's strengths, namely his emphasis on the interplay between social theory and empirical research.

8. For an earlier effort to reconcile functional and Marxian analysis see van den Berghe (1963).

References

Alexander, J. (1984) "Social-Structural Analysis", *Sociological Quarterly*, 25: 5–26.

Archer, M. (1988) *Culture and Agency*, Cambridge: Cambridge University Press.

Bernard, T. (1983) *The Consensus–Conflict Debate*, New York: Columbia University Press.

Blalock, H. (1962) "Occupational Discrimination", *Social Problems*, 9: 240–247.

Blalock, H. (1967) *Toward a Theory of Minority-Group Relations*, New York: John Wiley.

Blalock, H. (1990) "The Interplay of Social Theory and Empirical Research", in J. Clark, C. Modgil & S. Modgil (eds) *Robert K. Merton: Consensus and Controversy*, London: Falmer Press.

Blau, P.M. & Merton, R.K. (1981) *Continuities in Structural Inquiry*, London: Sage Publications.

Boudon, R. (1977) Review of L. Coser (ed.) "The Idea of Social Structure", *American Journal of Sociology*, 86: 1356–1361.

Brickley, P. (2003) "Robert Merton Dies", *The scientist.www.com*, http://www.biomedcentral.com/news/20030225/01

Clark, P.P. & Clark, T.N. (1982) "The Structural Sources of French Structuralism", in I. Rossi (ed.) *Structural Sociology*, New York: Columbia University Press.

Clark, J., Modgil, C. & Modgil, S. (1990) *Robert K. Merton: Consensus and Controversy*, London: Falmer Press.

Coser, L. (1975) "Robert K. Merton: The Man and His Work", in L. Coser (ed.) *The Idea of Social Structure: Papers in Honor of Robert K. Merton*, New York: Harcourt Brace Jovanovich.

Crothers, C. (1987) *Robert K. Merton*, London: Tavistock.

Early, G. (1998) "Performance and Reality: Race, Sports and the Modern World", *The Nation* (10–17 August): 11–20.

Eitzen, D.S. (1989) "Black Participation in American Sport Since World War II", in D.S. Eitzen (ed.) (3rd edition) *Sport in Contemporary Society*, New York: St Martin's Press.

Giddens, A. (1984) *The Constitution of Society*, Cambridge: Polity Press.

Giddens, A. (1990) "R.K. Merton on Structural Analysis", in J. Clark, C. Modgil & S. Modgil (eds) *Robert K. Merton: Consensus and Controversy*, London: Falmer Press.

Gimenez, M.E. (1982) "The Oppression of Women – A Structuralist Marxist View", in I. Rossi (ed.) *Structural Sociology*, New York: Columbia University Press.

Heydebrand, W.V. (1981) "Marxist Structuralism", in P.M. Blau & R.K. Merton (eds) *Continuities in Structural Inquiry*, London: Sage.

Hunt, M. (1961) "How Does It Come To Be So?" *The New Yorker* (28 January): pp. 39–59.

Jarvie, G. & Maguire, J. (1994) *Sport and Leisure in Social Thought*, London: Routledge.

Leonard, W. (1996) "The Odds of Transiting From One Level of Sports Participation to Another", *Sociology of Sport Journal*, 13, 3: 288–299.

Loy, J.W. (1969) "Game Forms, Social Structure, and Anomie', in R. Brown & B. Cratty (eds) *New Perspectives of Man in Action*, Englewood Cliffs, NJ: Prentice-Hall.

Loy, J.W. & Booth, D. (2000a) "Functionalism, Sport and Society", in E. Dunning & J. Coakley (eds), *The Handbook of Sport and Society*. London: Sage.

Loy, J.W. & Booth, D. (2000b) "Emile Durkheim", in J. Maguire & K. Young (eds) *Research in the Sociology of Sport*, London: JAI Press.

Loy, J.W. & McElvogue, J.F. (1970) "Racial Segregation in American Sport", *International Review for Sociology of Sport*, 7: 5–26.

Lüschen, G. (1984) "Before and After Caracas", in K. Olin (ed.) *Contribution of Sociology to the Study of Sport*, Jyvaskyla: University of Jyvaskyla.

Malinowski, B. (1945) *The Dynamics of Cultural Change*, New Haven, CT: Yale University Press.

McPherson, B., Curtis, J.E. & Loy, J.W. (1989) *The Social Significance of Sport*, Champaign, IL: Human Kinetics.

Merton, R.K. (1938a) "Science, Technology and Society in Seventeenth Century England", in G. Sarton (ed.) *Osiris*, Bruges, Belgium: St Catherine Press.

Merton, R.K. (1938b) "Social Structure and Anomie", *American Sociological Review*, 3: 672–682.

Merton, R.K. (1949) *Social Theory and Social Structure* (1st edition) Glencoe, IL: Free Press.

Merton, R.K. (1957) *Social Theory and Social Structure* (2nd edition) Glencoe, IL: Free Press.

Merton, R.K. (1968) *Social Theory and Social Structure* (3rd edition) Glencoe, IL: Free Press.

Merton, R.K. (1975) "Structural Analysis in Sociology", in P. Blau (ed.) *Approaches to the Study of Social Structure*, New York: Free Press.

Mills, C.W. (1959) *The Sociological Imagination*, Oxford: Oxford University Press.

Mouzelis, N. (1989) "Restructuring Structuration Theory", *Sociological Review*, 37: 613–635.

Mouzelis, N. (1995) *Sociological Theory What Went Wrong?* London: Routledge.

Petersen, R. (1992) *Only the Ball was White*, New York: Oxford University Press.

Radcliffe-Brown, A.R. (1952) *Structure and Function in Primitive Society*, Glencoe, IL: Free Press.

Sage, G. (1998) *Power and Ideology in American Sport* (2nd edition) Champaign, IL: Human Kinetics.

Schneider, J.J. & Eitzen, D.S. (1989) "The Perpetuation of Racial Segregation by Playing Position in Professional Football", in D.S. Eitzen (ed.), *Sport in Contemporary Society* (3rd edition) New York: St Martin's Press.

Smith C.W. (ed.) (1983) "Special Topic Papers: The Duality of Social Structures, Structuration, and the Intentionality of Human Action", *Journal for the Theory of Social Behavior*, 13(1): 1–95.

Snyder, E. & Spreitzer, E. (1989) *Social Aspects of Sport* (3rd edition) Englewood Cliffs, NJ: Prentice Hall.

Stinchcombe, A. (1968) *Constructing Social Theories*, New York: Harcourt, Brace and World.

Stinchcombe, A. (1975) "Merton's Theory of Social Structure", in L. Coser (ed.) *The Idea of Social Structure: Papers in Honor of Robert K. Merton*, New York: Harcourt Brace Jovanovich: 11–33.

Stinchcombe. A. (1990) "Social Structure in the Work of Robert Merton", in J. Clark, C. Modgil & S. Modgil (eds) *Robert K. Merton: Consensus and Controversy*, London: Falmer Press.

Sturrock, J. (ed.) (1979) *Structuralism and Since*, Oxford: Oxford University Press.

Sztompka, P. (1986) *Robert K. Merton*, New York: St Martin's Press.

Sztompka, P. (1990) "R.K. Merton's Theoretical System", in J. Clark, C. Modgil & S. Modgil (eds) *Robert K. Merton: Consensus and Controversy*, London: Falmer Press.

van den Berghe, P. (1963) "Dialectic and Functionalism", *American Sociological Review*, 28: 695–705.

Wallace, W.L. (ed.) (1969) *Sociological Theory*, Chicago: Aldine.

Willer, D. (1967) *Scientific Sociology – Theory and Method*, Englewood Cliffs, NJ: Prentice-Hall.

3
Reclaiming Goffman: Erving Goffman's Influence on the Sociology of Sport

Susan Birrell and Peter Donnelly

Erving Goffman was the consummate sociologist. Throughout our academic careers we had heard anecdotes about him, and when we started work on this chapter we sought out people who had known him. All their stories confirmed the ones we had heard – Goffman was always working, always observing, always making field notes. He is seen at 3:00 am in a Las Vegas hotel elevator, riding up and down, observing how people behave. Guests at a dinner party realize that he is no longer at the table – he is sitting in a corner taking notes. Although late for an appointment, he insists that his driver stop while he watches the public's response to a traffic accident. Lyman (cited by Smith, 1999, p. 18) noted Goffman's justification for this: 'sociology is something you do, not something you read about'.

With the appearance of his first book, Goffman (1959) not only announced his arrival as an important, if unorthodox social commentator, he also ushered in a new approach to sociology: a sociology of everyday life. He published 11 books, several of them still staples in undergraduate courses; most have never been out of print. He contributed to the fields of sociology, anthropology, social psychology, psychiatry, communication studies, and linguistics. His work is so accessible that he is one of the best known, and most widely read sociologists outside the academy.

Goffman was born in 1922, in Mannville, Alberta, Canada, as the second child of Ukrainian Jewish immigrant parents.[1] In 1939 he enrolled at the University of Manitoba as a Chemistry student, but left before completing the degree in order to work at the National Film Board in Ottawa, where John Grierson was developing the art of the documentary film as part of Canada's war effort. Dennis Wrong, who was also to become a well-known sociologist, also worked there, and persuaded

Goffman to join him in the Department of Political Economy at the University of Toronto where they studied sociology. He was influenced by one of his instructors, Ray Birdwhistell, and decided to pursue graduate studies at the University of Chicago – one of the best-known sociology departments in North America during the early 20th century.

Identifying the intellectual influences on Goffman is a difficult task, perhaps because his style of sociology was so different from anything that preceded it. However, a course at the University of Toronto that involved a close study of Durkheim's *Suicide*, the influence of several social anthropologists, and the University of Chicago's tradition of observational sociology, all left impressions on Goffman. His thesis supervisors Lloyd Warner, Everett Hughes, Anselm Strauss, and Herbert Blumer were leading American sociologists, and Blumer in particular was associated with the new approach of symbolic interactionism. The University of Chicago in the late 1940s was an exciting place to be for social scientists and visiting professors included Daniel Bell, Bruno Bettelheim, Kenneth Burke, C. Wright Mills, and David Riesman. However, as in most dynamic graduate programmes, peer influence is significant, and Goffman's 'circle of students' included Howard Becker, William and Ruth Kornhauser, Kurt and Gladys Lang, Bernard Meltzer, and Gregory Stone.[2]

Goffman received his Ph.D. in 1953, and went to work at the National Institutes of Mental Health in Bethesda, Maryland, where he carried out one year of fieldwork (claiming as his cover that he was 'an assistant to the athletic director') at St Elizabeth's, a 7000 bed psychiatric hospital in Washington, DC. *Asylums* (1961a) and *Stigma* (1963) are both grounded in his work there. He worked at the University of California, Berkeley, from 1957 to 1968 (where he supervised Scott's (1968) dissertation on the subculture of horse racing), and then moved to the University of Pennsylvania where he was named Benjamin Franklin Professor of Anthropology and Psychology. He died in 1982, at the age of 60, while President of the American Sociological Association.

In this chapter, we provide a brief outline of Goffman's theoretical approach and outline his contributions to the sociology of sport. We conclude by suggesting ways to reclaim Goffman's work for more critical analysis in the 21st century.

Goffman as theorist

Most researchers see Goffman as a generator of sensitizing concepts and insightful interactional principles rather than a social theorist. The significance of his sociology lies in his powers of observation and his ability to capture social life in particularly appropriate terms, such as 'impression management', 'role distance', and 'face-work'. Goffman's legacy is such that his work is not so much cited as taken for granted as a sort of sociological common sense.

Goffman's major substantive contribution to social analysis was his insistent focus on an overlooked aspect of social reality: the everyday, routine, and often trivial interactions that comprise the vast majority of social experience. In his attention to all forms of social encounters, Goffman argued that everyday interaction is the foundation of social order. As Goffman noted, 'My ultimate interest is to develop the study of face-to-face interaction as a naturally bounded, analytically coherent field – a sub-area of sociology' (1969, p. ix).

Goffman's model of the social order of interactions underpins all of his work. During his career he framed his insights within role theory (his famous dramaturgical model [1959]), game theory (his model of strategic interaction [1969]), and linguistic theory (the approach that underlay his final two books, [1974, 1981]), but his most familiar theoretical model is his dramaturgical model. A variation of social psychological role theory, Goffman's highly elaborated version furnishes a largely unacknowledged grounding for the move to performance theory and theories of performativity (Butler, 1993) so central to post-structuralist debates. Using the language of theatre, Goffman characterizes interactions as theatrical performances in which generally known 'scripts' for action are enacted by participants who take turns in their roles as actors and audiences. Actors are expected to have a large repertoire of roles from which to select the appropriate role for the situation, to present a creditable and idealized performance in that role, and to follow the normative script of the interaction. The audience must respond appropriately and appreciatively to the performances of others as they wait their own turn as actors. Within this metaphor, social life takes place in public, 'on stage', and in the even more interesting 'back stage' areas, the private areas where actors prepare for their performances by engaging in 'face work' or 'impression management' – the conscious act of maintaining the credibility of one's role.

Goffman's model of 'strategic interaction' uses games as the central metaphor for understanding the dynamics of interaction. This model is particularly applicable to the study of sport, where competitors enhance their competitive advantages through deception and misdirection. With the linguistic model that underlies his final work, Goffman (1974, 1981) provides a connection to discursive analyses being developed in several academic fields, including the sociology of sport. Regardless of the metaphor used, Goffman provides keen insights into the ways in which social order, and thus social hierarchy, is produced in everyday interactions through the work of committed social actors. All of his writing explores the rules that govern social encounters and the nuances of the interaction through which social order is produced and maintained. Most interactions are supportive, that is, actors work together to produce a smooth or 'supportive interaction'. They honour rules concerning the appropriate level of involvement, they guard against misunderstandings by sharing situation-relevant information, and they demonstrate appropriate respect for other actors. Honest threats to the social order, such as inept performances, too much 'role distance' (a disdainful detachment towards the role one is performing), 'flooding out' and other 'embarrassments' are met with 'remedial interactions' and attempts to restore order.

For Goffman, every interaction, no matter how apparently minor, is consequential: all interactions are important rituals that work to maintain moral order as well as social order. Acting out one's appropriate role in an encounter is not just about getting through the interaction without stumbling; more importantly, it is about honoring the role itself. Goffman (1967) outlines how properly observed rituals of deference (respect for others) and demeanour (respect for the role one is playing) maintain interactional order, and also reaffirm the moral order of interactions.

Failure to maintain smooth interaction – or worse, refusal to act in others' best interests – provides the opening for some of Goffman's more interesting analyses. One area of problematic interaction involves the socially stigmatized. In *Stigma* (1963), Goffman provides an analytical vocabulary for situations in which we do not grant to other individuals the deference they deserve. The best-known examples involve physical or mental conditions that are judged as visibly deviating from the norm. But analysis of stigmatization can also be used to understand the cultural treatment of members of unapproved groups such as women, people of colour, and the poor. At the other end of the spectrum, in contrast to the degradations aimed at stigmatized individuals, are interactions so positive and affirming that they work at a broader public level to confirm highly esteemed cultural values. Goffman's essay, 'Where the Action Is' (1967) develops these ideas around the cultural values of courage, integrity, gameness, and poise.

Finally, Goffman provides a model for understanding deception in social interactions. Because social actors generally assume that others also want to preserve the social order, they leave themselves open to manipulation by individuals who might subvert the agreements that sustain supportive interaction to use interactions strategically to gain advantage, such as by withholding or controlling important information or by disguising their identity. Some engage in 'strategic interaction' by constructing layers of 'containment' around their fellow participants so they will not see the real agenda or plan of action of the manipulator. Goffman (1969, 1974) provides a lively vocabulary to describe the variety of strategies and counter-strategies involved.

Strategic interaction is the very model for sport, where teams and athletes work to maintain their competitive advantage through deception, misdirection, feints, and dodges. As such, it provides a particularly clear example of the usefulness of Goffman's work to the study of sport. But, as we seek to indicate below, Goffman offers analytical entry into some rich conceptualizations of everyday life, and a vivid vocabulary that enriches our understandings of sport as a cultural form.

Erving Goffman and the sociology of sport

Goffman's presence was felt at the inception of the North American sociology of sport. In addition to his influence on Stone (1955), the essay that defined the sociology of sport (Loy, 1968) cited Goffman and several other analysts as having a potentially direct bearing on the field.[3] Sport scholars refer most frequently to Goffman's earlier work, which lays out his analytical model (1959), and which explores the concept of character (1967). Although Goffman has had limited *direct* influence on the sociology of sport, his *indirect* influence is widespread.

The usefulness of Goffman's dramaturgical perspective should be obvious since sport is both performance and competition (Stone, 1955). Sport clearly takes place in both the 'on stage' areas of the baseball diamond, basketball court, and soccer pitch, and the 'backstage' locker room and practice field. Indeed, the locker room's sanctity as a male, private staging area defines it as a quintessentially male space for the performance of male identities. A few sport studies have made use of Goffman's thesis that interactions work to establish social and moral order (Nixon, 1986; Muir, 1991).

Goffman's (1967) notions of deference and demeanour, and the way in which they may be manipulated in 'strategic interaction' (1969), underlie a small body of work regarding 'claims', 'credentialing', and 'trust'. Individuals work to have their claims (to be the person they purport to be, to have accomplished what they claim to have accomplished) accepted, particularly when such claims have to be taken on trust, at least for a period of time. 'Credentialing' among rock climbers, verification among rugby players, and verification and trust among both, show how claims are negotiated, manipulated, and exposed, in face-to-face interaction among actors (Donnelly, 1982, 1994; Donnelly & Young, 1988).

Goffman's concept of demeanor grounds his excursion into the study of character. The point that 'character is an exaggerated portrayal of demeanor' was reinforced by Birrell (1978, 1981, p. 365), who saw in Goffman's model an extension of Durkheim's ritual model. She explored Goffman's (1967) four motifs of character – courage, gameness, integrity, and composure – in the context of sport. Birrell and Turowetz (1979) explored Goffman's conceptualization of character tests in a comparative study of female gymnasts and professional wrestlers. Others who directly reference Goffman include Curry and Jiobu (1995) on sports gambling as an 'action' situation; Donnelly (2000b) and Frey (1991) on risk-taking; and Hughes and Coakley's (1991) important work on positive deviance or over-conformity to the sport ethic. Given the historical emphasis on sport as character building, it is surprising that more attention has not been paid to Goffman's interest in action situations.

Goffman's indirect influence has been most evident in studies of sport subcultures (Donnelly, 2000a). Initially, these studies used the idea of an individual's 'career' (from initial involvement to retirement) with special reference to Goffman's notion of the 'moral career' (Weinberg & Arond, 1952). Later studies examined wrestlers (Stone, 1972), horse racing (Scott, 1968), pool hustlers (Polsky, 1969), and international athletes (Stevenson, 1990). A strong tradition of studies of sport sub-cultures draws on more specific aspects of Goffman's work, focusing on identity (and its links to character), emotions, and roles (see Ball, 1976; Fine, 1987; Donnelly & Young, 1988; Snyder, 1994; Halbert, 1997).

Hart (1976) used Goffman's notion of stigma to explore how labelling women as inappropriate athletes helped to justify their exclusion from sport. The concept of stigma acknowledges the disproportionate power that individuals, differentially located in society, have to enact the presentation of their selves in certain settings. Stigma is an ideal concept for characterizing the state of gender relations in sport in the early 1960s. Hart's use of Goffman, and her acknowledgement of the social construction of identities, confirms her as one of the most sociological of early feminists in the sociology of sport, and indicated the potential of Goffman's work to ground more critical analyses.

With the exception of Birrell (1978), few sport sociologists have ventured beyond a type of 'analysis through labelling' to explore or test

Goffman's conceptual frameworks. In the following section, we argue that Goffman deserves renewed attention from sport studies scholars because his work connects in exciting ways with the new climate of critical cultural analysis that increasingly characterizes our field.

Reclaiming Goffman

No important scholar escapes critique and Goffman is no exception. The debates have focused on Goffman's methodologies, his position in the nexus between macro- and micro-sociologies, and his ideological perspective (Ditton, 1980; Winkin, 1988; Smith, 1999).

Early critics dismissed Goffman's methodology, suggesting that his work was unsystematic and unconventional, and that his style of writing was more that of an essayist than of a researcher. But few sociologists would advance the stylistic criticisms today. The increasing popularity of ethnographic methodologies, the move to discourse and textual analyses, the literary turn in the social sciences, and the emergence of case studies, life histories, narrative sociology, and other methods indicate that Goffman anticipated – or perhaps helped instigate – the removal of the methodological straightjacket of the past.

Critics have also found Goffman difficult to categorize theoretically. Marshall (1994) notes that, 'Sometimes he is seen as developing a distinct school of symbolic interactionism, sometimes as a formalist following in the tradition of Georg Simmel, and sometimes even as a functionalist of the micro-order, because of his concerns with the function of rituals (especially talk) in everyday life' (p. 204). His characterization as a micro-sociologist, and sometimes even as a psychologist, overly concerned with the minutiae of interactions, and with trivial matters (Gouldner, 1970), leads some to conclude he is not concerned with the macro-sociological concerns of power, social class, and social structure. Noting that Goffman accepted the criticism that he failed to address macro-concerns, Marshall (1994) summarizes his contribution as follows: 'He attempted ceaselessly to show that the interaction order was the bridge between the micro and the macro concerns of social life *and* sociology' (p. 204, emphasis added). Subsequent analyses of Goffman's work by those who represent critical perspectives (e.g. Birrell, 1981; Giddens, 1987) suggest that he made a significant contribution to the struggle to articulate micro- and macro-concerns (sometimes characterized as the 'agency–structure' debate). Studies in the sociology of sport which make the most comprehensive use of Goffman recognize that the details of social interaction were descriptively significant to the extent that they also shed light on macro-concerns.

The most troublesome criticism of Goffman for those hoping to reclaim him for critical analysis are the critiques of his ideological position. Gouldner (1970) has accused Goffman of being conservative, a sociologist of the middle class, and an apologist for capitalism (Gouldner, 1970). Others (Birrell, 1978; Gonos, 1980) disagree; Rogers (1980) argues that Goffman exposes the exercise of power, while Gonos suggests that, 'Goffman's work is a thorn in the side of bourgeois ideology' (Ditton, 1980, p. 3).

These critiques notwithstanding, given the critical and postmodern shifts that have occurred in the sociology of sport (see Ingham & Donnelly, 1997), we believe it is possible and desirable to reclaim Goffman as a relevant social theorist for sport, by connecting his inter-actionism with critical sociology, with discourse analysis, with feminist and other critical traditions, and with recent theories of performance and performativity.

Goffman's critical credentials in sociology were evident early in his career and had a widespread impact. Two works in particular, *Asylums* (1961a) and *Stigma* (1963), which examine the social construction of deviant identities, have explicit critical implications. Central to this is Goffman's concept of 'total institution' or 'any social organization (including prisons, mental institutions, monasteries, long-stay hospitals, boarding schools) in which the members are required to live out their lives in isolation from the wider society . . . [and] there is no possibility of any complete escape from the administrative rules or values which prevail' (Jary & Jary, 1995, p. 691). *Stigma* and *Asylums* gave rise to a wider critique of institutionalization and social control in the 1960s.[4] Goffman's insights are considered to have led to labeling theory which, in turn, led to a new deviancy theory in the UK in the early 1970s. For example, in a move that anticipates the critical cultural studies' move to Gramscian theories of hegemony and resistance, Goffman also documented – and celebrated – examples of inmate resistance at St Elizabeth's hospital. These latter steps, which combined the analysis of social interaction (labeling) with Marxist critical theory to consider the full political implications of labeling, clearly demonstrated the potential for making Goffman critical.

Ingham (1975) provides an early case for reclaiming Goffman's contribution to a critical sociology of sport, for the critical shift was just (in retrospect) becoming evident in North American sociology of sport (Ingham & Donnelly, 1997). Ingham's (1975) analysis of the occupational subcultures of athletes, which relied heavily on Goffman, articulated with the 'political economy' perspective on alienated labour in sport. Although Ingham carefully distances himself from what he considers Goffman's conservative ideology and his 'lack of concern with the transcendence of alienated existence' (p. 368), he found Goffman's concept of impression management a useful way to explore the effects of an athlete's socialization into the subculture of athletics and his/her performances for a variety of audiences in both front and back stage areas:

> The athlete is often confronted with a fundamental dilemma, whether to conform to the expectations of his peers [teammates], the expectations of the management, or the expectations of the public. Since each of these audiences may use different criteria for evaluation, the athlete becomes adept at the art of impression management. He is 'cool' for his peers, demeaned for the management, and dramatic for the fans. (p. 369)

Ingham's essay remains one of the best occupational analyses of athletes and, for our purposes, a powerful example of linking Goffman's analysis of social interaction to a much more critical analysis.

Unfortunately, such a combination of Goffman and critical theory did not reappear in the sociology of sport for almost twenty years. While working with William Julius Wilson at the University of Chicago on a study of 'the changing intersection of race, class, and state in the formation of the contemporary black subproletariat' (p. 223), Wacquant (1992) spent three years as a participant observer in a local boxing club. He found that the complex social world of the boxing club 'is created in connection with the social forces in the black ghetto and its masculine street culture, but it also shelters black men from the full destructive impact of those forces...[The experience] separated them from their peers and kept them alive as they tried to make sense out of life in dangerous neighborhoods devoid of hope or opportunity' (Coakley, 1998, p. 107). Wacquant employs a number of Goffman's concepts in his analysis of social interaction in the gym, again demonstrating the possibilities that result from linking interactionist and critical work.

Others have drawn looser connections between Goffman's work and more critical analyses. Hughes and Coakley (1991) hint that Goffman's concept of the 'total institution' might be usefully applied to sport. In many respects, from the closed (and close-knit) nature of the athletic world itself, to the total care environment experienced by (mainly professional) athletes (hotels, transportation, meals, etc., are all arranged for them), to the continual surveillance (by media, coaches, medical staff, the public, etc.) under which athletes find themselves, sport possesses many of the characteristics of a total institution. Our understanding of sport may benefit from such an analysis.

Goffman's later work, *Frame Analysis* (1974), *Gender Advertisments* (1979), and *Forms of Talk* (1981) anticipated the major shift in the sociology of sport in the 1990s towards media, textual, and discourse analyses. The earliest use of Goffman's concept of 'frames' focused on football hooliganism (Carroll, 1980); later studies examined the 1987 NFL strike (Schmitt, 1993) and the O.J. Simpson trial (McKay & Smith, 1995). This method of analysis is now so popular in sport studies that several anthologies showcase the approach (Birrell & McDonald, 2000; Andrews & Jackson, 2001).

Since one of the major justifications for sport participation has historically been its presumed character building qualities, it is surprising that so few sport scholars have engaged Goffman's (1967) work on action and character. Specifically, since Goffman's four elements of character – courage, gameness, integrity, and composure – can be seen as gendered, renewed attention to that framework might enrich critical feminist analyses on the production of gender ideologies and masculinities.

Courage and gameness are particularly implicated in the reproduction of masculinity. Courage and the implied risk-taking associated with it are culturally characteristic, more generally approved for males and may even be required as a test of masculinity. Displays of courage by women are sometimes met with more ambivalence. For example, when British mountaineer Alison Hargreaves was killed on K2, as a mother of young children, she was vilified in the media for taking such risks – a charge that has never publicly been laid against the fathers of young children. Likewise, gameness ('the capacity to stick to a line of activity and to continue to pour all effort into it regardless of set-backs, pain, or fatigue' [1961a, p. 219]), with its emphasis on toughness and bearing pain without complaint, has also traditionally been coded as a masculine attribute in North American culture. Research exploring the relations between risk, pain, injury and gender (Young & White, 1995), while affirming the masculine nature of gameness, has also identified this character attribute as increasingly salient in female athlete culture.

While integrity and composure appear less gendered, they also provide grounds for gendered performances in sport. In the past, when we still clung to the amateur ideal, athletes were expected to demonstrate fair play and integrity. As increasing commercialization of men's sports undercut that ideal, women's sport emerged as refreshingly immune. Recognition of stylistic differences in play between, for example, men's and women's basketball and ice hockey, prompted commentators to represent the culture and ethics of women's sports as salvation from the corruption and violence of men's sports. Others point out the double standards here, asking why this is a responsibility that belongs only to women, especially when men have profited so greatly from unsporting behaviour: 'It's not that women's athletic competition should turn into a blood sport, or that it's wrong to value cleaner, fairer, more principled play. But rather, women shouldn't be relegated to the ladies' auxiliary of men's sport – making less money and getting less attention, but proud in the knowledge that their play is uncorrupt' (Giese, 2000, p. 86). Finally, composure – 'self-control, self-possession, or poise' (1961a, p. 219), sometimes referred to as 'coolness' – is differently understood in men's and women's sport. Women are supposed to be poised, and some sports traditionally considered to be 'women's sports', such as gymnastics, figure skating, and diving, are designed to reward the performance of composure, tested in the most unnerving situations. While valued in men's sport, self-control is not necessarily expected, and displays of anger and losing one's cool, while punished, are understood as part of the natural exuberance of the male athlete. A more extended analysis of these contrasts would yield interesting insight into the continued gendering of sport performances.

Although Goffman would never have claimed the label of feminist for himself, some attempts to reclaim Goffman are evident in mainstream feminist sociology (Hochschild, 1990). Later in his career, he did examine gender relations through his principles of interaction in the essay 'The arrangement between the sexes' (1977) and in the visually rich *Gender Advertisements* (1979). Surprisingly, *Gender Advertisements* is not frequently cited in critical media analyses in sport, since it offers a catalogue of the methods through which the advertising world visually places women in subservience to men, and thus reproduces inequitable gender relations. Only Carlisle Duncan (1990) has built on this work, clearly seeing its usefulness for a ground-breaking analysis of sport photographs.

Hart's (1976) use of Goffman's concept of stigma has already been mentioned. Since the publication of *Stigma*, sociology has developed a much more sophisticated analysis of the politics of identity. Hart used the concept to theorize women as a marginalized group in sport, but it has clear utility for a critical analysis of other marginalized groups. For example, the US Golf Association's recent attempts to prevent a player with a disability from competing on the professional tour because he required a golf cart would clearly benefit from such an analysis, as would a more comprehensive view of sport for persons with a disability.

Finally, we note a clear line of theoretical development from the role theory of G.H. Mead, through Goffman's dramaturgical model, to the recent turn to performance studies and theories of performativity. In the first transition, Goffman's dramaturgical model moves away from more psychological models of role behaviour to a more sophisticated and stylized approach that locates role in a dynamic and complex cultural context marked by moral demands as well as social contingencies. Sport scholars would benefit from making that move with him.

For example, early attempts to explain women's low rates of involvement in sport focused on the notion of 'role conflict'. The role of athlete was presumed to conflict with a stereotypical notion of the 'feminine' role, producing debilitating conflict which kept women from sport. An analysis that built on Goffman's dramaturgical model, particularly his notions of 'role segregation', 'audience segregation', and that most felicitous of his phrases, 'the simultaneous multiplicity of selves' (1961b, p. 139), might have replaced this static version of social role-taking with a culturally situated approach that conceptualized identities as created and re-created in interaction with others. Furthermore, Goffman's concept of 'role distance'(1961b) might have injected a stronger sense of agency in this dynamic by replacing these debilitated would-be women athletes with more active cultural agents who could deploy role distancing techniques to solve the problem of different role expectations.

Perhaps most exciting is the recent rekindled interest in theories of performance and performativity. Although Goffman is generally a silent partner here, we see a clear connection, and some sport scholars have begun to work this rich vein for insight. As if responding directly to the limitations of earlier role conflict theories, Messner (2002) specifically invokes Goffman's dramaturgical perspective as the basis for his recent analysis of sport as a gendered practice. For Messner, the strength of the performance model is that it conceptualizes gender 'not as some "thing" that one "has" (or not), but rather as situationally constructed through the performances of active agents. The idea of gender-as-performance analytically foregrounds the agency of people in the construction of gender, thus highlighting the situational fluidity of gender...' (pp. 6–7). Rinehart (1998) is even more explicit in his recognition of performance as the central metaphor for sport in current analyses. Although he does not invoke Goffman, his introductory chapter on 'sport as performance' clearly draws on that tradition before extending the focus by conceptualizing sport as 'performance art' (p. 6).

But the most provocative theoretical connection might be forged by turning to the enormously influential work of Judith Butler (1993). Butler views gender as 'a cultural fiction, a performative effect of reiterative acts' (Jagose, 1996, p. 84). But as a discursive production, gender is also available for deconstructive resistant action. Performative disruptions such as parody – Butler's primary example is drag – deconstruct the common sense of the sex/gender/sexuality system by calling attention to the performativity of all gender enactments. In Butler's complex theory we see a much more sophisticated, post-modern version of a politics of performance that underlies Goffman's theories of interaction, particularly the idealizing imperatives of the performance ritual that make it available for manipulation, resistance, and disruption through strategic interaction. Closer attention to Butler on performativity might help us understand sport as both a gendered performance and an engendering performance.

Conclusion

A new trend is emerging in sociology – the insights of past theorists are being revisited to shed light on current research issues, and a number of sociological fields such as medical sociology and the sociology of gender are revisiting Erving Goffman. After assessing Goffman's contributions to the sociology of sport, we have attempted to show how Goffman may be overlain with more critical insights in order to add to our understanding of sport as a social phenomenon. Given the type of critical overlay we have advocated, the interaction order might take its place alongside the gender order as a significant element of analysis in the sociology of sport. As Schegloff noted, 'we have undoubtedly not yet finished learning from the work which [Goffman] has left us' (1988, p. 89).

Notes

1. Biographical information is primarily from Winkin (1988, 1999).
2. Riesman, Stone, and the Langs all carried out early studies in the sociology of sport; Reisman encouraged the field to grow; and Stone was very involved in its development.
3. Other analysts identified by Loy included Huizinga, Caillois, Piaget, and Veblen. Loy's appreciation of Goffman was passed on to many graduate students who worked with him at the University of Massachusetts in the 1970s, including Susan Birrell, Peter Donnelly, Rick Gruneau, Alan Ingham, and Nancy Theberge.

Birrell's (1978) doctoral thesis took the totality of Goffman's work as its subject, and remains the most systematic investigation in the field.

4. A number of commentators have suggested that it was, in part, Goffman's work which led to the widespread closure of many mental hospitals in the 1970s and 1980s. However, while critics of incarceration were calling for their replacement, the closures were usually carried out as a cost-cutting measure by governments without any replacement care.

References

Andrews, D. & Jackson, S. (eds) (2001) *Sport Stars*, New York: Routledge.

Ball, D. (1976) 'Failure in Sport', *American Sociological Review*, 41(4): 726–739.

Birrell, S. (1978) 'Sporting Encounters', unpublished doctoral dissertation, University of Massachusetts, Amherst.

Birrell, S. (1981) 'Sport as Ritual', *Social Forces*, 60: 354–376.

Birrell, S. & McDonald, M. (2000) *Reading Sport*, Boston: Northeastern University Press.

Birrell, S. & Turowetz, A. (1979) 'Character Work-up and Display', *Urban Life*, 8: 219–246.

Butler, J. (1993) *Bodies That Matter*, New York: Routledge.

Carroll, R. (1980) 'Football Hooliganism in England', *International Review of Sport Sociology*, 15(2): 77–92.

Coakley, J. (1998) *Sport in Society* (6th edition), Boston: McGraw-Hill.

Curry, T. & Jiobu, R. (1995) 'Do Motives Matter?', *Sociology of Sport Journal*, 12(1): 21–35.

Ditton, J. (ed.) (1980) *The View from Goffman*, New York: St Martin's Press.

Donnelly, P. (1982) 'On Verification', in A. Ingham & E. Broom (eds) *Career Patterns and Career Contingencies in Sport*, Vancouver: University of British Columbia.

Donnelly, P. (1994) 'Take My Word for It', *Qualitative Sociology*, 17: 215–241.

Donnelly, P. (2000a) 'Interpretive Approaches to the Sociology of Sport', in J. Coakley & E. Dunning (eds) *Handbook of Sports Studies*, London: Sage.

Donnelly, P. (2000b) 'Sticking My Neck Out', Presidential Address to the Annual meeting of the North American Society for the Sociology of Sport, Colorado Springs, CO, USA, 10 November.

Donnelly, P. & Young, K. (1988) 'The Construction and Confirmation of Identity in Sport Subcultures', *Sociology of Sport Journal*, 5: 223–240.

Duncan, M.C. (1990) 'Sports Photographs and Sexual Difference: Images of Women and Men in the 1984 and 1988 Olympic Games', *Sociology of Sport Journal*, 7: 22–43.

Fine, G. (1987) *With the Boys*, Chicago: University of Chicago Press.

Frey, J. (1991) 'Social Risk and the Meaning of Sport', *Sociology of Sport Journal*, 8(2): 136–145.

Giddens, A. (1987) *Social Theory and Modern Sociology*, Oxford: Polity Press.

Giese, R. (2000) 'She got Game', in P. Donnelly (ed.) *Taking Sport Seriously* (2nd edition) Toronto: Thompson Educational.

Goffman, E. (1959) *The Presentation of Self in Everyday Life*, New York: Anchor Books.

Goffman, E. (1961a) *Asylums*, New York: Anchor Books.

Goffman, E. (1961b) *Encounters*, Indianapolis: Bobbs-Merrill.

Goffman, E. (1963) *Stigma*, Englewood Cliffs, NJ: Prentice Hall.

Goffman, E. (1967) *Interaction Ritual*, New York: Anchor Books.

Goffman, E. (1969) *Strategic Interaction*, Philadelphia: University of Pennsylvania Press.

Goffman, E. (1974) *Frame Analysis*, Cambridge: Harvard University Press.

Goffman, E. (1977) 'The Arrangement Between the Sexes', *Theory and Society*, 4(3): 301–331.

Goffman, E. (1979) *Gender Advertisements*, New York: Harper & Row.

Goffman, E. (1981) *Forms of Talk*, Philadelphia: University of Pennsylvania Press.

Gonos, G. (1980) 'The Class Position of Goffman's Sociology', in J. Ditton (ed.) *The View from Goffman*, New York: St Martin's Press.

Gouldner, A. (1970) *The Coming Crisis of Western Sociology*, New York: Basic Books.

Halbert, C. (1997) 'Tough Enough and Woman Enough', *Journal of Sport and Social Issues*, 21(1): 7–36.

Hart, M.M. (1976) 'Stigma and Prestige', in M.M. Hart (ed.) (2nd edition) *Sport in the Sociocultural Process*, Dubuque, IA: Wm. C. Brown.

Hochschild, A. (1990) 'Gender Codes in Women's Advice Books', in S.H. Riggins (ed.) *Beyond Goffman*, New York: Mouton de Gruyter.

Hughes, R. & Coakley, J. (1991) 'Positive Deviance among Athletes', *Sociology of Sport Journal*, 8(4): 307–325.

Ingham, A. (1975) 'Occupational Subcultures in the Work World of Sport', in D. Ball & J. Loy (eds) *Sport and Social Order*, Reading, MA: Addison-Wesley.

Ingham, A.G. & P. Donnelly (1997) 'A Sociology of North American Sociology of Sport: Disunity in Unity, 1965 to 1996', *Sociology of Sport Journal*, 14(4): 362–418.

Jagose, A. (1996) *Queer Theory*, NY: New York University Press.

Jary, D. & Jary, J. (1995) *Dictionary of Sociology*, Glasgow: HarperCollins.

Loy, J. (1968) 'The Nature of Sport', *Quest*, 10: 1–15.

Marshall, G. (1994) *Concise Dictionary of Sociology*, Oxford: Oxford University Press.

McKay, J. & Smith, P. (1995) 'Frames and Narratives in Media Coverage of the O.J. Simpson Story', *Media Information Australia*, 75: 57–66.

Messner, M. (2002) *Taking the Field*, Minneapolis: University of Minnesota Press.

Muir, D. (1991) 'Club Tennis', *Sociology of Sport Journal*, 8: 70–78.

Nixon, H. (1986) 'Social order in a Leisure Setting', *Sociology of Sport Journal*, 3: 320–332.

Polsky, N. (1969) *Hustlers, Beats and Others*, New York: Anchor.

Rinehart, R. (1998) *Players All*, Bloomington, IN: Indiana University Press.

Rogers, M. (1980) 'Goffman on Power, Hierarchy, and Status', in J. Ditton (ed.) *The View from Goffman*, New York: St Martin's Press.

Schegloff, E. (1988) 'Goffman and the Analysis of Conversation', in P. Drew & A. Wootton (eds) *Erving Goffman*, Boston: Northeastern University Press.

Schmitt, R. (1993) 'Enhancing Frame Analysis', *Sociology of Sport Journal*, 10(2): 135–147.

Scott, M. (1968) *The Racing Game*, Chicago: Aldine.

Smith, G. (ed.) (1999) *Goffman and Social Organization*, London: Routledge.

Snyder, E. (1994) 'Interpretations and Explanations of Deviance among Collegiate Athletes', *Sociology of Sport Journal*, 11(3): 231–248.

Stevenson, C. (1990) 'The Early Careers of International Athletes', *Sociology of Sport Journal*, 7: 238–253.

Stone, G. (1955) 'American Sports', *Chicago Review*, 9: 83–100.

Stone, G. (1972) 'Wrestling', in E. Dunning (ed.) *Sport*, Toronto: University of Toronto Press.

Wacquant, L. (1992) 'The Social Logic of Boxing in Black Chicago', *Sociology of Sport Journal*, 9(3): 221–254.

Weinberg, S. & Arond, H. (1952) 'The Occupational Culture of the Boxer', *American Journal of Sociology*, 57: 460–469.

Winkin, Y. (1988) *Erving Goffman*, Paris: Editions de Seuil.

Winkin, Y. (1999) 'Erving Goffman: what a life?', in G. Smith (ed.) *Goffman and Social Organization*, London: Routledge.

Young, K. & White, P. (1995) 'Sport, Physical Danger and Injury', *Journal of Sport and Social Issues*, 19(1): 45–61.

4

Consciousness, Craft, Commitment: The Sociological Imagination of C. Wright Mills

John Loy and Douglas Booth

A prominent critic of American life and the orthodoxies of American sociology in the 1950s, C. Wright Mills today wears the mantle of the father of radical sociology (Scimecca, 1977, p. 111). Summing up Mills' life and work, Eldridge (1983, p. 112) pays tribute to his "innovative work in the sociology of knowledge"[1] and his intellectual influence on his contemporaries. He also acknowledges the range of studies completed by Mills "in what was, after all, quite a short working life" (Eldrige, 1983, p. 112). Mills' major works broadly relate to the study of power and social stratification. They include *The New Men of Power* (1948), *White Collar* (1956a), and *The Power Elite* (1956b). In the words of his principal biographer, Irving Horowitz, "Mills remains an engrossing figure for the social sciences and for American letters no less because of any uniquely inspiring concept or well-turned pithy phrase than because of his persistent belief that the qualities of intensity, purpose, and judgment must be brought front and center into the discourse of social research" (1983, p. 330).

C. Wright Mills: biographical sketch

Horowitz is not alone in noting Mills' intensity and purpose. Supporters and critics alike refer to these traits that were evident at an early age and that manifested in a man who felt "a deep alienation from America, its ethos, its politics, its way of life" (Miliband, 1968, p. 4). Born in Waco, Texas, on 28 August 1916, Charles Wright Mills[2] was the second child and only son in a middle-class Catholic family. He attended parochial and public schools in Sherman, Fort Worth and Dallas. Even as a boy, Mills "possessed a tenacious faith in his own abilities" and he never shied from "stand[ing] up to adults, teachers, and principals when he thought he was right" (Scimecca, 1977, p. 9). "Loneliness and intro-spection" characterized Mills during his school years. Support was rare and it invariably came from adults. " 'I have never known what others call "fraternity" with any group' ", he would later write, " 'neither academic nor political. With a few individuals, yes, but with small groups, no' " (Scimecca, 1977, p. 9).

Mills enrolled as a freshman at Texas A & M University in 1934; his father hoped that the rural military environment of the University would "make a man of the shy, withdrawn youngster" (Scimecca, 1977, p. 10). But after "one of the most miserable [years] of his life", Mills transferred to the University of Texas at Austin where he earned bachelor's and master's degrees in philosophy. One of Mills' philosophy professors had studied with George Herbert Mead at Chicago and introduced him to Mead's work and that of other pragmatic philosophers including Charles Pierce, William James and John Dewey. Another of his teachers had been an associate of Thorstein Veblen and exposed Mills to the works of this critical American sociologist. Scimecca (1977, p. 10) describes Mills' years at Texas as "a period of awakening":

> New ideas began to come alive for him. It was a time to grow, and, as is often the case, a time to rebel. C. Wright Mills ... played the intel-lectual rebel to the hilt [but] unlike most college students of the depression-ridden America of the late thirties, Mills never outgrew this role. His early years of isolation had left their mark, and Mills could maintain himself against any pressure that would try to limit his personal autonomy.

Mills left Texas in 1939 to pursue doctoral work in sociology at the University of Wisconsin. His senior mentor was Hans H. Gerth who had studied at the Franklin Institute of Social Research during the early Nazi era. Gerth mediated Mills' reading of the works of leading German sociologists, including Karl Mannheim and Max Weber. Before Mills completed his PhD in sociology at Wisconsin, he accepted an appointment as an assistant professor in sociology at the University of Maryland where he taught from 1941 to 1945. Tenure notwithstanding, Mills viewed his appointment as transitional and kept his intellectual and social involvement in university life to a minimum (Horowitz, 1983, p. 60).

In 1945 Mills accepted an offer from the University of Columbia where he remained for the rest of his career. Among his colleagues at Columbia were the renowned sociologists Robert Merton, Paul Lazarsfeld, Robert Lynd and William Goode, and the notable scholars Jacques Barzun, Richard Hofstradter and Lionel Trilling. Predictably, Mills alienated himself from friend and foe at Columbia. "His criticism of departmental colleagues, university-wide associates, and his own university administrators", writes Horowitz (1983, p. 83), "ultimately became the root source of a deeply felt hostility toward Mills".

Mills died after suffering a heart attack on 20 March 1962 at the relatively young age of 45 years. But his rather short professional career was productive and provocative. His thirteen published books made him a celebrity, although they were also a major source of the criticism that emanated from his peers (e.g. Domhoff & Ballard, 1968). Critics mostly focused on two aspects of Mills' work: "first, its relatively specu-lative empirical base and its populist tone, and secondly, its failure to relate systematically to other general theories of modern society" (Jary & Jary, 1991, p. 402). Mills' intellectual influence stems largely from his critical and highly readable *The Sociological Imagination* (1959). It pro-vides the foundation for the remainder of this chapter.

The crisis of sociology

At the heart of *The Sociological Imagination* is a hard-hitting attack on the tenets of American sociology in the 1950s. Mills is scathing about what he terms "grand theory" and "abstract empiricism". He singles out the work of Talcott Parsons as the exemplar of the deficiencies of grand theory – the "seemingly arbitrary and certainly endless elaboration of distinctions, which neither enlarge our understanding nor make our experience more sensible" (1959, p. 33). Nothing better reveals the limi-tations of grand theory, Mills continued, than the "partially organized abdication of the effort to describe and explain human conduct and society plainly". In the case of abstract empiricism, which he denigrated as "a style of social science...not characterized by any substantive propositions or theories" (1959, p. 55), Mills highlighted the work of his colleague Paul Lazarsfeld.

Mills' critique of American sociology in the 1950s was a precursor of what has become known as "the sociology of sociology" (cf. Friedrichs, 1970; Reynolds & Reynolds, 1970), and a presager of Gouldner's classic *The Coming Crisis of Western Sociology* (1970). Eldridge (1983, p. 114) contends that Gouldner's work "is very much in the tradition of Mills (with a very lengthy and much more considered discussion of Parsons)". In the thirty years since Gouldner raised the spectre of the crisis of sociology, a myriad of articles and books have referred to "sociology on the skids" (1995) in terms of its apparent decline, disintegration and demise (Huber, 1979; Rabow & Zucker, 1980; Touraine, 1984; Turner, 1989; Brotz, 1990; Turner & Turner, 1990; Berger, 1994; Horowitz, 1994; Feagin, 1999).

In a more positive vein, several key sociologists have provided more optimistic analyses of the state and status of sociology. Etzioni (1976) predicted the increasing importance of humanistic sociology; Smelser (1990) posited "a kind of peaceful pluralism as a visible motif" in contemporary academic sociology; and Hargens (1990) failed to observe any trends of decline. Similarly, Giddens (1995, p. 19) contended that while "sociology may have taken a beating since its heydey in the 1960s, its demise is much exaggerated". Moreover, he argued that while sociology may have fallen on hard times in America, British sociology was "doing *better* than in previous generations". Significantly, Giddens concludes his defence of the discipline by invoking C. Wright Mills:

> Sociology should rehone its cutting edge, as neo-liberalism disappears into the distance along with orthodox socialism. Some questions to which we need new answers have a perennial quality while others are dramatically new. Tackling these, as in previous times, calls for a healthy dose of what C. Wright Mills famously called the sociological imagination.
>
> (Giddens, 1995, p. 20)

Given Giddens' admonition, it is significant that Oxford University Press released a 40th anniversary edition of Mills' classic 1959 work, *The Sociological Imagination*. In the next section we highlight the major notions of Mills' conception of the sociological imagination and in our final section we discuss the relevance of C. Wright Mills' sociological imagination for work in the sociology of sport.

The sociological imagination

According to Mills (1959, p. 6), a social analyst must have a firm "grasp [of] history and biography and the relations between the two within society". This, he declared, is the "task" and the "promise" of the sociological imagination. His conception of the sociological imagination largely focuses on three interrelated notions: consciousness, craft and commitment. We highlight these in turn as an introduction to the sociological imagination in sport studies.

Sociology as a form of consciousness

Inherent in Mills's conception of the sociological imagination is the notion that sociology is a form of consciousness, as for example, a sociological awareness of "the personal troubles of milieu" and "the public issues of social structure" (p. 8). More explicitly, Mills argued that "the first fruit of this imagination – and the first lesson of the social science that embodies it – is the idea that the individual can understand his own experience and gauge his own fate only by locating himself within his period, [and] that he can know his own chances of life only by becoming aware of those of all individuals in his circumstances" (p. 5). Like Mills, Berger also conceives sociology as a form of consciousness. "The fascination with sociology", Berger (1963, p. 21) suggests in a Millsian manner, "lies in the fact that its perspective makes us see in a new light the very world in which we have lived all our lives".

In his analysis of the sociological imagination, based in part on an earlier interpretation proposed by Giddens (1982), Willis (1995, 1996) suggests that the sociological imagination consists of four *sensibilities*: historical, cultural, structural and critical. Given that Willis defines sensibility as "a keen appreciation or consciousness" (1996, p. 55), his schema is an ideal framework to illustrate sociology as a form of consciousness. Importantly, however, since sport is based on embodied social practices, we add a fifth sensibility, corporeality.

Historical sensibility

As previously noted, Mills' primary premise is that "social science deals with the problems of biography, of history, and of their intersections with social structures" (1959, p. 143). He felt that good sociology was historical sociology and he devoted an entire chapter to "Uses of History" in *The Sociological Imagination*. "The problems of our time, which now include the problem of man's very nature", Mills (1959, p. 143) insisted, "cannot be stated adequately without consistent practice of the view that history is the shank of social study, and recognition of the need to develop further a psychology of man that is sociologically grounded and historically relevant". And just as a historical sensibility provides a comparative view of social life so too does an anthropological, or cultural, sensibility.

Cultural sensibility

As Giddens (1982, p. 24) well notes, "the anthropological dimension of the sociological imagination is important because it allows us to appreciate the diversity of modes of human existence". Indeed, in "The Human Variety", another chapter in *The Sociological Imagination*, Mills stressed the point that the study of human diversity is critical to the social sciences. When Willis (1996) makes the point that cultural sensibility helps to dispel ethnocentrism in general and racism in particular (p. 65), and that it involves an awareness of cultural relativity, that is, that "cultures do not constitute a hierarchy from better to worse" (p. 66), he is in fact encapsulating many of the ideas put forward by Mills in the "Uses of History" and "The Human Variety".

Taken together, historical and cultural sensibilities make it possible to "break free from the straightjacket" of narrow and bigoted thinking (Giddens, 1982, p. 26). On the other hand, structural and critical sensibilities constitute key analytical approaches to the study of social stratification and social processes (Willis, 1996, p. 75).

Structural sensibility

Willis (1996, p. 76) explains the notion of structural sensibility, by way of contrasting the concepts of agency and structure:

> Do the actions of individual human beings (agents) create social structure, or does social structure constrain and create the actions of individuals? We can think of both agency and structure as being important but neither as being solely responsible for a social phenomenon. Rather, such a phenomenon is a result of a combination of agency and structural factors.

Interestingly, for all his references to them, Mills never developed theoretically rigorous concepts of structure and agency. His definitions of structure were simplistic (i.e. Mills, 1959, p. 134), while his conception of biography is somewhat ambiguous with respect to its relationship with human agency as a personal force. Although Willis implies, quite correctly, a complementary relationship between agency and structure, it should be noted that the nature of the relationship between these two main determinants of social outcomes, and the variety of formulations of the relationship, have long been subject to intense debate (see Bhaskar, 1979; Giddens, 1984).

Critical sensibility

In a sociological sense, critical does not denote negativity; rather it refers to being skeptical and reflective about social life. "In exercising a critical sensibility, sociologists try to uncover and expose the ambiguities, misrepresentations, distortions, and even falsehoods in competing explanations for a particular social phenomenon" (Willis, 1996, p. 83). Willis suggests that a critical sensibility forces one to address two basic questions: "How do we know?" and "How could it be otherwise" (1996, pp. 83–84). The first question requires an examination of evidence and epistemological issues, that is, how people come to have knowledge of the external world. The second question requires consideration of alternatives. "Human beings", Giddens (1982, p. 26) forcefully reminds us, "are not condemned to be swept along by forces that have the inevitability of the laws of nature. But this means we must be conscious of the *alternative futures* that are potentially open to us" (see also Mills, 1959, p. 174). Of course, just as Giddens (1982, p. 27) cautioned, "critique must be based on analysis".

Corporeal sensibility

Sports are sets of embodied social practices. At one level they involve physical movement but, more substantially, sporting bodies reflect a host of socially constructed values (e.g. discipline, health, self-improvement), and relationships of power (e.g. disciplined bodies, normalized bodies, submissive bodies). Moreover, they are highly visible markers of prestige and status. Interestingly, although Mills predates the study of the body as a fundamental social and academic issue, he was only too well aware of corporeal status. Part Three of his critically acclaimed book *White Collar* (1956a) examines at length the embodiment of style among the American middle classes. "As their label implies", Mills wrote (1956a, p. 241), white-collar people express their claims to prestige, "by their style of appearance".

In summary, from a Millsian perspective, any substantive sociological analysis of everyday life, especially leisure and sport, requires a strong sociological imagination. This in turn demands an adequate consideration of historical, cultural, structural, critical and corporeal sensibilities.

Sociology as a form of craft

Today, scores of textbooks afford senior students advice on general theory and research methods. Precious few, however, offer explicit explanations of the craft of sociology. Mills' "On Intellectual Craftsmanship", which appears as the appendix in *The Sociological Imagination*, is an important exception.[3] Scholars and students familiar with sociological investigation will find Mills' appendix overly mechanical and commonsensical. Nonetheless, it is an extremely useful "personal statement" of how he approached his task of fostering the sociological imagination. Here we describe the basic components of Mills' craftsmanship under the trilogy, tools, tactics and techniques.

Tools

Tools are the instruments that craftspersons use to create and shape the object of their work, including making possible the interpretation of data or information. Every academic discipline has its own tools and Mills identified three primary sociological tools: theory, empirical inquiry and language.

As we have seen, Mills opposed what he called grand theory where the outcome was merely "an arid game of concepts" (Mills, 1959, p. 34). Mills believed that sociologists – indeed all social scientists – must deal with specific problems and that grand theorists merely engaged in "cloudy obscurantism" (1959, p. 75). This did not mean, however, that he rejected theory per se. On the contrary, theory is an essential "formal moment within the work of social science" (1959, p. 48) that generates general conceptions about society in the service of specific problems: "elaborations of theories, systematic and unsystematic, promise to alert us to distinctions in what we may see, or in what we may make of what we see when we come to interpret it" (1959, p. 122). "Theories are theories", he said, only of a "range of phenomena" and "the working scientist must always keep uppermost a full sense of the problem at hand" (1959, p. 121).

Similarly Mills opposed raw empirical work that he called "thin and uninteresting". While empirical inquiry has its place, in helping "settle disagreements and doubts about facts", "reason", he insisted, "is the advance guard in any field of learning" (1959, p. 205). According to Mills, the real benefits of empirical projects lie in their design. Done well, he said, they will at least lead to new searches for data "which often turn out to have unsuspected relevance to [the] problem" under investigation (1959, p. 205). "The most economical way to state a problem is in such a way as to solve as much of it as possible by reasoning alone" (1959, p. 206). In short, "every working social scientist must be his own methodologist and his own theorist, which means only that he must be an intellectual craftsman" (1959, p. 121).

Lastly, sociological language was perhaps the tool of which Mills was most critical. He condemned its "turgid and polysyllabic" style (1959, p. 217) that he attributed to a fallacious attempt to build cred-ibility – "I know something that is so difficult you can understand it only if you first learn my difficult language. In the meantime, you are merely a journalist, a layman, or some other sort of underdeveloped type" (1959, p. 220). Mills had a simple remedy: clear, plain and precise English (Mills, 1959, p. 219).

Tactics

Mills recommended numerous tactics, or procedures, to facilitate the craft of sociological imagination. Here we single out those tactics intended to specifically expose the sociologist to broader points of view.

Mills believed that scholars should soak themselves in the literature – "to locate the opponents and friends of every available viewpoint" (1959, p. 214). Likewise, Mills noted the importance of scholars immersing themselves in the relevant intellectual, and social, environments that will encourage them to think rigorously about their work (1959, p. 201). For young scholars this meant "studying with the best professors and taking the finest courses" (Horowitz, 1983, p. 43).

Neither of these tactics meant gravitating to established and accepted viewpoints. On the contrary, Mills urged scholars to seriously consider extreme opposite positions, to search for contradictions, to undertake comparisons, and to examine positions through the eyes of alternative disciplines. "Often the best insights", Mills (1959, p. 213) advised, "come from considering extremes". By contrasting objects, Mills (1959, p. 214) continued, "you get a better grip on the materials and you can then sort out the dimensions in terms of which the comparisons are made". Similarly, "the idea is to use a variety of viewpoints:...ask yourself how would a political scientist...approach this" or an experimental psychologist or a historian. "You try to think in terms of a variety of viewpoints and in this way let your mind become a moving prism catching light from as many angles as possible" (1959, p. 214).

But of all his tactics, Mills devoted most attention to experience. Irrespective of their familiarity with the literature, Mills implored scholars to bring their life experiences to the fore in their intellectual work. "Do not be afraid", he wrote (1959, p. 196), "to use your experience and relate it directly to various work in progress". As he noted, sociologists do not study projects, rather they become tuned, or sensitive, to its themes that "they see and hear everywhere in [their] experience, especially, it always seems to me, in apparently unrelated areas" (1959, p. 211).

Techniques

Mills recommended creating a filing system based on ideas, personal notes, excerpts from books, journal articles, newspaper clippings, bibliographic items, outlines of projects and so forth. Just as "creative writers keep journals", so sociologists must open files that record events, experiences and ideas, and, critically, the implications of those recordings.

Mills especially advocated a separate file for history. "Every social science – or better, every well-considered social study – requires an historical scope of conception and a full use of historical materials" (1959, p. 145). The basic purpose of the file is to develop in young scholars "self-reflective habits" and to encourage them "to keep [their] inner world awake" (1959, p. 197). Most importantly, filing is a process of intellectual production: it requires labeling, classifying, organizing categories. Moreover, it requires continual maintenance, that is, rearranging categories as one develops new ideas, or makes new encounters and discoveries. Indeed, as well as a critical source of "stimulating the sociological imagination" (1959, p. 212). Mills refers to the file as "an index of intellectual progress and breadth" (1959, p. 199).

Sociology as a form of commitment

Motivated by what he saw as the injustices of the social order, Mills chose sociology as a career. In sociology he recognized a "profession that had the concepts and skills – and thus the responsibility – to expose and correct such injustices" (Goldsen, 1965, p. 88). Sociological problems, he noted, arouse curiosity, provoke thought and raise additional questions about a phenomenon (Willis, 1996, pp. 10–11). Mills believed that "the sociological imagination has its chance to make a difference in the quality of human life in our time" (1959, p. 226). The quest for sociological imagination "encourages the seeker not to take the social world for granted but to be reflective or critical about its nature and the place of the individual within it" (Willis, 1996, p. 134). Mills understood that reflection undermines taken-for-granted assumptions and compels people to confront their own understandings about how to behave in the social world. Reflection extends to analyzing one's own social location and the extent to which one's own experience is, or is not, typical for others similarly located in society (Willis, 1996, p. 136).

Mills passionately believed in the notion that men make history. He wanted people to take control over their own lives, and in this sense he was an advocate of the power of agency. In an academic setting he was particularly critical of intellectuals who abdicated their responsibilities as social critics and who failed to intervene in history. He reminded undergraduate students that, "the most admirable thinkers within the scholarly community . . . do not split their work from their lives. They seem to take both too seriously to allow such dissociation, and they want to use each for the enrichment of the other" (1959, p. 195). In this sense he encouraged students to think analytically about the social world in which they live. "Know that the human meaning of public issues must be revealed by relating them to personal troubles – and to the problems of the individual life" (1959, p. 195). Of course, Mills understood only too well that social critics confronted enormous difficulties in convincing the public of a position or asking the public to question what is typically portrayed as the national interest. Invariably the critic is labeled subversive, seditious and unpatriotic.

But it was his moral commitment, rather than concepts and skills, which made Mills such a powerful critic. And Mills' moral commitment was to reason and freedom (1959, p. 184). Humankind, Mills believed, would achieve control of its fate by knowledge and reason. This meant educating the public in the consequences of their action or inaction (Notestein, 1965, p. 50); and this became Mills' calling and chief vocation.

The relevance of C. Wright Mills for the sociology of sport

A number of leading sports sociologists, including Alan Ingham and Peter Donnelly, Richard Gruneau and Jennifer Hargreaves, make explicit reference to C. Wright Mills and his influence on their work. Gruneau (1983, p. 157, 1999, p. 122) refers to the influence of *The Sociological Imagination* in shaping his theoretical approach in writing *Class, Sports, and Social Development*; and Hargreaves (1997) cites the book as instrumental in her "conversion" from biological science to sociology as a masters student. It was, she writes alluding to corporeal sensibility, "the stimulus for me to explore the ways in which the physical (and sport, specifically) is linked to the social. It encouraged me to look for connections, to interrogate, to recognize contradictions, and self consciously to reassess sporting performances". Ingham and Donnelly (1997, p. 363) note that Mills' attacks on "grand theory" and "abstracted empiricism", and his discussion of "Intellectual Craftsmanship" were major influences on "the second generation" of North American sports sociologists. Mills alerted this generation to the possibilities of undertaking critical, probing and relevant social analyses of sport; he introduced them to passionate and committed scholarship; and he showed them how to reconcile scholarship with radicalism.

In this final section we briefly review two texts that we believe encapsulate Mills' sociological imagination, the intersections of biography, history and structure in general, and the historical, cultural, structural, critical and corporeal sensibilities in particular.

Sport, Power and Culture

There is little doubt that John Hargreaves' systematic analysis of power and sport in Britain reflects the five sensibilities in Willis' conception of the sociological imagination. In his foreword to the book, Stuart Hall highlights the historical and structural sensibilities of Hargreaves' analysis:

> The book is enriched by its historical framework, without which the topic makes little sense. Fortunately, the historical treatment does not simply provide a chronological and evolutionary frame for the study, but a context in which serious theoretical issues can be posed. These issues relate, specially, to the way sport has been articulated in different historical periods, to the relations between classes; to the role which sport has played in the re-education and re-formulation of the popular classes and to the 'stake' which sport represents in the general relationships of power in society.
>
> (1986, p. xi)

Discussions of popular culture, working-class culture and consumer culture, not to mention the cultural aspects of gender and ethnic divisions, and the role of media sport in the construction of national identity all provide clear evidence of the cultural sensibility. Critical sensibility informs *Sport, Power and Culture*, which Gruneau (1993, p. 102) calls the "best book-length piece of sport and social criticism" published in the 1980s. Lastly, his chapter titled "Schooling the Body" is an explicit analysis of corporeal sensibility. *Sport, Power and Culture* concludes on an overtly Millsian note:

> Those who are trying to formulate and implement a relatively progressive sports policy and who take sport seriously as an aspect of culture, are groping their way towards, and badly need an answer. What is certainly needed at the moment is critical reflection and creative thought. Logically, analysis is only the first step in what is, after all, a discursive process – that of policy formation. Policy cannot automatically be deduced from analysis: its formation is a creative process requiring imaginative leaps, and above all, a genuine interaction between policy-makers and subjects.
>
> (1986, p. 223)

One area where Hargreaves might fail from a Millsian perspective is biography. Yet, notwithstanding the absence of biography per se from *Sport, Power and Culture*, Hargreaves gives due consideration to the importance of agency, especially in the analysis of power relations.

According to Hargreaves (1986, p. 4), power relations are determined, in part, "by the kind of objectives agents pursue and by the strategies they employ to achieve them". A good example is his analysis of the "remarkable resilience" of animal sports, prize-fighting and folk football in the face of opposition from middle class reformers in the early nineteenth century. In their attempts to crush working class culture the latter promoted prohibitive legislation and even the use of troops and militia (Hargreaves, 1986, p. 31).

Admittedly, few historical sociology studies dealing with sport include biography.[4] By contrast, a biographical sensibility is apparent in Susan Brownell's *Training the Body for China* (*Sports in the Moral Order of the People's Republic*) (1995).

Training the Body for China

As a member of Beijing University's track and field team, Brownell won a gold medal in the heptathlon in the 1986 National Games of the People's Republic of China. She draws directly upon her experience as an athlete in examining the culture of sports and the body in China. Although Brownell is a cultural anthropologist, and although she makes no reference to Mills, we have no compunction about citing her work as an exemplar of Millsian sociology. First, as Mills himself noted, "cultural anthropology, in its classic tradition and current developments, does not seem to me in any fundamental way distinguishable from sociological study" (1959, p. 137). Second, Brownell, more than any other current social scientist studying sport, captures the totality of the sociological imagination, be it in terms of the intersections of biography, history and social structure in general, or historical, cultural, structural, corporeal and critical sensibilities in particular.

Brownell's attention to history appears in her overview of body techniques and public dramatization from polo at the imperial courts, to long gowns, queues and footbinding in the late Qing Dynasty, to conceptions of the Maoist body in the establishment of the People's Republic of China. Similarly, her comparative account of sex, the body and history in Chinese and Western sports also reflects a historical sensibility.

Given her formal training as a cultural anthropologist, it is fair to say that cultural sensibility is Brownell's major forte. The anthropological perspective informs her work and she acknowledges the personal influence of Victor Turner and John MacAloon. Her discussions of the relationships between body culture and that of class, consumer culture, public culture and sex/gender are particularly illuminating.

Given her training as an anthropologist, it is perhaps not surprising that Brownell's structural sensibility is less pronounced than her cultural sensibility. Nevertheless, she examines the ways in which power, in particular that emanating from the state and class and gender relations, shape body techniques. The title of her book, and the preceding discussion of her work, make it clear that Brownell has a heightened sense of corporeal sensibility. Indeed, we believe that her work stands as the most embodied account of sport, culture and society to date.

Brownell's critical sensibility is more often implicit than explicit. Nevertheless it is evident as illustrated by three of her chapter titles: "Those Who Work with Their Brains Rule, Those Who Work with Their Brawn Are Ruled"; "Bodies, Boundaries and the State"; " 'Obscene' Bodies, the State, and Popular Movements". Explorations of the tensions between men and women, Eastern and Western perspectives on sport, traditional versus modern ways, local versus global organizations, and between the communist revolution and free-marked economy, also offer evidence of her critical edge.

C. Wright Mills' *The Sociological Imagination* is the classic text in the tradition of radical sociology and it has had a large influence in sport sociology. The reasons are clear. As both the studies cited above demonstrate, sports sociologists who are attentive to the sociological imagination can only succeed in producing "an adequate view of the total society and of its components" (Mills, 1959, p. 211). And as Mills was at pains to point out, that is the essence of sociology.

Notes

1. Mills' work on the sociology of knowledge fused American pragmatism with European sociology (Eldridge, 1983, p. 111). He completed most of this work as a graduate student at the University of Wisconsin, before the age of twenty-five. It includes his doctoral dissertation published posthumously as *Sociology and Pragmatism* (1964) and five articles published between 1939 and 1943. The latter are reprinted in Horowitz (1964).
2. In college he adopted the initial C and his middle name Wright.
3. Alford (1998) and Becker (1998) are also exceptions. Both authors cite Mills, although neither refers to his appendix.
4. An early exception is C.L.R. James's *Beyond a Boundary* (1963).

References

Alford, R. (1998) *The Craft of Inquiry*, New York: Oxford University Press.
Bhaskar, R. (1979) *The Possibility of Naturalism*, Brighton, UK: Harvester.
Becker, H. (1998) *Tricks of the Trade*, Chicago: University of Chicago Press.

Berger, P. (1963) *Invitation to Sociology*, New York: Anchor Books.

Berger, P.L. (1994), "Does Sociology Still Make Sense?" *Review of Swiss Sociology*, 20(1): 3–12.

Brotz, H. (Jan./ Feb. 1990) "Why Sociology is Dead", *The Idler*, 27: 35–42.

Brownell, S. (1995) *Training the Body for China*, Urbana, IL: University of Illinois Press.

Domhoff, G.W. & Ballard, H.B. (1968) *C. Wright Mills and The Power Elite*, Boston: Beacon Press.

Eldridge, J. (1983) *C. Wright Mills*, London: Tavistock Publications.

Etzioni, A. (19 January 1976) "The Importance of Humanistic Sociology", *Chronicle of Higher Education*.

Feagin, J.R. (15 October 1999) "Soul-Searching in Sociology", *Chronicle of Higher Education*.

Friedrichs, R.W. (1970) *A Sociology of Sociology*, New York: Free Press.

Giddens, A. (1982) *Sociology – A Brief but Critical Introduction*, New York: Harcourt Brace Jovanovich.

Giddens, A. (1984) *The Constitution of Society*, Berkeley, CA: University of California Press.

Giddens, A. (1995) "In Defence of Sociology", *New Statesman & Society*, 7 April: 18–20.

Gouldner, A.W. (1970) *The Coming Crisis of Western Sociology*, New York: Basic Books.

Goldsen, R. (1965) "Mills and the Profession of Sociology", in I.L. Horowitz (ed.) *The New Sociology: essays in social science and social theory in honor of C. Wright Mills*, New York: Oxford University Press.

Gruneau, R. (1983) *Class, Sports, and Social Development*, Amherst, MA: University of Massachusetts Press.

Gruneau, R. (1993) "Theorising Power, Culture, and the Politics of the Body", in E. Dunning, J. Maguire & R. Pearton (eds) *The Sports* Process, Champaign, IL: Human Kinetics.

Gruneau, R. (1999) *Class, Sports and Social Development*, Champaign, Ill.: Human Kinetics.

Hargens, L.L. (Fall 1990) "Sociologists" Assessments of the State of Sociology, 1969–1984', *American Sociologist*, 200–208.

Hargreaves, J. (1986) *Sport, Power and Culture*, New York: St Martin's Press.

Hargreaves, J. (1997) "Speaking Volumes on C. Wright Mills's *The Sociological Imagination*", *The Times Higher Education Supplement*, 21 March: 21.

Horowitz, I.L. (1964) *Power, Politics and People*, New York: Oxford University Press.

Horowitz, I.L. (1983) *C. Wright Mills*, New York: The Free Press.

Horowitz, I.L. (1994) *The Decomposition of Sociology*, New York: Oxford University Press.

Huber, J. (Autumn 1979) "Comment: Where is the Cutting Edge of Sociology?", *Sociological Quarterly*, 20: 591–603.

Ingham, A.G. & Donnelly, P. (1997) "The Sociology of North American Sociology of Sport: Disunity in Unity, 1965 to 1996", *Sociology of Sport Journal*, 14: 362–418.

James, C.L.R. (1963) *Beyond a Boundary*, London: Hutchinson.

Jary, D. & Jary, J. (1991) *Collins Dictionary of Sociology*, Glasgow: HarperCollins.

Miliband, R. (1968) "C. Wright Mills", in G.W. Domhoff & H.B. Ballard (eds) *C. Wright Mills and the Power Elite*, Boston: Beacon Press.

Mills, C.W. (1948) *The New Men of Power*, New York: Harcourt, Brace & World.

Mills, C.W. (1956a) *White Collar*, New York: Oxford University Press.

Mills, C.W. (1956b) *The Power Elite*, New York: Oxford University Press.

Mills, C.W. (1959) *The Sociological Imagination*, Oxford: Oxford University Press.

Mills, C.W. (1964) [I.L. Horowitz, ed.] *Sociology and Pragmatism: The Higher Learning in America*, New York: Paine-Whitman Publishers.

Notestein, R. (1965) "The Moral Commitment of C. Wright Mills", in I.L. Horowitz (ed.) *The New Sociology*, New York: Oxford University Press.

Rabow, J. & Zucker, L.G. (1980) "Whither Sociology?", *Sociology and Social Research*, 65(11): 10–22.

Reynolds, L.T. & Reynolds, J.M. (1970) *The Sociology of Sociology*, New York: David McKay.

Scimecca, J.A. (1977) *The Sociological Theory of C. Wright Mills*, London: National University Publications.

Smelser, N.J. (Fall 1990) "Sociological Theory", *American Sociologist*, 275–282, "Sociology on the Skids." (Nov./Dec. 1995) *Utne Reader*, pp. 28, 30.

Touraine, A. (1984) 'The Waning Sociological Image of Social Life', *International Journal of Comparative Sociology*, 25(1–2): 33–44.

Turner, J.H. (1989) 'The Disintegration of American Sociology', *Sociological Perspectives*, 32(4): 419–433.

Turner, S.P. & Turner, J.H. (1990) *The Impossible Science*, Newbury Park, CA: Sage Publications.

Willis, E. (1995) *The Sociological Quest* (2nd edition) St Leonards, NSW: Allen & Unwin.

Willis, E. (1996) *The Sociological Quest* (3rd edition) New Brunswick, NJ: Rutgers University Press.

5

Theodor Adorno on Sport: The Jeu D'Esprit of Despair

David Inglis

Introduction

For many contemporary students of society and culture, certain thinkers are regarded as being somewhat beyond the pale, their work embodying wholly outmoded views and assumptions. It would be best, it is sometimes thought, if such authors and all their works were to be quietly condemned to the dustbin of history. One such figure is the German philosopher and sociologist, Theodor W. Adorno. Adorno is often represented as the supreme example of aristocratic elitism, gazing down from above with a lofty contempt for all matters 'popular'. So much so has this view of Adorno become an orthodoxy in academic circles in recent years that his very name has become a by-word for a cultural elitism that seems to be the epitome of modernist arrogance and hubris (see e.g. Fiske, 1989, p. 183). In the brave new post-modernist world in which we are purportedly living, it seems that the only lesson Adorno can teach us is to show how cultural analysis should not be done.

What then can Adorno possibly have to offer us for thinking about the nature of sports today? It is perhaps understandable why so many people dismiss Adorno's approach to sports and other cultural matters as being unworkable today. If one examines his scattered remarks on sports, one will find abundant evidence that Adorno is interested only in condemning sports and sports-people for their apparent mindless subservience to the capitalist system. One comes quickly to the conclusion that Adorno's position is a crude and reactionary cultural conservatism.

Such a conclusion is perhaps the inevitable result of a brief acquaintance with what Adorno has to say about sporting matters. However, the picture one will get on a more sustained engagement with Adorno's work, when one has digested precisely what he is trying to say, is a somewhat different matter. When the nuances and subtleties of Adorno's approach become clearer, one will realize that far from being utterly damning of cultural phenomena such as sports, Adorno holds a deeply ambiguous attitude towards them. Far from holding a wholly derogatory opinion of sports, Adorno wants not only to criticize the contemporary debased forms in which sports are manifested in today's capitalist society, but also to valorize and defend the possible, more free and liberatory, types of sports that could occur in a future society devoid of oppression and power.

In this chapter, we will first briefly outline the social and historical context of Adorno's work on cultural matters. We will then turn to what he has to say about sports in particular, and how this work has been misinterpreted by later authors claiming inspiration from his approach. In that regard, we will examine the importance of Adorno's writing style for his way of thinking about sport and culture in a utopian manner, before looking at how he attempts to see the utopian promise in contemporary sports, a promise hidden within the apparently unpromising manifestations of sports in capitalist society. We will conclude by showing how Adorno's approach remains crucial for thinking about sports, culture and society at the beginning of the twenty-first century.

Adorno and his times

Adorno (1903–1969) was one of the major members of the 'Frankfurt School' of critical theory, among whose other members were Max Horkheimer, Herbert Marcuse and Erich Fromm (Wiggershaus, 1995). The 'Frankfurt School' can be thought about as having a somewhat distinctive identity. In the first place, the various thinkers associated with the School were all attached, in one way or another, to the Institute for Social Research, a quasi-autonomous research centre set up within the University of Frankfurt in 1923. The Institute for Social Research was profoundly interdisciplinary both in its outlook and in the composition of its personnel, involving as it did specialists in fields such as philosophy, sociology, psychology and political economy. Second, the individual members of the Frankfurt School, although working often in very different fields of endeavour, generally had common elements in their respective bodies of thought. The overall intellectual tenor of the Institute was neo-Marxist, with one of the central themes of the thinkers therein being the elaboration of new and more supple forms of Marxist thought which would challenge the increasingly rigid and doctrinaire versions of Marxism being promulgated by the Communist parties of Western countries at the behest of Stalin's Soviet Union.

If an attempt to escape from such orthodox forms of Marxism is one defining aspect of the Frankfurt School, another was the particular socio-historical context in which its members had to operate. Throughout the later 1920s and earlier 1930s, the spectre of Fascism loomed over Germany, finally culminating in Hitler's rise to power in 1933. As most of the members of the Institute for Social Research were of Jewish extraction, this meant an immediate abandonment of Germany for the somewhat more welcoming environment of the United States.

Both the rise of Nazism and the shock of arriving in the New World created a profound impression on Adorno and his colleagues. The common theme to arise from both these experiences, and which would be registered very profoundly in their work, was the feeling that in modern societies, the individual was increasingly being swamped by the society around him or her. In their major work, *Dialectic of Enlightenment* (1944/92), written while the war still raged in Europe, Adorno and Horkheimer described this vision of the destruction of individuality and freedom in terms of the rise and eventual triumph of 'instrumental rationality'.

By this term they referred to the attitude whereby the most efficient means to an end is calculated, regardless of the cost to the individuals who might suffer in the process. Instrumental rationality, the form of thought which they believed was now dominant in the West, treated people as mere objects to be manipulated, rather than as autonomous, creative beings worthy of being treated with respect. The message of the book was that domination and power have unfortunately been an integral part of human societies since the very beginning of human life, but that now in the modern West, domination has become more extensive and more threatening to freedom than ever before. Domination does not so much operate in the service of a particular dominant class, the thesis that Marx had essentially put forward, but operates in the interests of the overall System, a capitalist system no longer based on free competition between individual capitalists, but oriented around the power of big business corporations each with monopolies in particular markets. In addition to that situation, just as in Nazi Germany the State increasingly interfered in and administered social life, so too in the West were individuals more and more coming under the power of Government. As a result, the glimmerings of individual freedom and autonomy that were just about discernible previously were now seriously in threat of being extinguished for ever.

From this point of view, if Nazi Germany was a totalitarian society, then the United States, which seemed to indicate what the Western society of the future would look like, was a quasi-totalitarian society. According to this perspective, there was not such a huge difference between the propaganda machine of the Nazis and the apparently 'free' mass media of radio, cinema and newsprint in America. These too were as propagandistic in their effects, lulling consumers into a false sense of harmony and pleasure, when actually the life-blood was being sucked out of them by the 'Culture Industries'. By this term, Adorno and Horkheimer (1944/92) meant the mass media and other forms of mass entertainment, such as large-scale sports events like baseball and foot-ball leagues. The Culture Industries sought to pacify the masses, lulling their critical faculties to sleep, and in so doing, accommodating people to the rule of monopoly capitalism (Adorno, 1996). It is this nightmarish vision of the totalitarian nature of 'the land of the free' that underpins all of Adorno's writings on mass culture in general, and sports in particular.

Sport and disenchantment

Adorno's theory of sports is embedded within his overall account of the rise of a social order characterized by extremely high levels of adminis-tration and control. Adorno is sometimes represented as having been one of the pioneers of the academic study of sport (Dunning, 1999, p. 242). Yet he is more often regarded as a figure who undercuts the very possi-bility of adequately investigating such phenomena by assuming a priori that all aspects of popular culture in the modern period are mere expressions of a quasi-totalitarian social order. The approach of Adorno, and his Frankfurt colleagues more generally, to sporting matters is often held to be characterized by a 'narcotic pessimism' (Andrews & Loy, 1993, p. 257). He appears to be the very epitome of the mandarin, disengaged, anti-popular cultural critic (Rose, 1978, p. 8). Why does Adorno's work seem to involve blanket condemnation of everything about the cultures of modernity, including their sporting elements?

In his written work, Adorno (1997a, p. 25) explicitly wishes to paint a picture of a ruinous dystopia, characterized by control and domina-tion. A key premise of his writing was that in the modern world "[t]here is nothing innocuous left". In one way, this statement means that all aspects of modern society, no matter how apparently trivial, are impli-cated in the form of domination, based around instrumental rationality, which underpins that society (Adorno & Horkheimer, 1944/92). Even phenomena as 'harmless' as games must therefore betray, in their very existence today, the marks of domination and unfreedom. As Adorno remarks, '[s]port itself is not play but ritual in which the subjected celebrate their subjection' (Adorno, 1996, p. 77). In the almost wholly administered world of monopoly capitalism, where cartels have eliminated the competitive market economy of the laissez-faire nineteenth century, 'sport permits competition ... to survive in a world in which competition has been eliminated' (Adorno, 1996, p. 77). Sport is now a brutalized form of activity that succeeds only in expressing the domination that underpins the rest of society. As a 'leisure' activity, it stands in relation to the realm of work as do all other leisure activities: 'free time is nothing other than a shadowy continuation of labour' (Adorno, 1996, p. 168). Sport in late capitalism is elevated into the principle of 'life itself', whereby competitive struggles are adulated at a period of complete stasis. In this way, the tension in an earlier phase of capitalism between periods devoted to leisure and work is now dissolved in place of a repetitive sameness (Adorno, 1996, p. 78).

Sport, then, is 'the colourless reflection of a hardened callous life' (Adorno, 1996, p. 78). This theme can be found at various points in Adorno's oeuvre. For example, in the article 'Veblen's Attack on Culture', we find Adorno (1967, p. 80) apparently agreeing with Thorstein Veblen's assessment of modern sports as 'outbursts of violence, oppression and the predatory spirit'. Further to this, Adorno claims that he extends Veblen's position by showing that sport today involves not only the desire of the person taking part to harm others, but also the wish of that person to harm himself or herself. In this sense contemporary sport is masochistic (1967, p. 81). This masochism is said to involve the subjected inflicting on their own bodies, through sporting activity, the domination already forced upon them by society (Adorno, 1996, p. 77). This 'repetition-compulsion' means that in modern society 'sport becomes a pseudo-praxis in which those who are practically active are no longer capable of helping themselves but now turn themselves once again into the objects they have already become' (Adorno, 1996, p. 78).

Sport thus seems to be both symptom and contributing factor to the disaster of dystopic modernity. The alienating conditions of life reduce 'relations between human beings to the good fellowship of the sporting community', where the latter is a perverted parody of the former (Adorno & Horkheimer, 1944/92, p. 165). Not only on the field of play but also among the audience of sporting events is this alienation made manifest. The 'dialectic of enlightenment' results in a highly technically controlled sporting event being accompanied by a reversion to spectatorial barbarity, as registered in the cries of the 'howling devotees of the stadium' (Adorno, 1996, p. 78). The barbarism inherent in modern sporting activities spreads to other areas of culture. The 'sportification' of culture is a crucial aspect of the development of the Culture Industries. Consumers compete with each other to view the latest offering that is the same as every other. The standardized structure of the cultural product, such as a film, is 'regulated as if by stopwatch' (Adorno, 1996, p. 74). Any enjoyment gained from such products by the spectator is equivalent to the pleasure garnered by the sportsman, that is, a form of pseudo-enjoyment that only mutilates (s)he who takes part in apparently spontaneous, but actually totally rigorously regulated, events (Adorno, 1996, p. 75). In general terms, then, the more domination that the contemporary period pays witness to, 'then all the greater becomes the might of sport in mass culture and the ... world in general' (Adorno, 1996, p. 78).

Looking at sport afresh

From a review of Adorno's above comments, it seems that his position is in effect a crudely elitist denunciation of sport and other cultural forms. There does indeed seem to be ample evidence to suggest that when Adorno examines sport from the premise that 'there is nothing innocuous left', he does actually start out from an assumption that 'everything is domination' and then finds that premise completely confirmed. Yet, the above statement simultaneously has quite another meaning beyond that of 'total domination'. It is also a demand that the apparently trivial and pointless be taken very seriously indeed. Games and other leisure activities are to be looked at as crucial aspects of modern society, not as mere side-shows or fripperies (Adorno, 1967, p. 80). The Frankfurt approach to cultural analysis, as with the concomitant approaches to philosophy, psychology and so on, was intended as a corrective to a vulgar materialist version of Marxism which viewed sports and leisure activities, in line with all other forms of 'culture', merely as epiphenomena of the economic base (Adorno, 1997b, pp. 43–44). In contrast to such vulgar materialism, the general modus operandi of the Frankfurt theorists was to take cultural matters seriously, as being worthy of attention in their own right.

Adorno did not believe that to engage thoughtfully with cultural phenomena meant that one should take them at 'face value', in the fashion of positivistic science (see below). Rather, the form of interpretation to be brought to bear on them was to be guided by the dictum that 'the splinter in your eye is the best magnifying-glass' (Adorno,

1997b, p. 50). That is, one must view cultural forms 'up close' but yet regard them askance. If we want to understand what Adorno is doing in his analysis of culture in general, and sport in particular, we would do well to remember this dictum. The orientation is to look at matters critically, with a somewhat jaundiced eye. However, to say that Adorno's position is wholly and unmitigatedly 'jaundiced' is to miss the point of his project (Hoberman, 1984, p. 248). This is so because, as we will now see, his metaphors of a nightmarish dystopian society are not random or accidental, but are crucial elements of his covert utopian analysis of modern culture.

Language and dystopia

A superficial reading of Adorno's position on sporting and other popular cultures gives the reader the impression that all is doom and gloom in the author's worldview. But Adorno's extreme linguistic rendering of a scene of dystopian horror is profoundly tied up with his utopian critique of the society that produces such a cultural nightmare. This can be seen more clearly if we remember that Adorno writes in a fashion that demands not to be taken literally. In his voluminous writings on philosophy, aesthetics and (especially) culture, Adorno was an unashamed ironist. Not only *Dialectic of Enlightenment* but also all the other cultural writings are saturated in irony (Rose, 1978, p. 11).

In part this was due to the intellectual tradition in which Adorno was immersed, a tradition that included such masters of the ironic as the philosophers Soren Kierkegaard and Friedrich Nietzsche (Rose, 1978, p. 5; Wiggershaus, 1995, p. 70). Furthermore, the youthful Adorno was influenced by the Austrian satirist Karl Kraus, whose lampoons of Viennese society in the 1920s were premised on a theory of language whereupon the truth of what was said was dependent on the form or 'presentation' (*Darstellung*) in which it was expressed (Buck-Morss, 1977, pp. 12–13). The idea that the very prose style in which social theory is expressed is crucial for the truth of the theory, is central to Adorno's understanding not only of sport in particular, but of modern culture more generally. How a theory of sport is written is therefore as important as what is actually being said about sport. Both the style of the presentation of the ideas and the substantive content of the theory are inseparable. Stylistics are therefore not just something to be used by the theorist when s/he feels like it; the very point of the theory is crucially dependent upon the way it is expressed. Therefore the use of irony by Adorno is no mere form of ornamentation in his prose, but figures as a crucial means of expressing what he wishes to express.

If one lives in a society characterized by total domination – the hyperbolic yet deeply ironic claim at the heart of Adorno's philosophy – then one must find ways of expressing that truth in a linguistic context marked by total domination. For Adorno, one of the great symptoms of the sickness of contemporary society was the domination of positivism, the doctrine that all aspects of human life could be explained on the basis of the natural sciences (Adorno, 1976). The fetishization of science over other forms of knowledge meant that the true nature of social reality was disguised under a cloak of apparent natural scientific 'objectivity'. As Adorno saw it, contemporary language, not just in academic discip-lines but in ever more areas of social life more generally, is 'positivist' insofar as it merely records abstract, reified 'data', rather than expressing the lived experiences that form, and are formed by, language (Adorno & Horkheimer, 1944/92, p. 164). The language of positivism, with which contemporary society is condemned to speak, both accepts and is wholly complicit in, domination. Thus if one wishes to express truth about the domination inherent in present society, one must find a language that will break through the static and obdurate linguistic terminology ascendant today.

The means of breaking through the barriers of accepted linguistic mores is irony. Irony and ironic expression are therefore crucial to Adorno's method of cultural critique, that of 'negative dialectics' (Adorno, 1973). The aim of a negative dialectical approach to a given subject is to show how there is disparity between the promises inherent in the concept of a thing and the thing itself. This is a manner of criti-cism bequeathed by the work of Marx, where the claims of liberty and individuality of bourgeois society are juxtaposed against the exploitative realities of that society. The chasm between appearance and actuality is the realm of the ironic, as irony reveals the pretensions of the claims of the existent and shows, albeit negatively, that things might be different from the way they are. Although Adorno believed that the latest phase of capitalist modernity comes dangerously close to obliterating the gap between illusion and reality (Adorno, 1997b, p. 211), he nonetheless held that that gap is the absolutely essential condition of authentic cultural critique. Such a critique has to be expressed in ironic terms, for ironic language is hyperbolic, and its overstatements allow the true nature of things to be glimpsed. The outrageousness of ironic language allows its substantive content a fleeting truth-value, a truth-value that points both to the nature of domination, and to how things might be, beyond a situation characterized by domination. Thus the hyperbole of dystopian language allows a brief glimpse into a future utopian realm where things are different from the ways in which they currently are. In essence then, Adorno uses an ironic prose style that paints indeed a very black picture of phenomena such as contemporary sports. He uses this exceptionally bleak vision to highlight just how much are sports and other cultural phenomena penetrated by domination and power today.

As a result, Adorno's writing, on sport as on any other area of culture, can be taken by the reader in one of two ways. The first possibility is that if one takes his claims literally then one will no doubt become highly offended by remarks about 'howling devotees of the stadium' and suchlike. But such a reading is – on the terms of Adorno's prose itself – a deadening literal misreading for it confuses the ironic form of his statements with their actual substantive content, that is, what they are really saying.

It is this misreading that is the basis for the kind of denunciations of Adorno that we saw above, namely that he is an out-and-out elitist who has nothing but contempt for such prosaic matters as sports (e.g. Hoberman, 1984). Yet Adorno is not ultimately a conservative but a Marxist, albeit one in some ways very different from the mainstream of Marxist thought. Unlike many Marxists, who state bluntly what they believe to be the case, Adorno is a master of irony and ambivalence, and it is those qualities that must be borne in mind if we are truly to understand what he thought about sports. Adorno's extravagantly negative statements on sports and other matters are, in their excessive negativity, quite explicitly designed as 'shock-tactics' which are intended to compel the reader to think in ways very different from accustomed (and hence dominated) modes of thought (Adorno, 1997a, p. 319).

To respond to such shock tactics and to see the world in the way they paint it, involves a second way of reading Adorno's prose, this time non-literally. If taken in the spirit Adorno intends, the image of howling stadium devotees will conjure up horrified responses on behalf of the reader, so that he or she may actively engage with the possibility that the contemporary epoch, for from being one of harmony and civilized consumer enjoyment, can actually be seen as one of brutality and degradation, a period of violence lurking under an appearance of unanimity and peaceful sporting pleasure.

Paradoxically, it is precisely the reader's awareness of the darkest depths of despair conjured up by Adorno's writing which fundamentally prevents us from reading his position as simply a form of conservative elitism. If Adorno's negative rhetoric was merely that, and had no fundamental implications for his position, then we would have to agree that Adorno's was indeed a conservative, intellectualist, anti-popular form of cultural analysis. But since the terminology deployed is designed to make the reader see phenomena in a very different light from his or her usual modes of perception, one cannot so easily dismiss Adorno's position as being simply a one-sided denunciation of cultural phenomena. The excessively negative rhetoric allows the object of analysis – be it sports or whatever – to be viewed in novel fashions. It is precisely the dystopian rhetoric about the object that allows the utopian element of the object to be revealed.

This awareness of utopian possibilities lying within the current form of the object under consideration is exactly what is lacking in the work of certain later writers, who are usually seen as embodying the essence of Adorno's approach to sporting matters. The two main authors in this regard are Bero Rigauer (1981) and Jean-Marie Brohm (1989). The latter (1989, p. 5) sums up the tenor of what could be called the neo-Adornian school in sports sociology:

> Apart from the act of labour, the dominant and fundamental way man relates to his [*sic*] body in state capitalist society is through sport – inasmuch as it is through the model of sport that the body is understood in practice, collectively hallucinated, fantasized, imagined and individually experienced as an object, an instrument, a technical means to an end, a reified factor of output and productivity, in short, as a machine with the job of producing the maximum work and energy.

At a superficial level, the message expressed here – that sports today are thoroughly permeated by domination, and that they operate in the interests of the capitalist economy – seems to be written in the spirit of Adorno's theory of sports and their relation to contemporary society. However, it would be a mistake to identify and denounce the work of the Master purely on the basis of the writings of his disciples. Both Rigauer and Brohm are often taken as exemplifying how Adorno-inspired work on sporting matters can go awry in a blaze of negativity (Morgan, 1994). Yet far from being characteristic of Adorno's method of ironic exaggeration, both of these later authors take Adorno's statements literally as the bases for their own interpretations of sport, rather than as the ironic exaggerations in the service of utopian critique that they are. Their work is thus only formally akin to Adorno's position. At a more profound level, their work has none of the richness of Adorno's ironic approach, forsaking it for the very monotone form of cultural critique Adorno wished to avoid.

Thus writers such as Brohm and Rigauer reproduce the extremities of Adorno's prose as substantive content, rather than utilising it as a means of teasing out the ambivalences inherent in sport today. Adorno's account of sport, as with his contributions to other areas of culture, should not be confused with the cruder work of his literally minded inheritors. These disciples misunderstand Adorno's ironic approach and in so doing forget that Adorno is a profoundly utopian thinker, albeit one whose utopianism is deliberately masked in a cloud of dark pessimism.

Sport and utopia

A truly conservative and elitist appreciation of a phenomenon such as sporting activity would regard that object in and of itself as intrinsically debased and unworthy of 'serious' consideration. But in Adorno's work, the negative rhetoric about sport does not correspond to a negative conception of the 'essence' of sport. Rather, the opposite is true: by emphasizing the current, negative state of this phenomenon, Adorno hopes to show that in its essence sport contains elements which are intrinsically positive, and that these elements could be realized in a possible utopian future.

For Adorno, sport is only debased in its contemporary expressions in capitalist modernity. This is the sense of the claim cited above that '[s]port itself is not play but ritual in which the subjected celebrate their subjection' (Adorno, 1996, p. 77). Adorno does not claim that at all times and places sport is ritualistic behaviour predicated on domination. Such a claim would be unacceptably monolithic, and utterly in contradiction with the principles of an authentically critical, dialectical approach to culture. Instead, it is only under present conditions that it takes on this reified form. In actual fact, sport's 'essence' – and thus its potential in a possible future characterized by non-domination – is of 'play', that is, free and purposeless bodily activity enjoyed for its own sake.

Adorno can be taken as holding that play is a form of activity which to a degree can stand beyond the realm of instrumental-rational activity. Adorno's comments on this topic are scattered throughout his work, and require some effort to reconstruct them. Morgan (1988) has carried out such a task, and it is partly on his account that we base the following remarks. Adorno was highly suspicious of all 'positive anthropologies', that is, theories of what human nature essentially 'is'. For Adorno, such directly utopian thinking is both far too abstract, ignoring the specific social and historical contexts in which people live, and also misleading, owing more to the fantasies of philosophers than a careful consideration of social and historical realities.

Because Adorno tried to avoid all such directly utopian theories of human nature, he should not be seen be as a straightforward apologist for a 'play-principle'. Nonetheless, he does accept such an idea in a mediated way. Sport is seen to contain within it a 'utopian' moment that looks forward to a time when humanity has escaped the coils of instrumental reason and the forms of domination that are concomitant with it. Even today, children's games hint at that possibility, as they provide a clue as to what a more equable society would look like. Played for their own sake, rather than as a means to a (repressive) end, the 'unreality [i.e. their non-instrumental nature] of games gives notice that [wholly instrumentalized] reality is not yet real. Unconsciously they rehearse the right life' (Adorno, 1997b, p. 228). In the same vein, Adorno locates emancipatory potential in the slapstick and nonsense of farceurs, clowns and circus performers, for their actions represent what is authentically 'human' (Adorno & Horkheimer, 1944/92, pp. 137, 143). Even in their most debased manifestations today as the 'sports' and 'entertainments' of mass culture, games and buffoonery stand testimony to how life could be, free of domination and based around principles where actions are carried out autonomously for their own ends, beyond the realm of domination. Games and buffoonish antics may currently be subordinated to the corresponding reified Culture Industry forms of 'sporting events' and 'entertainment', but because the emancipatory principle of autonomous play is inherently and indissociably part of these debased forms, then even today these forms are fundamentally ambivalent, exhibiting both deeply negative and highly positive characteristics.

There is thus always a utopian 'trace' lurking within the most apparently reified object. The aim of negative dialectical criticism to expose that otherwise suppressed kernel. Unlike some other versions of Marxian analysis, Adorno does not appeal directly to utopian principles when evaluating the present. His 'negative anthropology' forbids him from doing this as he believes that unmediated appeal to abstract utopian conceptions, within the context of a contemporary society characterized by almost complete domination, end up falling into a trap of utter abstraction, which destroys their emancipatory potential (Jarvis, 1998, pp. 70–71). However, although direct appeal cannot be made to such principles, indirect appeal can be made. The aim of a negative dialectical approach is to present the potential inherent in the concept a thing has of itself, with the debased nature of that thing in reality. The 'sports' of mass culture claim to be 'play', yet they are actually impregnated with the principles of instrumental reason. The claims made as to the 'playful' aspect of sport, however, point indirectly to a situation where sport might truly involve play rather than domination.

Thus we can see that there are two key components to Adorno's utopian analysis of culture in general and sport in particular. The first concerns his violent rhetorical condemnation of its contemporary manifestations. Such rhetoric is highly ironic and, as a result, exposes the gap between concept and actuality, between, for example, sport as it is now, and as it claims to be. The second component involves identifying how the claims contemporary sport makes for itself as a realm of freedom actually point to a situation where sport really could be organized around a non-dominating principle, that is, as 'play', The two components of Adorno's analysis are completely interdependent. The ironic rhetoric exposes the utopian potential, while the utopian potential – the intuition that things could be different – is the very reason for denouncing the present in terms of negative overstatement. Thus there is a very definite and deliberate ambivalence in Adorno's method of analysing sport – between destructive denunciation of what is, and constructive thinking about what could be. This ambivalence of approach maps onto the ambivalence of sport itself: sport could be concerned with freedom, but currently is a form of domination. The aim of critique is to show that future potential through censuring the present. The curse put upon sport is done with the hope of blessing it. The deliberate ambivalence of Adorno's approach towards the object of analysis thus marks it out as a fundamentally utopian analysis, rather than simply as an elitist form of cultural criticism and denunciation.

Conclusion

From the above, it should be clear that Adorno excoriates the guises sport takes today in order to think about what forms it might take in the future. Through a method characterized by the utmost negativity coupled with that of the most gratifying utopian intimations, he draws the conclusion that sport itself is an irreducibly ambivalent phenomenon. For Adorno, the modern period is one of extraordinary promise as well as great negativity. Sport thus figures as a realm marked both by the perversions of capitalist society, and by intimations of a better world beyond domination.

If one goes beyond a literal reading of what Adorno says about sports and other phenomena, one begins to see not only the subtlety of his position but also its potentially great power too. By adopting an Adornian perspective, contemporary sports, as with any cultural object to be analysed, is found to contain seeds of hope within a shell of despair. The core of Adorno's approach is that there is always a potential, redemptive element in a cultural object that looks towards a utopian future, buried within the unpromising husk of its present-day manifestations. Unlike many contemporary theorists of culture, Adorno does not wish to think about cultural forms and practices merely in terms of how they happen to be now; he also wishes to reflect on how they might be in the future. It is his utopian stress on 'things to come' that makes an interpretation of his work based on the view that he is undilutedly elitist and pessimistic wholly misleading.

For Adorno, the quintessence of an authentically 'critical' social theory of culture in general, and sport in particular, is the utopian element contained within the conceptual apparatuses of cultural critique. The very word 'critical' indicates a form of analysis that possesses a yardstick against which to measure the object of study. What a given phenomenon could be like should be juxtaposed on the way that object currently is. This yardstick is the product of reflection upon what a social and cultural order free from oppression and domination might look like. Without this element of utopianism, cultural analysis, of sport or of anything else, can find itself mired in the pure actualities of the present, rather than attempting to find the future potentialities inherent within the cultural phenomena it scrutinises.

This is a crucial insight for future studies of sports. If sporting activity is ever to have a chance of being free from oppression in practice, it will be necessary for students of sport to begin to think about how sports could be organized and played in freer and liberating ways. Only by holding up the lack of freedom and creativity at the heart of contemporary sports can we even begin to think about a better sporting world, as well as a better society more generally. To think a better future, however much the odds are against its realization, is the legacy of Adorno's social theory, and it involves students of sports and of other areas, in projects that think about how things might be, rather than merely passively accepting them as they are.

References

Adorno, T.W. (1967) *Prisms*, London: Neville Spearman.
Adorno, T.W. (1973) *Negative Dialectics*, London: Routledge.

Adorno, T.W. (1976) *The Positivist Dispute in German Sociology*, London: Heinemann.

Adorno, T.W. (1996) *The Culture Industry*, London: Routledge.

Adorno, T.W. (1997a) *Aesthetic Theory*, Minneapolis: University of Minnesota Press.

Adorno, T.W. (1997b) *Minima Moralia*, London: Verso.

Adorno, T.W. & Horkheimer, M. (1944/92) *Dialectic of Enlightenment*, London: Verso.

Andrews, D.L. & J.W. Loy (1993) 'British Cultural Studies and Sport: Past Encounters and Future Possibilities', *Quest*, 45: 255–276.

Brohm, J.-M. (1989) *Sport: a prison of measured time*, London: Pluto.

Buck-Morss, S. (1977) *The Origin of Negative Dialectics*, Hassocks, Sussex: The Harvester Press.

Dunning, E. (1999) *Sport Matters*, London: Routledge.

Fiske, J. (1989) *Reading the Popular*, Boston: Unwin Hyman.

Hoberman, J.M. (1984) *Sport and Political Ideology*, Austin: Texas University Press.

Jarvis, S. (1998) *Adorno*, Cambridge: Polity.

Morgan, W.J. (1988) 'Adorno on Sport: the case of the fractured dialectic', *Theory and Society*, 17: 813–838.

Morgan, W.J. (1994) *Leftist Theories of Sport: a critique and reconstruction*, Urbana and Chicago: University of Illinois Press.

Rigauer, B. (1981) *Sport and Work*, New York: Columbia University Press.

Rose, G. (1978) *The Melancholy Science*, London and Basingstoke: Macmillan.

Wiggershaus, R. (1995) *The Frankfurt School*, Cambridge: Polity.

6

Antonio Gramsci: Sport, Hegemony and the National-Popular

David Rowe

Introduction

The interest of the Italian Marxist philosopher Antonio Gramsci (1891–1937) in sport was, apparently, 'close to nil' (Guttmann, 1994, p. 6). Yet his ideas have been highly influential in the social analysis of sport. This chapter briefly introduces the man and his work, and explains the appeal of a Gramscian framework to social science scholarship in general and to sport in particular. The Gramscian concepts of 'hegemony' and 'national-popular' are given particular emphasis. The chapter concludes with a brief consideration of the trajectory and legacy of Gramscian thought in the social theorization of sport.

Brief biography

Antonio Gramsci was born on the Mediterranean island of Sardinia into a middle-class family, but one disrupted by his father's imprisonment on what are likely to have been politically inspired charges of public service corruption. His early life, therefore, was characterized by considerable deprivation as one of seven children mostly raised by his mother alone. Plagued with bad health arising from skeletal and abdominal disorders, he was a short, hunched-back figure who was encouraged to take an interest in politics by his elder brother. He became deeply politicized after the repression of Sardinian peasant unrest by mainland troops. Moving to the Italian mainland in early adulthood and studying linguistics and philology at the University of Turin, a combination of ill health, poverty and political commitments led him to drop out in 1915. A leading left wing activist, he played an important role in the formation in 1921 of the Italian Communist Party following the cessation of hostilities in the

First World War, becoming Party Secretary, a Communist member of Parliament and, among other political journalistic activities, editor of the Party newspaper *Unità*.

Gramsci had two children (one of whom he never saw because of imprisonment) with fellow Communist Julia Schucht. Arrested by Mussolini's Fascists in 1926, he was sentenced to a 20-year prison term two years later, the prosecutor summing up with the memorable injunction to the trial judge 'We must stop this brain working for twenty years!' Gramsci was, however, released a week before his death after a little over a decade of incarceration, and expired while in a 'secure' Rome clinic at the age of 46. His partner's sister, Tatiana, smuggled his compendious 33 notebooks out of the clinic and thence out of Italy by means of a diplomatic bag bound for Moscow (Gramsci, 1971, pp. xvii ff; Solomon, 1979, p. 265).

Gramsci's *Prison Notebooks* (1971) were published in Italian after the conclusion of the Second World War and the vanquishment of the Fascists. The notebooks are a difficult literary source to rely for several reasons. They are fragmented in nature, often in the form of jottings and multiple drafts. Gramsci, for reasons of ill health, surveillance of his work, and lack of library access, was constantly forced to change plans about the form and function of his writing. He was concerned that scholarship for its own sake would be a denial of his political responsibility as an active intellectual, denouncing '"Byzantinism" or "scholasticism" [as] the regressive tendency to treat so-called theoretical questions as if they had a value in themselves, independently of any specific practice' (Gramsci, 1971, p. 200). At the same time he tried to outwit the prison censor by using an elaborate system of code that, for example, led Karl Marx in some places to be referred to not by name but as '"the founder of the philosophy of praxis"' (Hoare & Nowell Smith, 1971, p. xiii). Reading Gramsci, therefore, is an exercise in which the author's intent and meaning is more than usually in question, and the reader is placed in the hands of translators and editors who have selected, reconstructed and re-assembled large tracts of his massive, shifting text. Some of the appeal of his work might, therefore, lie in its very openness to re-consideration, re-discovery and re-interpretation.

The English translation and publication of *Prison Notebooks* in the early 1970s was an important contribution to the international neo-Marxism of the time, with 'New Left' thinkers finding in Gramsci an invitation to break with orthodox, determinist forms of Marxism in favour of a more humanistic approach in tune with emerging cultural – especially youth – politics. The 'romance' of Gramsci's life (somewhat akin to that of the imprisoned Nelson Mandela), and his emphasis (as we will see below) on non-reductive cultural contestation and the necessity of intellectuals engaging with popular culture, were significant aspects of his appeal to social theorists. Gramsci's call to 'elaborate a popular culture' (1957, p. 85) – that is, to establish an 'organic' connection to the everyday lives of 'the people' – encouraged more sophisticated and reflexive analyses of many key areas of contemporary culture – not least among which is sport.

Social theory and Gramsci: grounds for a critique of sport

In discussing the application of Gramsci to sport, I will not attempt a comprehensive analysis of his thought. That would demand a highly abstract and detailed explication (of the role of intellectuals, for example, or of the workings of the political apparatus) that would far exceed this chapter's brief. Instead, I will canvass – rather crudely for purposes of clarification – competing theories of society from within sociology and preliminarily propose their application to sport. Most introductory discussions of sociology are framed around the differences between two grand theories of society – functionalism and conflict theory (especially in its Marxist form). The classical functionalist view of society is a system of organically interrelated parts with a tendency towards equilibrium, adapting to the needs of a changing environment and founded on a value consensus (e.g. Giddens, 2001). The emergence of the social institution of sport, from this perspective, can be explained as adaptation to modernization and industrialization. Physical play becomes more structured and regulated, it takes on many of the cohesive values necessary for society to exist (common purpose, mutual support, leadership, and discipline), especially in the schools, where children can learn socialization through sport. Sporting pursuits also develop into a modern industry that enables leisure time to be fruitfully and efficiently used. Workers (usually characterized as male) with discretionary leisure income pay expert professionals efficiently to perform – and in some case to get injured – on their behalf, helping to compensate for the boredom of their working lives.

This is something of a caricature of a functionalist perspective, but it importantly emphasizes the tendency of functionalism to assume the political neutrality of sport as a necessary institution that has evolved to take care of societal needs for the benefit of all.[1] Jay Coakley (1990, p. 23), for example, notes how a functionalist approach 'calls attention to the ways in which sport might serve *tension management* functions in society' by relatively harmlessly discharging aggression. The limitations of functionalist analysis of sport and of other aspects of society are obvious – a circular logic and a tendency to defend the *status quo* as inevitable and, unless dramatically proven otherwise, desirable.

A contrasting social theory stresses the centrality of conflict to the social order, emphasizing how society is shaped by the unequal distribution of power in society, leading in turn to inequalities of wealth, education and even life expectancy (Giddens, 2001). The foundation of this view of society, therefore, is an appreciation of structural conflict between social groups based on class, ethnicity, gender and other structurally produced unequal relations. From a conflict perspective, the social institution of sport would be viewed as the product of contending forces, each seeking to exercise control and maximize advantage over the various elements of physical play (like gaining access to commercial or public funding, or excluding 'undesirable' groups from sports clubs).

The greatest influence on conflict theory in the last four decades has been Marxism, which offers a theory of society as expansive as functionalism but founded on the pivotal importance of class struggle. An orthodox Marxist critique of sport would view the 'state of play' in anything but beneficial terms. From such a perspective, sport is represented not as a benign development of physical play but as an example of the development of the commodification of everyday life by capitalism, appropriating cultural pursuits, distracting the proletariat with sporting 'circuses', obstructing their revolutionary potential, turning athletes into 'robots' and spectators into disciplined, passive consumers, and creating further opportunities for capitalist exploitation and ruling-class domination (Lawrence & Rowe, 1986). An example of such a perspective (influenced by the Marxist philosopher Louis Althusser) is presented by Jean-Marie Brohm:

> Sport is dependent on the development of the productive forces of bourgeois society. Technical progress in sport closely follows the technological and scientific development of capitalism. Bourgeois sport is a class institution, totally integrated into the framework of capitalist production relations and class relations. Like other class institutions, such as the University, the Army etc.

> And, finally, as a phenomenon of the superstructure, sport is linked to all the other superstructural levels of capitalist society. The organizational unity of sport is ensured by the repressive grip of the bourgeois

state. Moreover, sport as ideology, transmitted on a huge scale by the mass media, is part and parcel of ruling bourgeois ideology.

(Brohm, 1989, pp. 47–48)

The problem with this uncompromisingly hostile approach to sport is as clear as that for an uncritically favourable functionalist perspective. Sport in a capitalist society is represented as beyond redemption and, as with other bourgeois social institutions, can only be 'reclaimed' by a proletarian revolution. For social theorists wishing to advance a critique of capitalism and its relationship to sport without producing such a rigid analysis, Marxist theories that either privilege the economic mode of production over all else or classify every social institution as 'captured' by bourgeois ideology do not offer a viable analytical foundation. Ironically, strong traces of a left-wing version of functionalism can be discerned in exaggerating the easy fit between economic relations and cultural forms and practices. Dominant ideology is shown to be imposed on the working class from above, and to have so infiltrated the state and civil society that it is reproduced not just institutionally but within our very own subjectivities in the very culture itself. Other than refining a rigorous doctrinal science to which most people, by its own logic, must be blind, such an analysis leaves little space for critical intellectual engagement.

It is here that the Gramscian alternative comes to the fore by offering a form of 'praxis' (a productive combination of theorizing and concrete engagement with key social issues and action) that is:

Criticism of 'common sense', basing itself initially, however, on common sense in order to demonstrate that 'everyone' is a philosopher and that it is not a question of introducing from scratch a scientific form of thought into everyone's individual life, but of renovating and making 'critical' an already existing activity.

(Gramsci, 1971, pp. 330–331)

Gramsci, it can be seen, encourages an intellectual philosophy that operates within the realm of the 'commonsensical' and the 'popular', and which enables the social analyst to work with the materials of everyday life in a relatively open yet critical way. In his concept of the 'national-popular', he proposes a way in which new and more progressive forms of common sense can be created out of articulating (i.e. fitting together) the national culture traditionally controlled by the state with the culture of the 'people', and by this means fashioning a powerful social and cultural bloc.

Intellectuals are seen by Gramsci as crucial to the success of any such social coalition, but not those of the traditional elite variety 'separated from the masses', but rather 'intellectuals who are conscious of being linked organically to a national-popular mass' (Gramsci, 1971, p. 204). While Gramsci had in mind 'intellectuals of a new type which arise directly out of the masses, but remain in contact with them to become, as it were, the whalebone in the corset' (p. 340), it is not hard to see how reading him encouraged scholars in conventional educational institutions to view themselves as 'organic' intellectuals intimately connected to the culture of 'the people'. The pressures for university teachers to be 'relevant' to the lives of the growing numbers of students and the increasing study of the popular in formal institutions were highly conducive to the adoption of Gramscian ideas.

Gramsci's humanism appealed especially to those Left-leaning social scientists and cultural critics made uneasy by the dismissal of the working class for being insufficiently revolutionary. Gramsci encourages intellectuals to 'feel' as well as to 'know', because 'One cannot make politics-history without this sentimental connection between intellectuals and people-nation', without which their relationships become 'of a purely bureaucratic and formal order', and intellectuals a kind of 'caste' or 'priesthood' (p. 418). Gramscianism, therefore, licenses critical analysts of sport to share – with reservations – the thrill of the sports stadium and the *frisson* of sports fandom.

Applying Gramsci to sport

The Gramscian perspective, then, shares some of the components of the orthodox Marxist critique of sport (for example, the pivotal role of class politics and conflict) but it differs in certain important respects. It does not see the ruling class as being in complete control of the working class, but instead as having to make important compromises with it. The meaning and practice of sport are viewed as contested by social classes and other social groupings, and the outcome of that contestation is seen as less certainly resulting, as tends to be the case in classical Marxism, with the inevitable defeat of the proletariat and other subaltern groups unless and until a comprehensive worker's revolution is achieved. Gramsci's most influential concept, hegemony, challenges this monolithic and determinist scenario by emphasizing that power relations have to be sustained by more than brute force and economic domination. They must be constantly re-made by securing 'common consent' through a process of (admittedly uneven) negotiation that always holds out the possibility of limited but nonetheless significant tactical victories for subordinate and subaltern groups. Sometimes, Gramsci argues, 'the leaders [*dirigenti*] of the dominant classes' simply get it wrong:

> Mechanical historical materialism does not allow for the possibility of error, but assumes that every political act is determined, immediately, by the structure, and therefore as a real and permanent (in the sense of achieved) modification of the structure. The principle of 'error' is a complex one: one may be dealing with an individual impulse based on mistaken calculations or equally it may be a manifestation of the attempts of specific groups or sects to take over hegemony within the directive grouping, attempts which may well be unsuccessful.
>
> (Gramsci, 1971, p. 408)

In other circumstances, disruption may occur when 'the great masses have become detached from their traditional ideologies, and no longer believe what they used to believe...a problem caused by the "crisis of authority" of the old generation in power, and by the mechanical impediment that has been imposed on those who could exercise hegemony, which prevents them from carrying out their mission' (p. 276). The 'hegemony' of the ruling class is not, then, seen by Gramsci as an inevitable condition but as a continuing 'work-in-progress' in which, while the *bourgeoisie* has many advantages in directing social values and controlling institutions, it has to take account of, and sometimes cede ground to, popular resistance. Gramsci is here discussing the major social upheavals that occur after war, but it is not difficult to see their relevance to less dramatic social contexts – in the case of sport this might be popular resistance to the regulation and even prohibition of certain sports for the English working class in the eighteenth and nineteenth centuries (Clarke & Critcher, 1985; Hargreaves, 1986) or, more recently, to the closure of a football club, the relocation of a sports franchise to another part of the country, or the takeover of a sports club by a media company (Gruneau & Whitson, 1994; Rowe, 2000).

These ideas of Gramsci have been a major influence on the sociology of culture and on the interdisciplinary field dedicated to working through the politics of everyday life by intellectuals operating both in and outside the academy – Cultural Studies (Turner, 1996). As John Clarke and Chas Critcher (1985, p. 228) note in relation to leisure, the concept of hegemony 'condenses, or crystallizes, a number of major themes about the processes of cultural domination and conflict'. It does so by treating national culture not as unitary but as comprised of many disparate and conflicting subcultures, and by stressing that the 'articulation' of all these cultural elements is no easy task.

Because Gramsci's analysis pays considerable attention to the 'ideological superstructure' (culture) rather than concentrating on the 'base' (economics), his work suggests many possibilities for the critical analysis of sport. Mechanical explanations of how capital has inevitably and irreversibly taken over sport can be challenged by more specific and reflexive critiques that do justice to the complexity of human society. Due account can also be taken of the specifically cultural dimensions of sport under prevailing patterns of 'culturalization' and 'mediatization' in image-saturated Western societies (Rowe, 2004). Forms of popular culture like sport, therefore, emerge within a Gramscian framework as important battlegrounds where social values and relations are shaped, represented and contested. Gramsci's concept of hegemony, by looking closely within a dynamic framework at how institutions are founded, actions interpreted, and ideologies generated, also suggests ways of overcoming some disabling dualities. In sociology, the problem of the structure/agency split (between society making people and people making society) can be at least partially healed through hegemony's emphasis on their simultaneous interaction.[2] In the interdisciplinary field of Cultural Studies the concept has been similarly used to heal the breach between structuralism (which stresses how human subjects are positioned within already existing structures of language, ideology and discourse) and culturalism (which emphasizes how social groups make their own culture and resist attempts to have it imposed upon them).[3]

Hence, from the mid-1970s onwards, as Garry Whannel (1992, p. 8) observes, 'Gramsci's concept of hegemony increasingly appeared appealing as an apparent resolution of the difficulty of forging an adequate synthesis of two productive but seemingly incompatible paradigms.' Importantly, given the concerns of this chapter, Whannel in his analysis of sports television goes on to note how sport has increasingly emerged not just as 'another site upon which rests a field of struggle over meaning', but, as argued by sports sociologists like John Hargreaves (1986), 'as sport has become more important as a component of the national culture, it has hence become more important to hegemony' (p. 9).

So, despite Gramsci's own lack of interest in sport (understandable given his many other areas of concern), his concept of hegemony has been applied extensively as a way of analysing the heightened role of sport within the 'national-popular' and, increasingly, we might suggest, the 'global-popular' (Miller *et al.*, 2001). As noted above, Whannel (1992), in situating his analysis of television sport and cultural transformation, recognizes the importance of Gramscian theory to the critical social analysis of sport since the 1970s. In constructing a canon of such work, the contributions of Hargreaves (J.A.) (1982), Gruneau (1983), Clarke and Critcher (1985), Hargreaves (J.E.) (1986), McKay (1991) and Tomlinson (1999) – as well as Whannel (1992) himself – would be included. Most (such as Tomlinson, 1999, p. 17) do not just deploy the Gramscian concept of hegemony as one among many implements within the theoretical toolkit (as with some of the more eclectic analytical perspectives), but explicitly acknowledge it as formative of their entire approach to the subject.

One influential early study is Richard Gruneau's (1983) *Class, Sports, and Social Development*, which addresses sport at the abstract level and in the specific Canadian context in a manner heavily influenced by the Gramscian perspective as interpreted by Raymond Williams (1977), supplemented by Williams's model of co-existent cultural forms that are (currently) dominant, residual (formerly dominant) and emergent (potentially dominant). Gruneau follows a Gramscian logic in acknowledging that sport is 'an area of social life that provides a sense of continuity and enjoyment for many members of the Canadian working class', and that the 'dominant moment in "modern" sport' offers some opportunities for that class to gain insights into its own domination (e.g. by perceiving the gap between the noble rhetoric of sport and its often ignoble commercial exploitation). However, these compensations and incomplete insights come at the cost of:

> The failure to acknowledge and understand the discontinuous nature of an emergent dominant form whose structures are in no way controlled by the underclasses, and whose acceptance represents a paradoxical cultural insertion into the hegemony of capitalist life.
>
> (Gruneau, 1983, p. 147)

This concern with domination and resistance in sport is also evident (with specific reference to the state) in edited collections from the same early 1980s period, with hegemony treated as a pivotal (though by no means uncritically accepted) concept (Cantelon & Gruneau, 1982; Hargreaves, 1982). These early works in the critical sociology of sport shade into the emergent field of Cultural Studies, and provide a platform for many others who adopt, in whole or in part, a Gramscian perspective (e.g. Clarke & Critcher, 1985; Ingham & Loy, 1993).

One of the most cited sociological works deploying Gramsci is John Hargreaves's *Sport, Power and Culture*. In his analysis of the development of sport in Britain, Hargreaves (1986, pp. 6–7) advances the thesis that 'sport was significantly implicated in the process whereby the growing economic and political power of the bourgeoisie in nineteenth-century Britain was eventually transformed into that class's hegemony in the later part of the century'. Here sport is regarded as an important aspect of class power relations, whereby cultural leadership replaces force as the major means of exercising control over 'subaltern and subordinate groups' in the context of a general 'recomposition of the working class'. This 'continuous work' of negotiating, forming alliances and fragmenting opposition is the means by which 'working class and other subordinate social categories (blacks, youth) are *won over* to sports rather than forced into, or manipulated into, involvement in them'.

Hargreaves argues that in the late nineteenth and early twentieth century period in Britain the foundation of 'the dominant class's hegemony over the working class' (pp. 57–58) was laid. At this time relatively uncoordinated physical activities were being consolidated into a modern institution, a development that for Hargreaves is not coincidental. Among other patterns he notes that, '[s]ports functioned to disproportionately attach the respectable elements among young working-class males to a variety of organizations, which aimed at integrating working-class people by engrossing their free time' (p. 77). This integrative role of sport, stressing the role of respectable leisure over disreputable 'hooligan' pleasurable pursuits, is an example of the working of the Gramscian concept of hegemony. For Hargreaves, the dominant class's interests were served by binding a large proportion of potentially disruptive, young working-class males to the social institution of sport largely administered at the grass-roots level by the lower middle and 'respectable' working class itself. This type of analysis appealed particularly to British sports scholars. For example, a special theme issue of *Sociology of Sport Journal* (1992) devoted to 'British Cultural Studies and Sport' contained contributions of a predominantly Gramscian nature.[4] The influence of hegemony theory on sports studies has been felt particularly strongly across the Anglophone world of sports studies, extending beyond Britain to the USA (e.g. Sage, 1990), Canada (Gruneau & Whitson, 1994) and Australia (McKay, 1991; Rowe *et al.*, 1997). The Gramscian approach to sport has also registered in many countries where English is not the first language, as evidenced, for example, in contributions to journals such as the *International Review for the Sociology of Sport*. But, as Gramsci was keenly aware, culture and intellectual life are perpetually shifting – not least for Gramscianism itself.

Conclusion: the trajectory and legacy of the Gramscian analysis of sport

Gramscianism has been in something of a decline in general Sociology and Cultural Studies, and sport theory has not been exempt from this trend. In brief, neo-Marxist theory, with its ultimate reliance on an explanatory class framework, has been strongly contested by the diffusive approach to power of Foucauldianism and the anti-determinist emphasis of postmodernism.[5] For example, Tony Bennett (1992, p. 29) has asserted the need to go 'beyond hegemony' because of the 'real limitations to the work that can be done from within the Gramscian tradition', finding in the analysis of the relationship of culture to power that 'Foucault is better to "think with" than Gramsci' (Bennett, 1998, p. 62). Gramscianism has been criticized in such works on a number of grounds, including class reductionism and determinism; Left functionalism (such as Hargreaves's (1986) account of the integrative function of sport quoted above); a tendency to premature analytical closure, and a lack of attention to key differences between cultural institutions by a simple assertion of the slippery concepts of hegemony and consent (Harris, 1992).

In theorizing sport this passing of the 'Gramscian moment' has registered in the displacement of class relations as the central problematic by a range of other sites of conflict – gender, race, sexuality, and so on. It is notable, for example, that in one edition of a journal carrying a special theme devoted to British sports studies (*Journal of Sport & Social Issues*, 1998), the influence of Gramsci is rather less to the fore. A starker example of gathering challenges to Gramscianism is the criticism of the published version of a presidential address to the North American Society for the Sociology of Sport (Messner, 1996). Michael Messner's article is symptomatic of the adaptability of the concept of hegemony to modalities of power other than class,[6] emphasizing the need to 'study up' on the linkage of sport, power and heterosexuality but also of avoiding the errors of the 'radical Foucauldians', 'sexual deconstructionists and queer theory' by stressing 'material, structured relations of power that shape language and ideology' (p. 227). From the standpoint of queer theory, Judy Davidson and Debra Shogan (1998, p. 359) complain that "Messner's address makes it acceptable to write about queer theory as long as the discourse reproduces the stable knowledge bases and political aims of a new hegemonic 'critical' sports studies", and that he is imposing an orthodoxy entailing 'systematic social analysis that proceeds from a Gramscian perspective of hegemony' (p. 360).

Here the ironic prospect of the hegemony of hegemony in sports theory is presented, with the corresponding need for Gramscians to assume intellectual leadership, win consent, and destabilize opposition from rival theoretical perspectives! There is no doubt that, as pointed out in the introduction to this chapter, the complexity and fragmentation of Gramsci's ideas create many interpretive permutations. Gramsci's theory can be accused, for example, of being too economically determinist and class reductionist, and also as being so vague as to be applicable to any phenomenon. It is also common for both his admirers and detractors to exaggerate Gramsci's impact on the social scientific study of sport. Nonetheless, his ideas have influenced much of the best social theory of sport in the last two decades, and continue to inform new work in the field (e.g. Budd, 2001). Above all, even a passing acquaintance with Gramsci has helped open up new critical space for scholars of the politics of popular pleasure. His concept of hegemony, in particular, helped sports theorists out of the disabling analytical trap of positing absolute, top down social domination against equally unfeasible notions of free play and autonomous people's culture. For sensitising sports theorists to the many sided play of power within and against social structures, Antonio Gramsci, to many an obscure and long-dead 'jailed Sardinian' (Hall, 1987, p. 16) who wrote little and cared less about sport, is a key social theorist of it.

Notes

1. As the chapters of this book illustrate, social theories of sport (or of any other social phenomenon) cannot be neatly parcelled up into entirely distinct positions. For example, the question of some similarities between structural functionalism and the figurational sociology of Elias is a matter of some debate (see Dunning, 1999), as is the presence of elements of functionalism within Marxist (including Gramscian) theory. The intention of this chapter is to acquaint the reader with Gramsci to a level where the interpretation of his work and its relationship to other social theorists can productively illuminate a more sophisticated social theorization of sport.
2. In a more orthodox sociological framework, Giddens's (1979) theory of 'structuration' has been designed to address this same analytical problem.
3. For the structuralism/culturalism debate, see Johnson (1979), Hall (1981).
4. The special issue also contains a hostile and querulous critique of Cultural Studies and hegemony theory by the American cultural anthropologist John MacAloon.
5. Foucault is often used (e.g. by Hargreaves (1986) in his discussion of sport and the disciplining of the body) somewhat uneasily in tandem with Gramsci. For

a consideration of the postmodern challenge to established critical theoretical paradigms, see, for example, Dunn (1998).
6. See, for example, the extensive use of the concept of 'hegemonic masculinity' in McKay *et al.* (2000).

References

Bennett, T. (1992) 'Putting Policy into Cultural Studies', in L. Grossberg, C. Nelson & P. Treichler (eds) *Cultural Studies*, New York: Routledge.
Bennett, T. (1998) *Culture*, Sydney: Allen & Unwin.
Brohm, J.-M. (1989) *Sport: A Prison of Measured Time*, London: Pluto.
Budd, A. (2001) 'Capitalism, Sport and Resistance Reflections', *Culture, Sport, Society* 4(1): 1–18.
Cantelon, H. & Gruneau, R. (eds) (1982) *Sport, Culture, and the Modern State*, Toronto: University of Toronto Press.
Clarke, J. & Critcher, C. (1985) *The Devil Makes Work*, London: Macmillan.
Coakley, J. (1990) *Sport in Society* (4th edition) St Louis, Miss.: Times Mirror/ Mosby College.
Davidson, J. & Shogan, D. (1998) 'What's Queer About Studying Up? A Response to Messner', *Sociology of Sport Journal*, 15: 359–66.
Dunn, R.G. (1998) *Identity Crises*, Minneapolis: University of Minnesota Press.
Dunning, E. (1999) *Sport Matters*, London: Routledge.
Giddens, A. (1979) *Central Problems in Social Theory*, London: Macmillan.
Giddens, A. (2001) *Sociology* (4th edition) Cambridge, UK: Polity Press.
Gramsci, A. (1957) *The Modern Prince and other Writings*, London: Lawrence and Wishart.
Gramsci, A. (1971) *Selections from the Prison Notebooks*, London: Lawrence and Wishart.
Gruneau, R. (1983) *Class, Sports, and Social Development*, Amherst, MA: The University of Massachusetts Press.
Gruneau, R. & Whitson, D. (1994) *Hockey Night in Canada*, Toronto: Garamond.
Guttmann, A. (1994) *Games and Empires*, New York: Columbia University Press.
Hall, S. (1981) 'Cultural Studies', in T. Bennett, G. Martin, C. Mercer & J. Woollacott (eds) *Culture, Ideology and Social Process*, London: Batsford/OUP.
Hall, S. (1987) 'Gramsci and Us', *Marxism Today*, June: 16–21.
Hargreaves, J.A. (1986) *Sport, Power and Culture*, Cambridge: Polity.
Hargreaves, J.E. (ed.) (1982) *Sport, Culture and Ideology*, London: Routledge & Kegan Paul.
Harris, D. (1992) *From Class Struggle to the Politics of Pleasure*, London: Routledge.
Hoare, Q. & Nowell Smith, G. (1971) 'Introduction' to Gramsci, A., op cit.
Ingham, A. & Loy, J. (eds) (1993) *Sport in Social Development*, Champaign, IL: Human Kinetics.
Johnson, R. (1979) 'Three Problematics', in J. Clarke, C. Critcher & R. Johnson (eds) *Working Class Culture*, London: Hutchinson.
Journal of Sport & Social Issues (1998) 'Power/Resistance/Sport' Theme Issue, 22(3), 235–316.
Lawrence, G. & Rowe, D. (eds) (1986) *Power Play*, Sydney: Hale and Iremonger.
McKay, J. (1991) *No Pain, No Gain? Sport and Australian Culture*, Sydney: Prentice Hall.

McKay, J., Messner, M. & Sabo, D. (eds) (2000) *Masculinities, Gender Relations, and Sport*, Thousand Oaks, CA: Sage.

Messner, M. (1996) 'Studying up on Sex', *Sociology of Sport Journal*, 13: 221–37.

Miller, T., Lawrence, G., McKay, J. & Rowe, D. (2001) *Globalization and Sport*, London: Sage.

Rowe, D. (2004) *Sport, Culture and the Media* (Second Edition), Buckingham, UK: Open University Press.

Rowe, D. (2000) 'No Gain, No Game? Media and Sport', in J. Curran & M. Gurevitch (eds) *Mass Media and Society* (3rd edition) London: Edward Arnold.

Rowe, D., McKay, J. & Lawrence, G. (1997) 'Out of the Shadows: The Critical Sociology of Sport in Australia, 1986–1996', *Sociology of Sport Journal*, 14(4): 340–361.

Sage, G. (1990) *Power and Ideology in American Sport*, Champaign, IL: Human Kinetics.

Sociology of Sport Journal (1992) 'British Cultural Studies and Sport' Theme Issue, 9(2), 103–219.

Solomon, M. (ed.) (1979) *Marxism and Art*, Brighton: Harvester.

Tomlinson, A. (1999) *The Game's Up*, Aldershot: Ashgate.

Turner, G. (1996) *British Cultural Studies*, Boston: Unwin Hyman.

Whannel, G. (1992) *Fields in Vision*, London: Routledge.

Williams, R. (1977) *Marxism and Literature*, Oxford: Oxford University Press.

7
Sport, Colonialism and Struggle: C.L.R. James and Cricket

Brian Stoddart

C.L.R. James was born in Trinidad in 1901 (the same year as Chairman Mao) and died in London in 1989. During an intellectually rich life he witnessed a myriad of events that interacted to produce in him a unique standpoint on life, art, sport and politics (Buhle, 1986; Stoddart, 1990; Worcester, 1996). He

- was influenced by the birth and demise of the Soviet Empire.
- was marked by the revelations about Stalinism.
- observed the zenith and the disintegration of the British Empire.
- experienced the rise of Cold War America and suffered the excesses of McCarthy.
- was close to the centre of Pan Africanism.
- was in the vanguard of postcolonialism.
- posited culture and cricket at the heart of politics.

Throughout that same life James watched the West Indies enter world cricket as students and become undisputed world champions. More significantly, he identified that cricket rose as an inherent part of the Caribbean postcolonial struggle through both race and politics. Consequently, he had a strong influence over the social analysis of sport but, ironically (given the title of his best known work), within some specific cultural boundaries.

Three aspects of James' work should be noted here, and not only because they are reflected in the approach taken to writing this piece.

First, and unlike most other subjects in this collection, James' approach to cricket/sport was principally autobiographical so that his 'theoretical' approach was a 'lived' one, essentially. His views on the intersection of cultural practice, race, rank and caste were formed by his own experiences or observations. In some senses it was ethnographic work, but he would not have described it as such.

The second aspect flows from this. Again unlike most subjects here, James' 'theory' cannot easily be lifted from its cultural *milieu*. His view of the Caribbean is not one he would have seen as automatically transferable to any other setting. He was a 'theory arising from practice' observer, rather than a 'theory being applied to a situation' one.

Then, thirdly, there is the deep paradox that James himself recognized as embedded in his work on both cricket and Marxism. He saw his deep love for cricket (and literature) at odds with his desire for social and political change in that cricket was an 'establishment' game seeking to preserve into the industrial and post-industrial ages a set of social relations more appropriate to a pre-industrial time.[1] In that, he recognized the power of cricket (and sport in general) as a reifying agency, but one whose charms he could not resist. His cricket writing, then, attempted to justify his acceptance of the game and to find a 'revolutionary' strain within it. That paradox and/or challenge has been an ongoing problem for many Caribbean intellectuals.

Understanding these three aspects alone helps explain most of James' strengths and shortcomings in any attempt to apply his principles to the wider sports world.

That book

When it appeared in 1963, *Beyond a Boundary* was starred immediately as the greatest cricket book ever written. The first edition dust jacket signaled the book's difference and, cautiously, suggested its significance:

> A great nuggetty goldmine of a book...a grandly exciting cricket book, but something much more...it was through English cricket and English literature that he and his people have made their most fruitful and most enduring contact with the essence of English life.

To a seventeen-year-old New Zealand schoolboy and cricket fanatic, the book seemed misplaced in the sports shelves of the Ashburton library. Every other cricket book he knew recalled a tour, deified a player, celebrated a great moment or rejoiced the grandeur of English cricket along with the style and standards it had exported to its empire (Cardus, 1945; Stoddart, 1993). In New Zealand, cricket was conducted to English standards and the icons (buried in a pitiful international playing record) were people like Martin Donnelly, a graceful strokemaker who went to Oxford, had a career and treated the game as a pastime.

The problem with the book at that time for that reader was that it drew on many issues and experiences other than cricket. While there was a dim general awareness that cricket was located in cultural practice – after all, English comics like *Lion* and *Tiger* carried uplifting stories about cricket as a social training ground – this book revealed much more.

For a start, the book was about the 'West Indies' in which James grew up, which he left, to which he returned to and then left again physically but never spiritually (Farred, 1996). With the limited exception of England, because of the postwar wave of Caribbean migration (Welsh, 1997), 'West Indies' as a cultural and political construct was then little, if at all, known around the cricket world. West Indies was known for its playing style, but the culture within which that style was shaped constituted unknown territory. The book's wider references to Caribbean affairs, then, made it a bewildering read for anyone unschooled in the region's rich history. Family, education, politics and learning ran through the book in a breathtaking display of intellectual power.

Then, there were indications that in the Caribbean some aspects of cricket's 'shape' were socially questionable – other cricket literature portrayed the game as a bastion of fair play and honourable thought. Here, people were regarded as much if not more for who and what they were (or were not) than for their cricket field achievements. From there, James argued that cricket was as powerful a force in moulding Caribbean society as any political movement, economic force, religious entity or educational system. Cricket was a system around which society played itself out.

There should be a suspicion, then, that references to the 'greatest cricket book' came from reviewers seeing 'different' as 'great' or even as 'so complex it must be great' but, appearing when it did, the book opened several analytical lines in cricket and in sports more widely. Significantly, intellectual weaknesses in the book took a long time to appear and some, at least, did so only when political and ideological tastes changed. The best example is that of women. Very few appear in the book because it was a man's world that was being deconstructed. Those women who did appear, however, were extremely powerful and, in many regards, their influence underpins much of the world portrayed. At one non-sports conference, an eminent historian commented that my analysis of some Caribbean cricket aspects was 'very gendered' – overlooking, it seemed to me, the central point about exclusion/inclusion and discrimination as a whole.[2]

The Other

For many in the imperial and post-imperial world by 1963, West Indies was still unknown as a social entity, as distinct from a cricketing one. England had lost the 1950 test series to them at home, but the overwhelming images were of Caribbean migrants celebrating in carnivalesque fashion, dashing batsmen and energetic bowlers, all with flashing smiles. These were cricket's happy jesters, in the common view.[3] In places like New Zealand, a tour by West Indies just a little later seemed to confirm those images. At that point, a decade or so before the book's appearance, West Indies cricket success was explained, where it was explained at all, largely by reference to greatly talented individuals whose sheer skills overcame a lack of a team approach, as understood in the purely Anglo world. In New Zealand, as in the rest of the Anglo world, the quiet team player had emerged from the English style canon as *the* most valued player. For West Indies, that appeared not to be the case.

James exposed that imagery as superficial, and revealed a world where cricket was marked by the past in a way that would never leave that specific cultural game form. The theme may be seen clearly in James' other writings that are, by and large, ignored by analysts of sports culture. *The Black Jacobins*, for example, is an exquisite re-examination of the Haitian slave revolt that he transmutes from a sporadic, instinctive uprising to a cool political plan (James, 1980). Slaves think for themselves and fix upon a determination, in James view, as opposed to the 'instinctive uprising in the face of tyranny' argument that had prevailed before. There are interesting parallels in changes to our understanding of the French Revolution, of course. It is interesting to note, too, that the 'subaltern School' of South Asian studies that appeared during the 1980s went to great lengths to prove the same point, yet never referred to James (Guha & Spivak, 1988). That might be something of a *motif*: James as an unknown, sometimes unrecognized force.

In the literature, 'The Other' refers largely to cultures other than those located in the so-called 'metropolitan' world and James fits that. However, his work also referenced a different Other in the cricket world, the unknown players. Most previous cricket literature dealt with international and first class levels with rare, and idealized, excursions into the English village cricket world (Macdonnell, 1941; Parker, 1978). James showed us very different people.

In Telemaque, for example, he found the exemplar for his views on colour, class and cricket. Telemaque played for Stingo in Trinidad, a team for 'plebeians'as James put it, a black club with no social status.

A waterfront worker and trade unionist, Telemaque was a good all-round player never selected in the island team but who should have been. Through him, James pondered the politics of selection based on other than playing skills. Did cricket's Trinidadian ruling elite overlook Telemaque because of his labour activism? Who knows, but the impression was there, and in James we find some of the greatest insights into the power of *representation*.

Over twenty years after having read *Beyond a Boundary* for the first time (but having read it many times since), I was reminded of Telemaque and representation. My team in Barbados, a black team akin to Stingo, played a final at the island's cricket headquarters. For some obscure reason, the girlfriend of one player was refused entry to the main grand-stand. At a wake following the loss of the match, the player-boyfriend attributed her exclusion to the 'white bastards' who ran the cricket association. Many thought the boyfriend, a powerful batsman, should have played for Barbados just as Telemaque should have played for Trinidad fifty years earlier. The representation of power and classification was as strong as it had been when James was playing and observing.

James creates many such reflections. For example, just one black man has played for Australia in over a century of international cricket, and he was not an indigenous Australian (what work has been done on cricket in that community owes much to James, because the politics of race have been as powerful there as in the Caribbean). Sam Morris played one test for Australia in the late nineteenth century before retiring, becoming a groundsman and going blind. He is as unknown as Telemaque, and all references identify him as the son of Barbadian 'immigrants' (Cashman *et al.*, 1997). It seems highly unlikely that his parents were 'immigrants' within ten or twenty years of emancipation. More likely, they arrived in Australia in another form of bondage: that of transported convicts. Fittingly, Morris lived long enough to witness West Indies's first tour of Australia in 1930–1931 when the Barbadian fast men, George Francis and Herman Griffith led the bowling and their fellow islanders, Derek Sealy and Lawson Bartlett were leading batsmen (Bassano & Smith, 1990). All descended from slaves. My interest in Sam Morris comes directly from James' demonstration of the power that lies within individual stories.

In some ways the James pointers remain unheeded in the West. Sports sociology and history are fixated on metropolitan practice, and forays into the Other are rare, certainly when compared with other fields of inquiry.[4] That is natural, in some ways – we need to understand our own cultural forms, after all. However, James would have suggested that the inner workings of those forms are often best explained by reference to something very different: come to know thyself by looking at others. Even in cricket, though, his advice has been ignored because West Indies, India, Pakistan and the rest are regarded mainly by Western rather than local terms (Roberts & James, 1998). Most sports historians and sociologists are not as widely read or experienced as James, and their work reveals that.

The history

James pointed out, through people like Telemaque, that West Indian cricket was marked irrevocably by the history of the society within which it took root. The passage from slavery and beyond, from subjugation to self-respect was not only spelled out in cricket. Implicit in the book was the idea that cricket, as a social system, was *responsible* for carrying the memories and patterns of slavery long past the days of its official bonds, and of the political reconstructions that marked Caribbean societies through the first half of the twentieth century. He echoed Gramsci's 'cultural' Marxism in that view, but the Italian was far from seeing the reifying social effects of sport recognized by James (even though sport was a powerful tool in Fascist Italy (Bosworth, 1996).

All Caribbean cricket work emanates from James, and through it runs one important, central condition: while slavery was abolished in the first third of the nineteenth century, cricket helped carry the pattern of social relations established during slavery well into the twentieth and, even, the twenty-first century. That was most evident in James' famous account of the campaign to have a black man appointed West Indies captain. The good news was that it occurred in 1957, the bad news that it might have been for the wrong reasons or, at least, on the basis of the wrong criteria (not that James alludes to the point).

Even when West Indies first toured England in 1900, black players predominated but whites held firm control over authority positions. That situation continued into the 1930s and 1940s when very few white players were good enough to be selected. In the years preceding 1957, the captain was frequently the only white team member. Non-white West Indians 'read' in that circumstance the abiding presence of a mentality descended from plantation slavery when 'Massa' controlled all aspects of life. At a time of growing political independence, how could that continue?

By 1957 the West Indian Cricket Board of Control was still dominated by whites even though white players were scarcely in evidence. The

Board's solution, urged by James (a direct activist in the debate) was to appoint Frank Worrell as captain. He was black, but atypical. Born in Barbados, he was never comfortable there and transferred to Jamaica but played much of his cricket in England where he gained a university degree. In that, then, he was West Indies captain but based largely in England so that the representation, obviously, was of the Board selecting someone who was non-white but projected 'white' qualities (whatever they might have been). What could not be argued were his playing and leadership qualities, and his success was palpable.

Nonetheless, James avoided much of what his own analysis might have told him: was the election of Worrell a black 'victory' or, more controversially, another control set piece constructed by the minority elite descended from earlier dominant days? This question must not be seen as a criticism of Worrell, whose record speaks loudly, but as a question of James for not following his own logic.

Beyond the captaincy lay the broader issue of access to cricket for all social groups, and the history that was much more powerful. From the outset, access in all Caribbean sites had two major dimensions. First, there was the question about whether or not a player could join a club at all then, and secondly, which club could it be? The reason was simple: each club was coded by a matrix of class, status, colour, occupation and even religion. James' explanation of the differences between Queens Park, Shamrock, Constabulary, Shannon, Maple and Stingo in Trinidad is probably the most famous section in *Beyond a Boundary*. What these clubs preserved were the social patterns that had evolved during and after slavery. That was inevitable, sociologically, as we know now, but it was not the real thrust of the James message. He showed that sport would *always* be associated with class, economy, politics and identity. The importance of that message was that it ran completely counter to the dominant views, in 1963 and well beyond, of sport being a classless, apolitical and harmonious state within which players and spectators alike shrugged off their everyday baggage.

Incidentally, James underlined a significant analytical point here, through his demonstration that he *knew* to which club he belonged. That is, it was not just that other people told him where to go, he understood clearly his structural place and that, of course, was little different from slavery days. One Barbadian black batsman, who went to a school where whites were among his teammates, told me that the day he left school he knew exactly which club he must join. He and his white friend and opening partner walked out the school gates, went in different directions and never again played together. This too evokes

Gramsci in that self-ascription has been a major force within the social structuring of sport but is still little understood or recognized, even.

The principle spreads well beyond Caribbean cricket fields, and an understanding of James is invaluable in sports ethnography. Playing in Australia, I was struck frequently by how opposition teams characterized my university teammates socially and culturally. Those teammates responded in kind. Memorably, there was one serious standoff between my university's 'privileged, upper class snobs' (as characterized by the opposition using stronger language) and a team of 'ethnic, working class yobbos' (as depicted by my teammates just as colourfully). Without James, it would have been difficult to explain this fracas arising from an insignificant cricket match. Given Jamesian insight, it was a case of identity and ascription, clearly! At more elevated levels, James helps find a way into the different social typologies constructed about each other by cricket-playing nations, especially in playing or administrative crises – cultural differences abound at those moments, as in Australia–India interaction, for example (Stoddart, 2000).

The significance of James' break through in this general area has been immense in West Indies, as the Garry Sobers and Everton Weekes stories confirm. Both were immensely successful internationally, and became West Indies icons. Yet they reached those heights by chance. Both were born into poor families on plantation lands and, as such, had insufficient social standing for entering the Barbados Cricket Association that supplied the island team and enabled West Indies selection. Thousands of poor black players like them were excluded in that system, so an alternative competition arose in the 1930s. Sobers and Weekes played first for teams in this sub-class league. Powerful white figures then engineered places in the 'senior' competition for them, Weekes joining Army and Sobers the Police (he was placed in the band even though he did not play an instrument). Both succeeded. The point was that their success still depended upon white orchestration and navigation of the social system (revisiting the Worrell point). That dependency caused trouble throughout their careers and years after his retirement Weekes told me, with bitterness, that he had to 'pay his dues' to get where he had.

James drew far less attention to other excluded groups such as the Indians and the Chinese. These groups were introduced to Trinidad and what was then British Guiana (now Guyana) during the later nineteenth century to fill the labour vacuum resulting from the abolition of slavery. What emerged was just as exclusionary a structure as that with emancipated blacks, and the cricket contours were reproduced. Indians and Chinese had their own leagues and found it difficult to gain West Indies selection (Birbalsingh & Shiwcharan, 1988).

In part, this gap in James' analysis proceeds from a more socially monolithic projection of the West Indies than might have been anticipated. He hints at differences, as in the politics of regional selection, but never really explores how those differences proceeded from cultural variety. Michael Manly, a later prime minister of Jamaica, repeated the weakness in his Caribbean test cricket history that was really a book about Jamaica (Manly, 1988). The important lesson for sports cultural theorists is that theories based upon one cultural construct cannot easily be transferred to another. This is a major weakness in some cultural studies works taken from their English context and transferred elsewhere on the assumption that the underpinning frameworks must be the same.[5]

The final irony of all this in the post-independence period was that West Indian white players experienced similar selection difficulties as others had earlier. In fact, one white Barbadian who probably should have played for West Indies, but never did, was the son of the man who engineered Everton Weekes his Army place. James would have understood the poignancy of that situation and, for that reason alone, must be seen as a pioneer in identifying sport as influential in forming social stratification.

The politics

James went first to England in the company of Learie Constantine who was there to play professional cricket but who ended up in the House of Lords. That is clear proof in itself of the link between Caribbean cricket and politics. What the pair found in England was a gap between what cricket and literature 'told' them about English culture, and what English cultural practice actually did. Put simply, the cricket canon was about unity and cooperation while they experienced division, derision and discrimination. The solution to as well as the source of that contradiction lay in politics.[6]

The principal legacy of the link lies in the sporting campaign against South African apartheid. In cricket, but for West Indies' unshakeable stand the ban on South Africa would not have lasted so long and, perhaps, not even begun. The focus here is not that campaign against South Africa, but the source of and support for West Indies' stand, because it may be attributed directly to James. What South Africa represented to Caribbean activists was the continuation of a racially dominant regime reflecting the power that had permeated Caribbean slavery.

Particularly, activists recognized sport as central to the South African power structure in a way that activists elsewhere did not. In Australia and New Zealand, where the Anglo code prevailed, the idea of separating sport from politics was strong. In West Indies, observers knew the connection between sports form and social structure more intimately. That was the point of James' work.

From there it is an easy step to the politics of sports organizations. Given that cricket was a significant cultural force, control of the game was an important site for struggle, of which the captaincy issue was just one aspect. In Barbados, the difficult circumstances for Sobers and Weekes sprang from a white, dominant class control of the Barbados Cricket Association long after the group had declined as a playing and/ or political force.

James gave us an excellent beginning point for an analysis of why sports politics have been so important at two levels: the domestic, and the global. Domestically, it reveals why people work so hard to maintain sports organizations as conservative social forms. Young people have often found themselves at odds with sports organizations over dress, general appearance, behavioural forms and even training approaches. James would have understood why a West Indies player made one appearance with Rastafari dreadlocks, then appeared next with close shaven hair – he had to conform.

Though James wrote about the International Olympic Committee long before its modern commercial crassness, he would have understood present patterns perfectly. The IOC sees itself, on one hand, as a multinational company devoted solely to the cause of sport without reference to politics and, on the other practices, openly, politicized and patterned decision-making (Jennings & Simson, 1992). James would have recognized the difference between the perceptions of the IOC and its realities, between its pronouncements and its practices. He would certainly have done so more cuttingly than some analysts who remain firmly bedazzled by Olympic superficiality (Hill, 1992).

He would have understood, too, the reasons for the International Cricket Council encountering difficulty dealing with match fixing, its largest ever problem. A complex matter, it has one core feature. The issue was ignored persistently because of the cultural distance between the leading countries. The ICC continues to believe that the global cricket's universal social practices are those of the Anglo tradition. This, despite touring players from earliest days commenting on crowd behaviour in the subcontinent and the Caribbean as very different from that at 'Home'. Put (perhaps too) broadly, Anglo crowds are largely passive watchers, those elsewhere bring to bear a more active culture. In those circumstances, gambling was natural. Current difficulties may be explained simply: if no problem is recognized, then no solution is required until, as happened with the Indian police inquiry, the issue moves from the sports to the civil arena.

James, then, was among the first to recognize the inextricable link between sport and politics, and the sophistication of his analysis remains. Once more, however, it could be that his linking of politics and the popular culture has not been taken up fully by later commentators on sports politics, again because the increasingly transnational nature of the work drives attention away from the cultural specificity that does so much to explain the link in the first place.

The changes

One major limitation is James' largely static landscape. Surprisingly, given his analytical sophistication, the 'take' on evolution and change is not so sure as that on social relations through cricket. By 1963, he was writing about a cricket organizational form that had not shifted since the century's turn whether it was the Caribbean regional cricket councils, the overarching regional Board or what was then the Imperial Cricket Council. James dealt with shifting relational patterns within an enduring structure. The patterns of power inside and between those bodies had shifted scarcely, either. His concern was with the struggle of the dispossessed inside the machine.

Given that, how useful is James in trying to analyze the modern game? At one level he would have a major problem. His characters are steeped in cricket's history and meaning. Telemaque, asked to express his disappointment, noted merely that these 'things' happen, with the 'things' redolent with the social context of the game. Moreover the characters, including James himself, 'knew' where they belonged even if they did not like the situation allotted to them. Culturally, the game had deep meaning from the smallest Caribbean community level through the collective West Indian psyche.

James might think the game has now been decultured in several ways. Steve Waugh is unusual in that he understands the game's culture and its place in Australian collective memory. Waugh's arrangement of a team visit to Gallipoli en route to England for the 2001 Ashes series might have linked cricket and warfare uncomfortably, but showed that he understood cricket not only as a game for several Australian generations, but also as a curious, largely inexplicable touchstone to national development. James would have understood that, but not the over-emphasis on the commercial dimension.

He would have appreciated, especially, some postcolonial dimensions of the modern game. England captained by someone called Nasser Hussain and including Owais Shah and Uzzam Iqbal would have delighted him as at an earlier point did players like Basil D'Oliveira, Roland Butcher, Norman Cowans and others. (It would be interesting to hear James on why the Caribbean migration impact upon English cricket now seems supplanted by the subcontinental one).

His analysis cannot explain the current traffic in players. Keppler Wessels, Graeme Hick, Andy Caddick and Andrew Symonds represent an ability to treat a game out of cultural dimension, in that they played for specific countries for reasons ranging from the economic to the opportunis-tic.[7] That is why contemporary observers have difficulty assigning meaning to contemporary cricket, because it is devoid of meaning and context (espe-cially following the match-fixing scandals). If anything, reading James emphasizes that heartless state, simply by showing what really was at stake in the Caribbean game. An important side point is that the cultural passion for cricket continues most strongly in India and Pakistan and there are clear postcolonial reasons for that, as shown by writers ranging from Ashis Nandy (1989) to Emma Levine (1996)[8] and, notably, Ramachandra Guha (2002).

That takes us to the modern Caribbean game specifically. Inevitably, after fifteen years of dominance, West Indies declined in the early to mid-1990s. Such is James' power over the critical view that the decline is regarded widely as both a playing problem and a social decay. What has been lost, it is thought, is a unifying purpose for cricket in the Caribbean (Stoddart, 2003). Talented athletes eschew the game not just because of economic opportunities offered by American college sports, but also because cricket has lost its symbolism, its meaning. That has been traced to changing family patterns, global culture, lack of coaching and an array of other reasons.

Over all this hangs the spectre of change and, as I have suggested, James does not handle that well. His cricket was fixed in an era when the goal was the overthrow of a colonial regime. His successors work within a more complex world where Caribbean purpose, possibilities and plans are less clear-cut. The symbolic power of a Patrick Ewing or an Ato Bolden is not that they have gone to different sports, but that they have gone to different worlds from the one inhabited by James (even though he spent a long time in the United States – his lack of reference to American sports is striking or, at least, his devotion to the British one during that exile was telling). Even for James, that is, understanding sorts from outside his 'host' culture proved difficult to interpret socially.

The impact

The most immediate impact of *Beyond a Boundary* was that when scholars turned their attention to the social dimensions of cricket, they did so with necessary reference to James' textured take on the Caribbean.

That impact was felt directly in the Caribbean. Arriving in Barbados in 1985, I was welcomed warmly by historians keen to support my work, for a reason curiously apart from the natural collegial atmosphere. One colleague commented that it was valuable to have an outsider investigate 'their' game, because that game took them to areas of the island's history too difficult to contemplate. They shared the global fear of having a game they loved produce unpleasant dimensions.

It was a variation on the theme that historians of sport encounter often: resentment at a 'sacred' social activity being subjected to critical inquiry with the risk that the foundations might be revealed as made of clay. In the Caribbean it was understood that the base was clay, but believed that the edifice was made of marble. It was time for the clay to be revealed. While James began the analysis, more work was required.

For that very reason, however, the work produced has a patina of 'sameness'. Powerful as the Jamesian code is, it has proved difficult to escape. Caribbean cricket accounts reflect strongly James' original typologies: intersections of colour, caste and class predominate, as do issues of stratification despite many aspects of the original typologies having passed. A good example comes in writings about the great Vivian Richards: by his own story and stories told by others, Richards exemplified the struggle for recognition and the parameters of power (Richards, 1991). In Richards' case it is enriched by the references to Rastafari, but is still grounded in the Jamesian dialectic.

That is not to say that the dialectic is limited or *passé*. Newer work on Caribbean cricket subcultures, such as the Indian populations, invaluably refers to James (even though he ignored those sections). Nonetheless, newer Caribbean cricket 'problems' are proving difficult to confront because of the powerful history exercised by James.[9] That became evident during West Indies' 1990s playing slide. Much analysis concentrates on what might now be seen as the flimsy 'globalization' arguments: middle class youth eschew the game for faster, more *de rigueur* activities such as windsurfing, while poorer classes turn to more potentially lucrative activities like basketball and athletics. Cricket is too slow and too inconclusive to attract contemporary youth.

The less visited and less palatable possibility is that the very social core that made cricket such a powerful force, and upon which James focused unerringly, has receded fast. It is not so much that slavery and its aftermath have been forgotten, but that the direct impacts upon social practice has been overlain by so many other forces, especially in Caribbean societies taking such different economic and political directions (Paget & Buhle, 1992). An increasing Caribbean problem, then, is that the cricket woes must be explained by the masters of the postcolonial regimes rather than blamed upon the pre-independence forces. That is an extremely difficult problem with which to grapple, and is not one where James is useful immediately: in a curious way, it is the parallel of the 1985 context where someone else might deal with it more readily.

In the non-Caribbean setting, James has been just as powerful and, in some ways, might just be a little more enduring than in the setting that produced his work. Since the Second World War, for example, Australia has become an increasingly multicultural community. Yet the evidence of that multicultural change has been almost non-apparent in cricket. No Australian Aboriginal cricketer has yet played for Australia and none appear likely to do so immediately. Further, almost no Asian-Australians appear currently in the first class game. In junior ranks there is an appearance now of non-Anglo names. The Jamesian analysis provides a good way into this paradox: cricket is a reflection and a manifestation of a particular 'world' that uses the game to help survive wider sweeping social changes. Tinkered with though it is, the playing form and ritual practices resonate with an earlier age atmosphere and social form that do not match automatically the cultural *milieu* in which a newer version of the Australian citizen is raised.

Curious reflections are possible in communities like Malaysia. While Malaysia has a cricket subculture, its strength and weakness is that the game has been dominated historically by the Indian community, more specifically by the Sri Lankan Tamil community, that came to the country as indentured labourers and who became prominent in industries like the railways. Cricket was a marker for that community so that Chinese were drawn in rarely, and Malays became involved only where they could dominate socially and politically. That is almost quintessential James.

The same might be said of New Zealand where the English model and cultural setting, described so well by James, have persisted so strongly. Only recently has New Zealand turned to Australia rather than England for coaches, even though Australian cricket production methods have led the world for many years. New Zealand preferred 'English' coaches (one of mine was an 'Englishman' of Guyanese origin) in the face of a demonstrably failed English cricket culture. As James might have said, that indicates more about the culture of the production of the game than about the game itself.

Outside the cricket world, however, James has had a remarkably small impact upon the analysis of sports practice. In a way, that is a testament to the very power of his work, a curious point that may be explained thus. James' power lies in tying closely the game and the social milieu within which it arose. The inevitable logic must be, then, that the analytical power of such a view is bound by its social construct so, remove the construct and remove the power. Put more precisely, if James' model is applied to a game located in another social construct then its real meaning will be reduced. Baseball moves to a very different cadence as people like Roger Angell tell us (Angell, 1984). Players like Ty Cobb, Babe Ruth, Jackie Robinson and Joe DiMaggio were constituted by worlds remarkably different from those of George Headley, Learie Constantine, Everton Weekes and Frank Worrell.

Conclusion

The measure of any work is within the power of its impact, and on that score there is no doubt that James is the single most important analytical work on cricket. It is now aided by others such as Ashis Nandy (1989) on Indian cricket and Mike Marquesee (1995) on the decline of England, but James started the process. What he showed was that a cricket culture can be explained fully only by deeply learned reference to the culture and location within which it is found. When read in association with Gramsci, Stuart Hall, Anthony Giddens and the like, it provides an enormously powerful understanding of the role of modern sport.

It will be apparent that his 'reading' of the Caribbean game, and its line into the 'game as we have transformed it' analytical framework, changed forever the way in which people would view that specific cultural form and cricket more widely – it provided the imperative to understand the culture as part of any attempt to understand the social implications of the game in that setting (Stoddart & Sandiford, 1998). At the same time, applying the Jamesian cadence of cricket into a British colonial/ postcolonial world has been much easier than putting it into other sports in different settings, even other colonial ones. Perhaps one of the strongest lessons has been the need to understand the locally specific in an age where the escalating tendency has been to 'read' the global. Curiously enough the globalization debate, represented by people like Tom Friedman (2000) and Sam Huntington (1996), provides excellent reasons as to why the work of people like James must continue to be read. He provides as an additional insight the power of perseverance and resistance within localized cultures, no matter the pressures upon them.

For my own part, I could not have had nearly as rich an understanding of the place of sport in many cultures around the world had I not read and re-read James. Now, of course, therein lies a possible paradox of my own: if James has to be seen in the locally specific, then how can I have used his work in so many different settings? The answer is simple enough. Like all good and meaningful theoreticians, whether they work from within or towards a specific culture, James provides enormous insight into human behaviour, attitudes and ideals. He does not provide an analytical template, but he provides a way of seeing, and that is what can be applied more universally. Had it not been for James, then, I would not have understood why I was so moved, almost every day for a year, as I passed by Frank Worrell's grave in the grounds of the Cave Hill campus of the University of the West Indies – it was a powerful and constant reminder of how cricket (for which read sport in general) had been and, in some locations continues to be much more than a game.

Notes

1. I was reminded of this a few years after my first reading of *Beyond a Boundary*. Malcolm Caldwell, radical English historian of and commentator upon southeast Asia, gave a seminar at the end of a tiring Australian tour, and perked up only when the conversation turned to the fortunes of the Surrey County Cricket Club. He acknowledged freely the point that, as with James, there was a contradiction between his Marxist position on southeast Asian politics and his devotion to a conservative county cricket structure. Caldwell was murdered in Cambodia in 1978.
2. The conference was the 'Histories in Cultural Systems' meeting, 1991, organized by Greg Dening for the Humanities Research Centre of the Australian National University (Dening did not make the comment).
3. At least one Caribbean radical now sees this view as a positive part of a 'transformative' process by which West Indies made cricket their own: Tim Hector, 'Crisis in Society and Cricket – Women to the Rescue', http://www.candw.ag/ ~jardinea/ffhtm/ ff990625.htm, 25 June 1999.
4. Two rare examples are Whiting (1989) and Krich (1990).
5. Contrast the recent sophisticated work of Rowe (1999) with his collaborative work with Geoffrey Lawrence (Lawrence & Rowe 1986).
6. An excellent Indian example may be seen in Guha (1998).
7. All these players were born in one country but represented another, cutting away at a traditionally 'nationalist' sentiment underlying international cricket.
8. Peter Wollen (1995/96) comments that Nandy, in his analysis of Indian cricket, attempts to combine a rejection of modernity with a commitment to a transformed future. I am indebted to Vinay Lal for alerting me to this range of work.
9. A good demonstration of this may be seen in Beckles (1998).

References

Angell, R. (1984) *The Summer Game*, New York: Ballantine.

Bassano, B. & Smith, R. (1990) *The West Indies In Australia, 1930–1931*, Hobart: Apple.

Beckles, H. (1998) *The Development of West Indies Cricket: Vol. 2 – the age of globalization*, Kingston: University of the West Indies Press.

Birbalsingh, F. & Shiwcharan, C. (1988) *Indo-Westindian Cricket*, London: Hansib.

Bosworth, R.J.B. (1996) *Italy And The Wider World, 1860–1960*, London: Routledge.

Buhle, Paul (ed.) (1986) *C.L.R. James: His Life and Work*, London: Allison & Busby.

Cardus, N. (1945) *English Cricket*, London: Adprint.

Cashman, R. *et al.* (1997) *The A-Z of Australian Cricketers*, Melbourne: Oxford University Press.

Farred, G. (1996) 'The Maple Man', in G. Farred (ed.) *Rethinking C.L.R. James*, Oxford: Blackwell.

Friedman, T.L. (2000) *The Lexus and the Olive Tree*, New York: Farrar, Strauss and Giroux.

Guha, R. (1998) 'Cricket and Politics in Colonial India', *Past & Present*, 161 (November 1998).

Guha, R. (2002) *A Corner of a Foreign Field: The Indian History of a British Sport*, London, Picador.

Guha, R. & Spivak, G.C. (1988) *Selected Subaltern Studies*, New Delhi: Oxford University Press.

Huntington, S.P. (1996) *The Clash of Civilizations and the Remaking of World Order*, New York: Simon & Schuster.

James, C.L.R. (1963) *Beyond a Boundary*, London: Hutchinson.

James, C.L.R. (1980 revised edition [originally published 1938]) *The Black Jacobins*, London: Allison & Busby.

Jennings, A. & Simson, V. (1992) *The Lords of the Rings*, London: Macmillan.

Krich, J. (1990) *El Beisbol*, New York: Prentice-Hall.

Levine, E. (1996) *Into The Passionate Soul of Subcontinental Cricket*, New Delhi: Penguin.

Macdonnell, A.G. (1941) *England Their England*, London: World.

Manley, M. (1988) *A History of West Indies Cricket*, London: Deutsch.

Marquesee, M. (1995) *Anyone But England*, London: Verso

Nandy, A. (1989) *The Tao of Cricket*, New Delhi: Penguin

Paget, H. & Buhle, P. (eds) (1992) *C.L.R. James's Caribbean*, Durham: Duke University.

Parker, J. (1978) *The Village Cricket Match*, Harmondsworth: Penguin.

Richards, V. (1991) *Hitting across the Line*, Sydney: Macmillan.

Roberts, M. & James, A. (1998) *Crosscurrents*, Sydney: Walla Walla and Mobitel.

Rowe, D. (1999) *Sport, Media and Culture*, Buckingham: Open University Press.

Rowe, D. & Lawrence, G. (eds) (1986) *Power Play*, Sydney: Prentice Hall.

Stoddart, B. (1990) 'C.L.R. James: a remembrance', *Sociology of Sport Journal*, 7(1): xx.

Stoddart, B. (1993) 'Cricket, Literature and Culture: windows on the World', 1992 Barry Andrews Memorial Lecture, *Notes and Furphies*, 30 April.

Stoddart, B. (2000) 'Identity Spin', *South Asia*, XXIII, Special Issue, *Midnight To Millenium: Australia-India Interconnections*.

Stoddart, B. (2003) 'Cricket Matters: The International Game and Public Opinion' – The Tenth Frank Worrell Memorial Lecture, University of the West Indies.

Stoddart, B. & Sandiford, K. (eds) (1998) *The Imperial Game*, Manchester: Manchester University Press.

Welsh, S.L. (1997) '(Un)Belonging Citizens, Unmapped Territory', in S. Murray (ed.) *Not On Any Map*, Exeter: University of Exeter Press.

Whiting, R. (1989) *You Gotta Have Wa*, New York: Vintage.

Wollen, P. (1995/96) 'Cricket and Modernity', *Emergences*, 7/8.

Worcester, K. (1996) *C.L.R. James: a political biography*, New York: State University of New York.

8
Anthony Giddens: Structuration Theory, and Sport and Leisure[1]

John Horne and David Jary

For my sins, I am a Spurs supporter

(Giddens, 1998)

Introduction: Anthony Giddens, a global sociologist

Anthony Giddens has been described as 'the most prominent British sociologist of our time'. For Lemert (1999, p. 183), 'he may well be the sociological social theorist who has most radically, and successfully, revised the language of social science'. Since 1971, Giddens has written or edited over 30 books. There are literally thousands of articles and chapters, as well as around a dozen full-length books, discussing and applying his work and he has become the most cited contemporary sociologist. His work has been taken up and applied across the social sciences. His conception of 'The Third Way', influenced the 'New' Labour Government of Tony Blair and has been courted by Former US President Clinton and an array of European leaders. In 1999 he presented the prestigious Reith Lectures on BBC Radio on the theme of globalization. It is apparent that Giddens has established himself as a prominent 'public intellectual' and a world sociologist (see also Bryant & Jary, 2000). In this chapter we set out to consider the existing and potential contribution of Structuration Theory and the writings of Anthony Giddens to understanding the role of sport and leisure in late modern, global society.

Anthony Giddens was born in 1938 in Edmonton, North London. His Masters thesis at the London School of Economics was on 'Sport and Society in Contemporary England'. He then joined the Department of Sociology at the University of Leicester – where, coincidentally, Eric Dunning and Norbert Elias, later to become prominent for their contribution to the figurational analysis of sport and leisure, were also in post. An early published article (Giddens, 1964) was on 'the concepts of play and leisure', but there was no direct follow-up to this. Instead he turned his attention to general theory and the study of class and power, beginning with an exegesis of classical theory and continuing with his formulation of structuration theory, culminating in the publication of his magnum opus, *The Constitution of Society*, in 1984. A second major phase in his work has been his focus on globalization (Giddens, 1990a) and self-identity (Giddens, 1991). From 1969 until 1997 he was at Cambridge University, becoming Professor of Sociology in 1985. Whilst at Cambridge he also helped found the hugely successful Polity Press. In 1997, his role as a public intellectual having taken-off in a big way, he returned to the London School of Economics (LSE) as its Director, and has greatly raised the profile of the school as the UK's leading social science institution. As a public intellectual and at the LSE he has followed his conviction that the social sciences can make a major difference in social affairs. He has recently been labelled as 'the last modernist' (Mestrovic, 1998), because of his refusal to sanction the cultural relativism and cultural pessimism associated with some versions of post-modern theory. While recognizing the many problems facing modern global society, he retains a confidence in the future as long as human agency can be properly applied. He is opposed to the notion that globalization is the kind of one-way street – 'Americanization', 'McDonaldization', 'winner-take-all society' and so on. Instead – this he presents as 'utopian realism' – he sees opportunities for the enhancement of individual life style and life chances, and the achievement of a more democratic culture, as the outcome of global processes.

It is a puzzle that when Giddens' thinking has been applied so widely elsewhere, why it has not been more widely employed in the study of sport and leisure. It is undeniable, as Jarvie and Maguire (1994, p. 4) state, that 'Structuration Theory has not yet pushed itself to the forefront of the sociology of sport and leisure'. One explanation may be the dominance of other previously established theoretical perspectives in the sociology of sport and leisure, including Figuration Theory and Marxian and Gramscian theory. A further factor is that apart from ephemeral pieces (e.g. Giddens, 1990b) he has himself written little, specifically, on sport and leisure. However, a number of prominent sport and leisure theorists and researchers *have* made significant use of his work, including Gruneau (1983) and Jarvie and Maguire. We have ourselves previously discussed Giddens' potential contribution to the study of sport and leisure as part of critique of figurational sociology (in Jary & Horne, 1994) but we now prefer to emphasise the complementarity between has ideas and other leading approaches to the study of sport and leisure. Emphasis will be placed on:

- the utility of the synthesis and reformulation of sociological approaches to agency and structure provided by structuration theory – especially the concept of 'duality of structure'.
- Giddens' more recent work on self-identity, 'reflexivity' and relations between the local and the global, central to an understanding of the late modern social condition.

We will not be arguing that Giddens has all the answers; we address criticisms of his approach. However, we will argue that the sociology of sport and leisure would benefit from greater attention to his work.

Structuration Theory

Giddens' writings on Structuration Theory (Giddens, 1979) can best be seen in relation to the 'perspectival wars' of the 1960s and 1970s in sociology. Both the 'orthodox consensus' – supplied by functionalism – and the rival 'action' approaches were criticized from a variety of perspectives. Giddens sought to provide in their place a reformed social theory based upon an ontology transcending existing dualisms, especially agency-structure. Instead, Structuration Theory reconceptualizes the dualism in terms of an ontological 'duality' in which agency and structure are seen as intertwined. In this schema, individuals are both reproduced by and reproduce/transform structure. As Giddens expresses it: according to the notion of the 'duality of structure', the structural properties of social systems are both the *medium* and *outcome* of the practices they organize.

For Giddens, using a particular sense of 'structure', structure(s) involve 'resources' as well as 'rules'. They 'recursively organize' social reality (including time and space). They are the properties of practical actions and thus have real effects (e.g. particular institutions), but they are in themselves 'virtual', existing only through these actions and as 'memory traces'. In identifying such a social ontology as the theory of structuration, Giddens does not imply that there is only one *substantive* theoretical position that fits this ontology – various candidate theories might be so grounded. As Cohen (1994, p. 649) states, 'Structuration Theory provides an 'ontology of potentials' rather than an ontology of fixed social traits.'

Parallels have been drawn between key aspects of Giddens' structuration theory and Bourdieu's thinking (see also Bryant & Jary, 1991). Central to this is Bourdieu's concept of 'habitus', 'transpositional dispositions' structuring structures and action but doing so without presuming either a consciousness of end or a determination by structure. Like Giddens, Bourdieu wants to remove the historic split between structure and agency and there is also a shared emphasis on a 'reflexive' sociology. Giddens, however, can be seen as a more accessible, more systematic theorizer than Bourdieu, and more global in scope. Bourdieu perhaps scores in terms of a direct application of his theory to sport and leisure (especially Bourdieu, 1978, 1984). But his account of sport and leisure in terms of positional/ class advantage is narrower than that potentially provided by Giddens.

A further theorist also often mentioned in the same context as Giddens on agency and structure is, of course, Norbert Elias, whose opposition to *homo clausus* is a similar notion to Giddens' conception of 'duality of structure'. It is possible, though Giddens says not (see Bryant & Jary, 1996), that Giddens was directly influenced by this. However, Elias places far less emphasis on sociology itself as a historical agency than either Giddens or Bourdieu, preferring to emphasize a more empiricist 'object adequacy' of sociological accounts. Compared with Elias or Bourdieu it is Giddens who is most willing to range holistically and globally and to speculate. For us, such future-orientation is a major virtue in sociology. Furthermore, the concept of the 'civilizing process' with which Elias's work is most associated, though a creative concept in stimulating the historical study of the development of competitive team sports – the so-called 'sportization process' – has limitations. As Clarke and Critcher (1985) remark, as well as mock fights and mimetic excitement, sport and leisure also embrace health, grace, beauty and much else.

Consistent with Structuration Theory as a general ontology of potentials, Giddens' theory of modernization and social change greatly adds to the value and interest of his overall view. His account of modernity grows from a critique of functionalist and evolutionary theory and Marxism (especially Giddens, 1981). An emphasis on the interaction of agency and structure also means an emphasis on 'contingency', that nothing is predetermined, there is no historic universal class (see also Jary, 1991). But key general features of modernity are identified that include the stretching of social relations across time and space, and a disembedding and reembedding of social institutions of which globalization is the outcome.

Three 'syntheses' provided by Structuration Theory

In our earlier articles on theories of sport and leisure (e.g. Horne & Jary, 1987; Jary & Horne, 1994) we contrasted the work of Gruneau (1983),

Hargreaves (1986), Cultural Studies researchers and the Figurational approach. It is characteristic of Giddens' work that it is built on a mix of others' theories and insights and can be seen as a synthesis of great potential value to sport and leisure theorists. We argued that Structuration Theory could provide the sociology of sport and leisure with three interrelated syntheses of existing social theories (Jary & Horne, 1994):

1. an improved general model of 'structure and agency' (more specifically, a model of agency, structure and particular social structures) taking on board, but modifying, important relatively recent additions to sociological theory deriving from ethnomethodology and structuralism, and (via the work of Goffman and the time-geographers) also providing an enhanced framework for discussion of 'time-space' and the interrelations between macro and micro levels of analysis (Giddens, 1979, 1984).
2. an invaluable non-deterministic paradigmatic formulation of 'authoritative' (political), 'allocative'(economic) and 'cultural' dimensions of social order and social change, the virtue of which is to allow a blending of Marxian and more orthodox concepts and issues (especially see Giddens, 1984) and focus on a 'dialectic of control', the ever present possibilities of political, economic and cultural contestation.
3. a synthesis of theories of modernity and globalization linked also with a general account of self-identity and new forms of identity politics – 'life politics' as well as 'emancipatory politics' – and the new social movements associated with these (especially see Giddens, 1990a, 1991, 1992).

What these syntheses amount to (according to Giddens, 1990a) is a 'critical theory without guarantees' uncosseted by 'providentialism' and requiring empirical research to back it up.

Applications of Giddens' approach in theories of sport and leisure

Whilst Frank's (1990) discussion of 'the body as medium and outcome' is obviously influenced by Giddens' core concept of duality of structure, where Structuration Theory has been used in sociological studies of sport and leisure, it has mainly been used to underline a theory of power relations in which, unlike elitist and some Marxist theories of power, a 'dialectic of control' exists in all social systems. As Giddens (1984, p. 15) states, 'power is integral to agency: action logically involves power in the sense of transformative capacity'. Power is the central dynamic of social life and hence is central to the analysis of all social practices, including sport and leisure. In this model of power, while dominant groups have access to superior resources to achieve outcomes, subordinate groups never completely lack resources to resist or redirect domination.

Such a view underpinned many of the writings about sport as a social institution emanating in the early 1980s. Richard Gruneau's (1983) analysis of sport in Canada argued for an approach that recognized both the power of dominated as well as dominant social groups to shape cultural and ideological practices, including sport and leisure. John Hargreaves (1986, pp. 3–4) identified power as a relationship involving struggles over resources and outcomes, which 'is diffused and circulates throughout the social body'. Later on he identifies a 'neo-pluralist convergence arising from the work of Giddens, Foucault, and Touraine'. He draws attention to the importance of bases of action other than class, that power is 'dispersed and negotiable', and that 'subordinate groups possess a great deal more autonomy and capacity to develop strategies than once assumed' (Hargreaves 1992, p. 277). In studying masculinity and sport, Michael Messner (1993, p. 13) also adopts a formulation of power that is Giddenesque: 'Sport must...be viewed as an institution through which domination is not only imposed, but also contested.'

In Horne & Jary (1994) we cited other significant examples where sport and leisure is analysed in this way, including the important examples of a 'bricolage' of 'oppositional' styles (e.g. Mods and Rockers) provided by the Birmingham School of Cultural Studies in the 1970s, directly challenging the idea of an 'homogenizing' culture. We have also (Jary *et al.*, 1991) presented football fanzines as an example of cultural contestation with the corporate commercialization of soccer. Sugden and Tomlinson (1998) have expressed similar conceptions of power in analysing the politics of world soccer.

John Bale (1995) reviewing Jarvie and Maguire's (1994) review of theories expresses surprise that, although including chapters on Bourdieu and Elias, they did not accord Giddens the same treatment. However, Jarvie and Maguire can be seen as in fact drawing a good deal upon Giddens' thinking. They recognize 'the immense contribution that Giddens has made to contemporary sociology' identifying the 'common hallmarks' of 'good sociology' as including attention to: (i) 'the meaningful interplay between individuals' lives and structural contexts' (ii) 'the necessity to ask questions about structured process...concretely situated in time and space' (iii) 'the unintended as well as the intended outcomes of various social transformations' (p. 256). They also emphasize, as for Giddens

(iv) the multi-dimensional relative autonomy of four interconnected features of the world-system (capitalist economy, nation state system, modern technology and the world military order) (v) that it is 'more meaningful to talk of postmodernism as a phase in the development of a more radicalized modernity' (p. 224) (vi) that it is 'difficult to understand local or national experiences without reference to global flows' (p. 230) and (vii) that 'Global practice still lies within the province of human actions' (p. 256).

It is plain, then, even from this brief summary, how Giddens' work can be important for the sociology of sport and leisure. In the remainder of this chapter we will explore further the relevance of his thinking by consideration in more detail of some of the central concerns of his late writings on 'radicalized modernity', 'reflexivity' and 'risk society'; on globalization; on self-identity and 'lifestyle'; and on the new politics and the role of social science in relation to this.

Key concepts in the later phase of Giddens' sociology

'Radicalized modernity'

'Radicalized modernity' is the term (Giddens, 1990a, 1991) employed in opposition to conceptions of 'post-modern society' to emphasize that: (i) radical doubt is *inherent* in modernity, and institutional pluralism rather than epistemological pluralism accounts for a sense of fragmentation; (ii) tendencies to integration and disintegration are *both* evident in a process of globalization of culture; (iii) though challenged, the self is not dissolved or dismembered – rather the possibilities for reflexive self-identity are enhanced; (iv) the pressing nature of global problems can underpin truth claims; (v) empowerment is a feature of modern society, not merely powerlessness; (vi) 'post-modernity' might be used to refer to a subsequent movement beyond the institutions of modernity, but this has not yet occurred.

Reflexivity

Though complex and much debated (especially see Beck *et al.*, 1994) the core conception of reflexivity as used by Giddens is clear enough and bound up with 'radicalized modernity'. As expressed by Giddens (1991, pp. 38–39):

With the advent of modernity, reflexivity...is introduced into the very basis of system reproduction...[T]radition can be justified, but only in the light of knowledge which is not itself authenticated by tradition...The reflexivity of modern social life consists in the fact that social practices are constantly examined and reformed in the light of incoming information about these very practices, thus constitutively altering their character...[O]nly in the era of modernity is the revision of convention radicalized to apply in principle to all aspects of human life.

The 'reflexivity' of knowledge and reflexive monitoring by individuals and institutions leads to new bases of 'self-identity' in which 'the self becomes a reflexive project'. For example, 'because of the openness of social life today, the pluralization of contexts of action and the diversity of 'authorities', lifestyle choice is increasingly important in the constitution of self-identity and daily activity' (Giddens, 1991, p. 5). However, in a world in which everything is open to scrutiny, including epistemology, nothing is certain, 'ontological uncertainty and insecurity' also increase. More generally, whilst emphasizing the potentially positive outcomes of reflexivity, Giddens is acutely attuned to both benign and not so benign 'leakages' into society of scientific and social scientific knowledge and the role these have played in creating a sense of late modernity as a 'juggernaut' and a 'runaway world' (Giddens, 1990a).

'Risk society'

The concept 'risk society' (as developed by Beck, 1992, and taken up by Giddens) captures the new context of risk and trust that emerges in the circumstances of the new reflexivity. Compared with 'traditional' social systems, 'active trust' in proliferating abstract and expert systems and in 'pure relationships' is required in a context in which the basis for trust is uncertain and trust when granted remains conditional. Not only is the capitalist world economy centred on risk, but our perception of 'late modernity' also is of a society subject to many forms of 'manufactured' risk. Many new contexts emerge for political debate over the application of science, often without obvious resolution, for example, new developments in science and technology associated with the body (cloning, genetic manipulation, drug technologies, etc.), some of these with implications for sport and leisure. Often it is difficult to distinguish between high risk/high consequence risk from low risk/low consequence risk or the various mixes of these, so complex have our choices and decisions become. And crucially, and not least in our sporting and leisure involvements, our own identities are also caught up in risk. Not only is leisure in general everywhere increasingly reflexive and a matter of personal decision, connected with 'risky' narratives of self, so also, as first suggested by Simmel, do high risk sports and 'adventure' appear to gain increasing appeal with each advance of modernity as people learn to play with risk and excitement (Elias & Dunning, 1986).

Globalization

In framing his analysis of globalization, Giddens counters the globalization sceptics and takes up what others have described as an unreservedly 'transformationalist' position (Held *et al.*, 1999). Compared with critics of the concept he argues that globalization has to be understood as an undoubted new phase and the existential reality of late modern society. As the subtitle of his recent book based on the Reith Lectures (Giddens, 1999) proclaims, crucial to Giddens' view is that: 'globalization is reshaping our lives'. It is a phenomenon operating both 'inside' and 'outside' the individual. Unlike some other contributors to the debates about globalization Giddens views globalization as multidimensional in scope. Economic developments are important but so too are political, cultural and technological developments. In all of this, the transmission of information permitted by developments in systems of communication – including the development of the 'weightless' but symbol-led economy – are especially important and Giddens shares much with the arguments of Castells (1996) about the development of a 'network society'. The differential impact and the, perhaps increased, inequalities of this new global society are, of course, also apparent, posing some problems for Giddens' theory. But the facts of this transformation are undeniable, with among the most important issues – for leisure as well as more generally – being the precise relation between the global and the local.

Self-identity and lifestyle

For Giddens, an utterly central aspect of modernity and globalization is that the question, 'How shall I live?' has to be answered in day-to-day decisions about how to behave, what to wear and what to eat (Giddens, 1991, p. 14). The self becomes a 'reflexive project' understood by individuals in terms of their own sense of, and ways of telling, personal identity and biography – the construction of 'narratives of self'. It is in this context that the concept of 'lifestyle' becomes especially important, not least in relation to leisure. As Chaney (1996, p. 86) sums up – and this might be Giddens writing – 'Lifestyles ... are processes of self-actualization in which actors are reflexively concerned with how they should live in a context of global interdependence.'

Applying Giddens

How more specifically then might our understanding of modern sport and leisure be advanced using Giddens' perspective and concepts on modernity and globalization? Three areas will be particularly considered.

Lifestyle and the ludic

Although the concept of lifestyle has, to some extent, been corrupted by the commodification of self-hood through marketing strategies emphasizing mere style at the expense of deeper meaning, for Giddens meaning is central to 'lifestyle'. Giddens' is an avowedly analytical approach, yet empirical research into how people understand the exploration of identity in the choices and tensions of mass consumption confirms much of his suggestive theorizing (e.g. Crouch & Tomlinson, 1994; Lunt & Livingstone, 1992). David Chaney (1996, p. 38) is especially convinced that 'we need something like a concept of lifestyle to describe the social order of the modern world'. He argues that the crisis of authority in modernity is not only the 'stuff' of intellectual discourse but also 'can be seen to motivate the investments in meaning and identity that constitute so much of everyday lifestyle practice' (p. 83) including leisure. Lifestyle 'sites' display both the reassurance of authority and the principle of ambivalence (or anxiety) in consumer culture. Hence shopping for 'style' may reassure, but lifestyles may also 'be practical means of living with ambivalence' (p. 84). Lifestyles also become a precondition of the cultural innovations of post modernism – evident in the fluid 'neo-tribal' often at-a-distance forms of association described by Maffesoli (1994).

Understood as existential projects, rather than as the consequences of marketing projects, lifestyles have normative and 'aesthetic' implications. Lash and Urry (1994) argue that the transition from 'organized' to 'disorganized' capitalism is associated with a new 'aesthetic reflexivity' that becomes 'the very stuff of post-organized capitalist economies of signs and space' (Lash & Urry, 1994, p. 59). They find it 'surprising' that Giddens does not more fully analyse the monitoring of the self and the body involved in sports and leisure, but the potential is clearly there (Giddens, 1990a, 1991, 1992) for others to do so. Concurring with Giddens' mix of emphasis on reflexivity but critique of post-modernism, Tucker (1993), notes the importance placed by Giddens on play, aesthetics and cultural memory, although he too sees room for greater development of these aspects, especially 'liminality' and 'aesthetic innovation'. He notes how Winnicott, whose 'ego theory' Giddens employs, points to the value of 'transitional space' in individual development. Like others, he also suggests that, in general, 'emotion' requires further attention, as the 'missing link' between agency and structure. For Tucker, Giddens' treatment of the 'ludic' remains too often simply a prelude to rational cognitive development. Critiques like Tucker's or Lash and Urrys' are valuable. However, none of what they want from research and theory is incompatible with structuration theory. Hetherington (1998), for example, employs Giddens as a lead into his discussion of 'spaces for identity': liminality, travel, 'escape attempts' and so on.

The globalization of sports and leisure forms

If we turn to the institutional forms of contemporary sport and leisure, the relevance of Giddens' thinking is again apparent in a number of areas, especially to an analysis and understanding of the global diffusion of modern sport and leisure forms.

Much of the spread of European sports and leisure forms in the 19th and 20th centuries occurred in the wake of economic and political forms: sport in particular followed Empire. Cheaper and more rapid means of transport and travel also made international sport possible on a regular, increasingly global, basis. The International Olympic Committee was formed in 1894 and the modern Olympics are a pertinent example of what Giddens suggests is a general feature of radicalized modernity and globalization, the reworking or invention of a 'traditional' form to meet the needs of modernity. The influence of global capital on the rise of 'culture industries' and the global stretch of modern media of communication obviously have major importance, including the emergence of modern global sports and leisure corporations such as Coca-Cola, Nike or McDonalds.

Rather than simply seeing economic and cultural imperialism – Westernization, Americanization, McDonaldization, and so on – as characteristic of globalization, what Giddens' model of globalization suggests is that the process is unlikely to be all one-way but rather will be multi-dimensional, involving bottom-up as well as East-West and North-South transfers and blendings of forms (cf. Harvey *et al.*, 1996). Giddens' conception of the 'dialect of control' and a dialectic of the local and the global in these terms is used by Jarvie and Maguire. On the one hand, the 'spectacularization' of media manufactured 'sports' such as WWF and Gladiators, and the global merchandising of top teams and top stars to the detriment of local interest in local players and sports teams leads to phenomena such as Manchester United having more supporters in China than in the UK. On the other, Asian martial arts and Australian Rules football are examples of many once local sports forms now on a world stage. Numerous to-and-fro borrowings in leisure forms are evident for example in music and dance – for example, jazz, Afro-Cuban and modern 'world music'. Whilst a universal commodification process – and US domination in some areas – is highly apparent, so too is a *proliferation* of sport, media and leisure forms. Nike's persuasive slogan 'just do it' may be intended to entrap consumers in Nike images but there are wider dimensions to the freedom of 'just do it' in modern leisure, with obvious alternatives and resistance to McDonaldization or Nikeization (see Jary, 1999). The need to explore the balance of power in the dialect of control in sport and leisure is plain. One tendency is the domination of global media corporations such as Rupert Murdoch's News International. On the other hand, a great variety of choices remain between different sports and leisure activities, and different identities. There is ample evidence that modern sports have the capacity to both 'condense' and transform complex symbol systems, including national and political ideologies in open-ended ways (e.g. James, 1963; Tomlinson, 1998). We previously noticed the examples of 'oppositional' styles within cultural consumption provided by cultural studies theorists. Although an intensification of the embrace between corporations such as Coca-Cola and McDonalds and sports and leisure organizations is apparent, this is not invariably a winning combination. The global ambitions of cultural corporations seeking economies of scale in the manufacture of taste is opposed by local knowledges that diffuse, subvert and appropriate commodities and services for 'alternative' styles. Giddens' conceptualizations are potentially highly useful in framing the significant issues.

Lifestyle, life politics and leisure

For Giddens, whilst there has been a loss of trust in conventional forms of democracy, therein lies the possibility for an extension of democracy via the new politics that flows from the significance of lifestyle. He distinguishes between a tradition of 'emancipatory politics' (in which activists seek to improve the organization of collective life to enhance individual autonomy) and 'life politics'. While emancipatory politics is a politics of life chances, life politics is a politics of lifestyle (1991, p. 214). The latter does not 'primarily concern the conditions which liberate us in order to make choices: it is a politics of choice. Life politics relate personal identity to ethical/aesthetic agendas. Associated with new social movements – in Beck's terms a new 'subpolitics' – and through these with 'Utopian Realist' possibilities of social transformation, the new subpolitics includes the politics of the body and gender, multiculturalism, and environmental issues. In sport, for example, women's participation, as players and spectators has become an important issue. There is the basis for a more open-ended critical sociology of sport and leisure forms to arise from an extrapolation of the 'utopian realist' possibilities identified by Giddens, located within his three syntheses of sociological theories.

Criticisms of Giddens

Before moving to a general conclusion, three sets of general criticisms of Giddens's work can be briefly noted. These relate to:

- Problems with his conception or operationalization of 'agency and structure' – his model of 'duality of structure'.
- His 'failure' to ground his commentaries in empirical research sufficiently.
- Alleged evolutionary/or idealist elements in his thinking.

All three of these have some purchase, but none of them are fatal. The first (e.g. Mouzelis, 1993) concerns the charge that the more 'concrete' conceptions of social structure are understated in his work as the result of his particular notion of structure, leading to an 'agency bias'. The second (see Bryant & Jary, 1991) has some force but there is a trade-off between general theory and empirical depth in Giddens that can perhaps be justified by the range and perceptiveness of Giddens' theorizing and the 'reflexive' and 'critical' role he sees for sociology. The third criticism, also related to Mestrovic's jibe that Giddens' is the 'last modernist', accuses Giddens of being simply a continuation of Enlightenment optimism and discredited modernist theories of development. The more specific charge of idealism (e.g. Rustin, 1995) relates to his faith in the effectiveness of ideas and agency as against constraining structures and thus also involves the first critique. However, in our view, there is no basis for suggesting that Giddens gets into fundamental difficulties on any of the three counts. It is arguable that no theory can be expected to entirely resolve the methodological issues surrounding agency and structure – as Lemert suggests, there will perhaps always be a 'black hole' (including the unconscious, perhaps the aesthetic). As Giddens himself suggests, research, to be practical, will often bracket structure while studying agency and vice versa. Despite the criticisms, we want to argue that Giddens provides the best available general framework to relate flexibly to the difficulties involved. Moreover, Giddens' multi-dimensional view of globalization has the virtue of providing suggestions for focused empirical enquiry into institutions and local-global relations even when he does not actually himself provide this analysis.

Conclusions

Giddens once described his role as firing critical salvos into contemporary debates in social theory. He continues to do this both as a sociologist and as a public intellectual. Admiration for his work has been widespread and his works have been widely discussed and applied as guides to research. On the other hand the criticisms of his work have also been numerous. The latter has sometimes been the case when the implications of Giddens' work for the study of sport and leisure have been discussed. There are still relatively few studies in sport or leisure that explicitly refer to Giddens or Structuration Theory. Yet many studies on sport and leisure would benefit from a fuller articulation with general social theory that Structuration Theory could provide. More particularly, at the start of a new millennium, Giddens' conception of reflexivity and 'lifestyle' can be argued as increasingly useful not just in understanding people's involvement and participation in leisure and sports activities, but in linking these activities with the wider global social order of late modernity.

Epistemologically Giddens is 'post-empiricist', moving between the relativism of postmodernists and the realism of conventional sociology (Stones, 1996). Structuration Theory provides a general framework for handling the issues involved in the current impasse between realism and relativism. It is also the basis for 'a critical theory without guarantees', a 'utopian realism' in which one may look for beneficial extrapolations of 'favourable' social tendencies. In this way Giddens' work poses questions with respect to reflexivity in lifestyles and the centrality of social science to reflexivity in wider social formations. We would argue that Giddens' handling of issues of individual relationships and personal experiences, using concepts central in structuration theory – not least his valuable emphasis on an ever present 'dialectic of control' and the more general view that power is not only an enabling and a constraining concept – can be centrally useful to sports and leisure sociologists, especially in a context in which modernity/post modernity is experienced as dialectical relations of liberation and disorientation, exhilaration and anguish.

Note

1. This chapter was drafted in the late 1990s.

References

Bale, J. (1995) Review of Jarvie & Maguire (1994), *The Sociological Review*, 43(4): 604–606.

Beck, U. (1992) *Risk Society*, London: Sage.

Beck, U., Giddens, A. & Lash, S. (1994) *Reflexive Modernization, Politics, Tradition and Aesthetics in the Modern Social Order*, Cambridge: Polity.

Bourdieu, P. (1978) 'Sport and Social Class', *Social Science Information*, 17: 819–840.

Bourdieu, P. (1984) *Distinction*, London: Routledge.

Bryant, C. & Jary, D. (eds) (1991) *Giddens' Theory of Structuration*, London: Routledge.

Bryant, C. & Jary, D. (eds) (1996) *Anthony Giddens*, 4 vols, London: Routledge.

Bryant, C. & Jary, D. (eds) (2000) 'Anthony Giddens', in G. Ritzer (ed.) *The Blackwell Companion to Social Theory*, Malder, Mass: Blackwell.

Castells, M. (1996) *The Rise of the Network Society*, Oxford: Blackwell.

Chaney, D. (1996) *Lifestyles*, London: Routledge.

Clarke, J. & Critcher, C. (1985) *The Devil Makes Work*, London: Macmillan.

Cohen, I. (1994) 'Structuration Theory', in W. Outhwaite & T. Bottomore (eds) *Blackwell Dictionary of Twentieth Century Social Thought*, Oxford: Blackwell.

Crouch, D. & Tomlinson, A. (1994) 'Collective Self-Generated Consumption', in I. Henry (ed.) *Leisure in Different Worlds*, Eastbourne: Leisure Studies Association.

Elias, N. & Dunning, E. (1986) *The Quest for Excitement*, Oxford: Blackwell.

Frank, A. (1990) 'Bringing Bodies Back in', *Theory, Culture and Society*, 7: 131–162.

Giddens, A. (1964) 'Notes on the Concepts of Play and Leisure', *Sociological Review*, 12(1): 73–89.

Giddens, A. (1979) *Central Problems in Social Theory*, London: Macmillan.

Giddens, A. (1981) *A Contemporary Critique of Historical Materialism*, London: Macmillan.

Giddens, A. (1984) *The Constitution of Society*, Cambridge: Polity.

Giddens, A. (1990a) *The Consequences of Modernity*, Cambridge: Polity.

Giddens, A. (1990b) 'Gazza's Goal Slump', *Times Higher Education Supplement*, 21 December.

Giddens, A. (1991) *Modernity and Self-Identity*, Cambridge: Polity.

Giddens, A. (1992) *The Transformation of Intimacy*, Cambridge: Polity.

Giddens, A. (1998) Book Review in *The Guardian*, 13 June: 8.

Giddens, A. (1999) *Runaway World*, London: Profile Books.

Gruneau, R. (1983) *Class, Sport and Social Development*, Amherst: University of Massachusetts Press.

Hargreaves, J. (1986) *Sport, Power and Culture*, Cambridge: Polity.

Hargreaves, J. (1992) 'Revisiting the Hegemony Thesis', in *Leisure in the 1990s*, Eastbourne: Leisure Studies Association.

Harvey, J., Rail, G. & Thibault, L. (1996) 'Globalization and Sport', *Journal of Sport and Social Issues*, 20(1): 258–277.

Held, D., McGrew, A., Goldblatt, D. & Perraton, J. (1999) *Global Transformations*, Cambridge: Polity.

Hetherington, K. (1998) *Expressions of Identity*, London: Sage.

Horne, J. & Jary, D. (1987) 'The Figurational Sociology of Sport and Leisure of Elias and Dunning: an exposition and critique', in J. Horne, D. Jary and A. Tomlinson (eds) *Sport, Leisure and Social Relations*, London: Routledge & Kegan Paul.

James, C.L.R. (1963) *Beyond a Boundary*, London: Stanley Paul.

Jarvie, G. & Maguire, J. (1994) *Sport and Leisure in Social Thought*, London: Routledge.

Jary, D. (1991) 'Society as Time Traveller', in Bryant & Jary (1991) *Giddens' Theory of Structuration*, London: Routledge.

Jary, D. (1999) 'The McDonaldization of Sport and Leisure', in B. Smart (ed.) *Resisting McDonaldization*, London: Sage.

Jary, D. & Horne, J. (1994) 'The Figurational Sociology of Sport and Leisure Revisited', in I. Henry (ed.) *Leisure*, Eastbourne: Leisure Studies Association.

Jary, D., Horne, J. & Bucke, T. (1991) 'Football Fanzines and Football Culture', *Sociological Review*, 39(3): 581–598.

Lash, S. & Urry, J. (1994) *Economies of Signs and Space*, London: Sage.

Lemert, C. (1999) *Sociology After the Crisis*, Boulder: Western.

Lunt, P. & Livingstone, S. (1992) *Mass Consumption and Personal Identity*, Milton Keynes: Open University Press.

Maffesoli, M. (1994) *The Time of the Tribes*, London: Sage.

Messner, M. (1992) *Power at Play*, Boston: Beacon Press.

Mestrovic, S. (1998) *Anthony Giddens*, London: Routledge.

Mouzelis, N. (1993) 'On Figurational Sociology', *Theory, Culture & Society*, 10: 239–253.

Rustin, M. (1995) 'The Future of Post-Socialism', *Radical Philosophy*, 74: 17–27.

Stones, R. (1996), *Sociological Reasoning*, London: Macmillan.

Sugden, J. & Tomlinson, A. (1998) 'Power and Resistance in the Governance of World Football', *Journal of Sport and Social Issues*, 22(3): 299–316.

Tomlinson, A. (1998) 'Power: Domination, Negotiation and Resistance in Sports Cultures', *Journal of Sport and Social Issues*, 22(3): 235–240.

Tucker, K. (1993) 'Aesthetics, Play, and Cultural Memory', *Sociological Theory*, 11(2): 193–211.

9

Civilizing Games: Norbert Elias and the Sociology of Sport

Richard Giulianotti

Norbert Elias's status as an influential sociologist was secured only in the late 1970s, when the first volume of his magnum opus, *The Civilizing Process*, was finally published in English. By that stage, already over 80 years old, Elias had given an extraordinary lifetime's service to the discipline of sociology.

Since the late 1970s, Elias's sociological approach has acquired a very 'established' position within the sociology of sport and leisure, most obviously in the UK and the Netherlands. His status was initially underpinned by his conviction – highly unusual among leading sociologists – that sport and leisure pastimes are important social phenomena. Elias's message has been more significantly extended by his followers, many of whom remain unswervingly faithful to his writings, and to the collective belief that Elias's genius has been unduly ignored by academics, past and present, across the humanities. To date, Elias's ideas have tended to be rather uncritically applied to sports-related social processes. Conversely, I seek to provide a brief, critical reading of Elias's perspective, and its contribution to the sociology of sport. We begin, however, with a short biographical sketch of Elias.

Elias: a short biography

Norbert Elias was born in Breslau in 1897 into a bourgeois Jewish family and served in the German Signal Corps during the First World War. Afterwards, he enrolled at the University of Breslau as a medical and philosophy student; though dropping medicine under pressure of work, the natural sciences continued to influence his thinking. In 1925, he moved to Heidelberg to study sociology, coming under the brief influence

of Alfred Weber (brother of Max Weber) and Karl Mannheim. He followed
Mannheim to the University of Frankfurt in 1929 but, as the Nazis came
to power in Germany, Elias fled to Paris in 1933 and then to England
two years later. After securing an allowance from a local Jewish foundation,
Elias spent three years in the British Museum's library writing *The
Civilizing Process* in German. His father died two years later, and his
mother perished in Auschwitz, probably in 1941, a fate that haunted
Elias for the remainder of his life. Although briefly employed at the
London School of Economics, Elias was interned in 1940 as a German
'alien'. After the war, Elias survived by giving guest lectures and talks
before accepting his first permanent position, aged 57, as lecturer in
Sociology, at the University of Leicester in 1954.

At Leicester, Elias published several articles and reworked a postgraduate
thesis by J.L. Scotson into *The Established and the Outsiders*. *The Civilizing
Process*, still untranslated, was read more widely, particularly in Holland.
Elias retired in 1962 and accepted a chair in Ghana for two years. Returning
to Leicester, he started work with Eric Dunning on sport sociology,
and strengthened his influence on younger colleagues. He published
The Court Society in 1969, and *What is Sociology?* in German in 1970. Elias
moved to Amsterdam in 1975, then Bielefeld in 1978, before returning
to Holland in 1984. Throughout his 'retirement' and until his death in
1990, at the age of 93, Elias was highly productive, building an international reputation. *The Civilizing Process* and *What is Sociology?* appeared
in English; and he completed the manuscripts for *The Loneliness of the
Dying, Involvement and Detachment, The Society of Individuals, The Symbol
Theory, Time: An Essay, Mozart: Portrait of a Genius, The Germans*, and his
autobiography, *Reflections on a Life*. He published regularly in journals
like *Theory, Culture and Society*, and, with Eric Dunning, wrote *Quest for
Excitement*, his major statement on sport and leisure.

While more detail has still to come out, this extra-ordinary life and
charismatic intellect can help to explain the loyalty and partisanship
among Elias's adherents. Informal comments from some academics who
encountered Elias confirm that his 'forceful personality' and uncom-
promising views could also alienate colleagues and students (see Mennell,
1992, pp. 22, 24; van Krieken, 1999, p. 33). Similarly, to some neutrals,
Elias's followers nurture a sense of embattled isolation, typically com-
plaining that their work is misrepresented or purposefully misconstrued
by 'opponents'. Ironically, some Eliasians display a lack of discursive
restraint or critical detachment that Elias (1987, p. lxix) more generally saw
as bedevilling the human sciences, in comparison to the more advanced,
natural sciences.

Figurations, process sociology and game models

Elias's work is rooted in his 'figurational' or 'process-sociological' reading of human societies. Process sociology views societies as figurations of people who are knitted together through lattices or webs of interdependence. 'Figuration' is a 'generic concept for the pattern which interdependent human beings, as groups or as individuals, form with each other' (1987, p. 85). This is a relational theory, encompassing as broad a range of social forces, developments and trends as possible. Diverse power balances and tensions exist within figurations, such as in families, schools, workplaces, civic formations and states. Consequently, Elias dismisses the 'false dichotomy', between structural or macro theories and interactionist or micro theories, that underwrites much sociological thinking. However, the idea of 'social figurations' effectively constitutes Elias's conception of 'social structure'; at times he uses the words interchangeably.[1] In this way, social structures are understood in a relatively microsociological sense, as consisting of people or not at all, rather than in the more structuralist, neo-Durkheimian sense, which views structures as obdurate phenomena that are more than the sum of their individual parts. This does not mean that Elias sustains a rank individualism. Indeed, within the historical context of heightened individualism throughout the 20th century, Elias's assertions on social figurations may be viewed as counter-intuitive. He is especially critical of the *homo clausus* image of humanity, whereby individuals experience themselves as somehow separated or hermetically sealed off from the rest of the world. Elias (1978a, p. 118) argues that people do not just 'go through processes'; they are themselves 'processes', and this has some potential parallels with relatively de-centred post-structuralist readings of the human subject.

Elias (1978a, pp. 71–103, 130–131) employs 'game models' to illustrate his notion of figurations. Games are more than 'models' of social existence; they are microcosms of the fundamental nature of social life. His game models include real ones such as four people playing cards or a football match between two sets of teams. In the latter, the game is in 'constant flux'; to understand and enjoy proceedings, players and supporters must 'follow the fluid figuration of each team'. At the heart of games are negotiations of power, trials of strength, between individuals. Such competition 'is the basic situation encountered whenever people enter into or find themselves in relations with other people ... They form a normal part of all human relationships' (1978a, p. 73). Power is a social resource rather than a material entity; it exists only through social relationships. Game models help to illustrate the falsity of dichotomizing 'individuals' and 'society'. As Elias notes, we do not contextualize player actions by speaking about their 'background' or their 'society'. Instead, the didactic power of game models helps us to understand, and literally to see, the interdependencies of all players. Elias (1978a, p. 74) illustrates the 'bi-polarity' or 'double-binds' within power relationships through the old master and slave analogy: while the master is clearly more powerful, he (*sic*) depends on the slave for that power to continue. In the most one-sided games, dominant players still depend upon inferior opponents for the 'contest' to proceed. Elias's 'game models' are therefore clearly distinct from 'game theory', a strain of 'rational choice theory', which also employs social relations between players as a metaphor for social life. While, like Elias, rational choice theory illuminates player interdependencies, process-sociology prioritizes the fluidity of the game, 'the progressive interweaving of moves', rather than the rational calculations of individuals (1978a, p. 97). Yet, somewhat confusingly, Elias slips beyond metaphor into a realist claim, implying that social relations *are* games, particularly when discussing 'players' within party oligarchies and democratic frameworks of power. This simplifies his argument, setting his claims within the manageable parameters of a game involving only players. But, it draws the reader into making a philosophical act of faith (agreeing that the world is a game), as well as over-simplifying the reality of social relations: do all 'players' agree on the rules and objectives of the game, on who can play, and whether there really is a game going on at all?

To elucidate the complexity of modern societies, Elias employs an arithmetical approach that centres upon a calculation of the number of possible relationships that individuals enter into relative to the number of other individuals within the figuration. Complex societies will have greater numbers of interdependent individuals. This is consistent with Elias's other argument (following Durkheim, discussed below) that more 'civilized', modern societies have more complex divisions of labour, involving the specialized work of more and more people. Yet, to continue the game analogy, we may argue that a contest's complexity does not simply depend upon player numbers nor the calculation of executed moves. In some sports, trends towards 'despecialization' mean that the division of labour is much more flexible, and players must fulfill a number of roles. Elias might explain such developments through the enskilling or civilizing of individual players, who learn a portfolio of roles, but this still calls into question his arithmetical approach to game relationships.

Figurational sociology has definite methodological implications for the social sciences. Elias dismisses the common academic practice that allows disciplines like sociology, psychology and biology to partition and protect their spheres of thought and influence. These subjects must recognize their 'relative autonomy' as interdependent phenomena if a more advanced understanding of human societies is to be achieved (1978a, p. 96). Elias does distinguish epistemologically the concerns of the natural and social sciences because the structure, language and dynamics of human groups can change rapidly and differ markedly over time and space. Nevertheless, artificial disciplinary barriers must be broken down to explore how the various biological, psychological and sociological aspects of human life interweave. While, as we shall see, this cross-disciplinary approach has enabled a useful Eliasian contribution to the study of the emotions, it does still seem to be dominated by sociologists, thus according sociology a Comtean primacy. Elias's adherents have yet to produce a serious cross-disciplinary research programme within sport studies, or to evolve a major, advanced statement on delicate research issues, such as elite athletic performance, that otherwise tend to divide the natural and social sciences. Part of the problem here may lie in some Eliasians' general tendency towards writing repetitively, reproducing established arguments on specific sports-related issues, rather than realizing a deeper ambition, in building more creatively upon Elias's points of departure.

The civilizing process: emotions, manners and violence

The Civilizing Process provides Elias's most important sociological legacy. In brief, the civilizing process describes the developments by which, from the 16th century onwards, socially accepted standards of conduct, etiquette and sentiment underwent major transformation in Western Europe. Originating in court society, the civilizing process was subsequently shaped by the rising bourgeoisie of the 18th and 19th centuries, and then incorporated more 'respectable' sections within the urban working classes. From here, the civilizing process is more easily explained according to its micro and macro claims, although the deep interdependencies of the two must be stressed.

In microsociological terms, the civilizing process involves individuals exercising greater degrees of bodily and emotional self-control. Since the Middle Ages, standards of social conduct and etiquette surrounding bodily functions, eating practices, sexual habits, and violence have become increasingly intensive and constraining for greater numbers of people. Bodily emissions are studiously controlled, while sexual and sleeping habits are more privatized. Higher standards of 'civility' are reflected through our heightened 'thresholds of repugnance', our 'disgust functions', which lead to our moral criticism of, and indeed physical revulsion towards, breaches of corporeal taboos. Conscience-formation and patterns of personal restraint have become more elaborate, while time-regulation has become more orderly and less fluctuating (1992, p. 147). Our experience and performance of these 'civilized' standards is mediated by our 'habitus', viewed by Elias as our 'second nature' or psychic structure that we share with others from our social group.[2]

Interrelated, more macrosociological trends have shaped the civilizing process across the long term, and these include: economic growth, an increasingly complex division of labour, the greater use of money in social and economic relationships, the formation of states, and the rise of 'functional democratization'. Each trend highlights the growth of more chains of social interdependency and the more rational organization of human relationships. Following Weber, Elias (1987, pp. 76–77) notes that state formation is underwritten by the state's claim to a monopoly on violence and taxation. Police and armed forces function to protect people from each other, hence everyday violence is less readily experienced or feared. Functional democratization facilitates longer-term social stability: powerful groups (such as the court society) accommodate pressures 'from below' (such as the early bourgeoisie and, later, the working classes) and reconcile themselves to growing state powers. The 'parliamentarization' of English society through the 18th century is linked by Elias (1986, in Elias and Dunning, pp. 27–28) to the 'sportization' of games since both sports and parliamentary contests involve non-violent battles between competing groups according to rules of procedure. Elias and his followers emphasize the 'double-bind tendencies' that exist between social classes or other groups within power relationships. Thus, the lower orders can pressurize higher social groups to refine their customs and practices. However, the broad tendency is towards a civilizing process that gradually influences, rather than emerges from, the lower orders (including those colonized by the West); hence, Maguire (1999, p. 43) refers to the upper classes and 'a gradual seepage of their distinguishing models of conduct into other strata'.

Elias discusses the 'we–I' balance that mediates individual-societal relations. Within relatively 'civilized' societies, this balance tends to involve relationships between individuals and nation states. In discussing the historical development of the 'we–I' balance, Elias does slip into evolutionist and somewhat functionalist terminology. Pre-state 'tribes' (like the American Indians) are seen as hindered by the 'drag effect' in their social habitus, prevented from being successfully integrated within the nation state, and instead slip into a 'fossilization' of their collective habitus (1991a, p. 212). Elias is understandably critical of some of the 'decivilizing' consequences, notably xenophobia and warfare, that are evident in modern 'we–I' balances. Indeed, given the high personal toll that he suffered as a result of warfare, genocide and state persecution, the 'civilizing process' is a remarkable testament of faith in the potential of modern human societies. In universalistic mode, Elias envisages a point at which the 'we–group' identity of individuals will extend beyond nation states 'towards the plane of mankind' (1991a, p. 232). This long-term trend should raise the 'we–I' balance to a new level, resulting in greater individualization (such as through stronger human rights) and the integration of global state institutions. The implication here is that individuals will effectively acquire an Eliasian sociological imagination, coming to see themselves within a global figuration, thus resulting in the transnational organization of institutions to fulfill benevolent missions.

An important component of the civilizing process concerns Elias's reading of the interplay between natural and social processes for individuals. This interdependency enables Elias to explain sport's role, as a social outlet, for 'instinctual, affective and emotional impulses'. All societies provide some kind of emotional counterbalance for the constraints of everyday life. Societies that are relatively restricted in civilizing norms contain more ordinary, routine outlets for these instincts, as battles, physical struggles, personal risks and dangers are more prevalent. Where civilizing norms are more constraining, these instincts are more routinely suppressed, but are afforded 'mimetic' outlets, such as through the performing arts, sports and games, or periods of 'controlled decontrol' (such as holidays). Mimetic activities facilitate the experience of the emotional intensity of battle or personal risk-taking within relatively safe, civilized, cultural contexts.

> Sport allows people to experience the full excitement of a struggle without its dangers and risks. The element of fear in the excitement, although it does not entirely disappear, is greatly diminished and the pleasure of the battle-excitement is thus greatly enhanced.

Yet sport does not fulfill a purely cathartic function, as an outlet for emotions that cannot be sublimated through other, more routine aspects of social life. Instead, Elias argues that modern sports events can generate and heighten our emotional arousal. Emotional tensions are not always resolved by the end of play. Hence, the sports event may see spectators and participants entering the stadium in a relatively relaxed frame of mind. As the contest proceeds, more emotional arousal may occur, perhaps through intensified competition or the generally physical nature of play. At the end, at least one team may still experience strong emotions, perhaps of frustration or anxiety, regarding the game and the result.

In his conception of 'established-outsider' relations, Elias (and Scotson, 1965) complemented the civilizing process by a further study on the social construction of inequalities. 'Established' social groups and networks are defined by their greater power over 'outsider' groups through their monopolization of many resources, such as the economy, violence, personally rewarding work, ethnic and gender advantages, personal relations with state employees, and so on. The civilizing process and established-outsider relations are processual and in interdependent states of flux. Consequently, the civilizing process is not unidirectional nor something that may be simply read off from the individual's social stratification in time or space. 'Decivilizing spurts' may occur even after long civilizing periods, while individuals of very similar background may display different standards of emotional and bodily control due to significant differences in socialization or interdependency networks. The civilizing process does not represent a deliverance from absolute barbarity, since individuals in all civilizations undergo socialization into the meaningful suppression or transformation of drives and impulses (1986, p. 45). Nevertheless, while he viewed the civilizing process as applying generally to European nations, Elias (1994a) did distinguish its more obvious manifestation in England and France from its relative failure in Germany, which evidenced stronger, more problematic 'decivilizing spurts' and the rise of Nazism.

The emergence of modern sport is closely tied to the social relations between the British upper and middle classes ('the established') and groups lower in the social order at home and abroad ('the outsiders'). Through the rituals of sport, the 'civilized' social habitus of these established groups was employed to demarcate them from 'uncivilized' outsiders. Cricket and tennis, for example, were imbued with various aristocratic or upper middle-class codes of civilized behaviour regarding rule-following, team-work, obeying one's captain and accepting the adjudication of an 'impartial' sovereign figure (the umpire). In reflecting the 'double-bind' of interdependency between these social groups, while the established classes demarcated themselves through play, sports events were typically staged before the outsiders or included these 'uncivilized' groups as participants. In playing cricket in the village or overseas, the established classes retained their patrician role before locals, and drew these 'outsiders', through an informal variant of 'functional democratization', into observing and practicing these 'civilized' mores. This process-sociological account has similarities with cultural studies and Marxist analyses regarding sport's function in incorporating the lower orders into the social practices and cultural mores of hegemonic British elites.

Elias applies his theories in relatively conventional fashion to examine the social development and figurational dynamics of sport. In *Quest for Excitement* (co-authored with Dunning), Elias is concerned to explain the social changes that have marked the transformation of many games and pastimes from Antiquity through to the Middle Ages into modern sporting practices. The most obvious historical contrast is afforded by the much greater toleration of physical violence in sports and games in the past compared to contemporary times. For example, the Greek *pankration* (a brutal form of pugilism) was imbued with warrior ethics, was highly violent, often resulted in death, and lacked the differentiation of fighters according to weight or height. The Roman gladiatorial games and circuses were also deadly combat dramas. Latterly, according to Elias and Dunning (1986), the 'folk football' played in Britain through to the late 19th century was a popular and often violent pastime. These games lacked the formal codification of playing areas, possessed only rudimentary rules, and facilitated regular outbreaks of violence. Serious injuries and deaths were not uncommon as some folk football games were little more than semi-institutionalized fights between rival groups or communities (Elias & Dunning, 1986, p. 179). Pugilism and folk football underwent intensive civilizing during the 19th century, to produce respectively the Queensbury rules of boxing, and specific football codes. Dunning (1977) notes that this civilizing of sporting pastimes was rooted historically in the rising games ethics of English public schools from the mid-19th century. Headmasters and teachers sought to exercise discipline more effectively by inculcating the relatively bourgeois values of muscular, gentlemanly Christianity among their wealthier, usually aristocratic pupils. Hence, the civilizing of sports was a development interdependent to the wider 'functional democratization' of English society, whereby the ruling classes came to accommodate greater pressures 'from below' (the bourgeoisie).

The civilizing process has been employed by Elias and his followers to explain British football-related violence. Elias (1986, p. 57) explains football violence as an 'outsider syndrome, as a form of behaviour and feeling characteristic of young outsiders when they are able to congregate and to form a huge crowd'. Latterly, Eric Dunning and colleagues at the University of Leicester forwarded a developmental explanation of football hooliganism. They argued that the development of the civilizing process precipitated an overall decline in violence within British football crowds, most notably just after 1945.[3] Contemporary football hooliganism emerged from the early 1960s onwards, when greater numbers of 'rough' working-class males gained prominence within crowds. Greater media and political concern about violence reflected higher thresholds of repugnance across UK society, but these moral panics drew 'rough' fans into football at the expense of more respectable spectators. Latterly, intensified fan violence during the 1980s highlighted broader 'decivilizing' aspects of British society (the Falklands war, paramilitary warfare in Northern Ireland, violent industrial disputes, urban riots) and the apparent diminution of functional democratization. The process sociologists' insisted that rough, lower working-class males were behind most fan violence, due to their lower levels of functional interdependency, and their encounters with less civilized social mores during childhood socialization (Dunning *et al.*, 1988). Nevertheless, the process-sociologists guard against empirical refutations by claiming that 'rough' middle-class fans may also be involved, thereby reflecting some 'decivilizing' trends within the upper echelons (Dunning *et al.*, 1991, p. 474).

Figuring the criticisms

Elias's arguments certainly possess a grand theory appeal, through his attempts to resolve the micro–macro debate, establish a meta-narrative on human history (the civilizing process), sort out the nature–nurture debate (such as through his analysis of the emotions), and theorize the ontology of social life (viz. figurations and webs of interdependence). Within the sociology of sport, the civilizing process and the sociology of the emotions, as interrelated research problems, have been turned particularly towards the analysis of violence. It is here that many criticisms emerge. We shall begin with a consideration of more conceptual criticisms before addressing substantive and empirical weaknesses.

An opening, fundamental question is whether we can regard Elias as contributing a genuine social theory. Symptomatically, Elias makes few impressions in textbooks and compendia for modern social theory courses. Figurational sociology has been criticized for being descriptive and untestable. By seeking to explain everything it may explain nothing; in this regard, it shares the problems of other untestable perspectives, such as rational choice theory (see Smelser, 1992). These problems are very obvious in relation to the 'civilizing process': whenever the chance emerges to test the theory through refutations, such as through episodes of modern violence, Elias points us towards 'decivilizing' tendencies. Yet, for its initiates, once the basic tenets are grasped, figurational sociology is easily reproduced, and provides a comforting recourse for the routine 'explanation' of anything. Elias also displays a lack of critical reflexivity through his minimal referencing of sociologists and other scholars who clearly influenced his thinking and terminology (most obviously Weber, Durkheim and Parsons). In downplaying these 'interdependencies', Elias provides us with a paradoxically individualistic and *homo clausus* self-portrait. It is also in this light that we might address any claims by Eliasians that Anthony Giddens (1984), through his 'structuration theory', effectively clones the process sociology of Elias, with whom Giddens once worked. The two sociologists do appear to share strong continuities in their respective, post-dualist readings of social structure. However, Giddens is clearly more influenced by other theoretical standpoints, notably ethnomethodology which he tends to acknowledge.

Second, Elias's followers have been at pains to demonstrate that they are not social evolutionists, particularly in their use of the term 'civilization'.[4] However, Elias's language and reading of colonial histories can suggest otherwise. The esteemed anthropologist Jack Goody (2001) recalls meeting Elias in Ghana in 1962, and being struck by Elias's ignorance of the local culture and his Weberian reading of 'simpler societies'. Elias uses highly normative terms – like 'semi-petrified', 'fossilization', 'drag effect' and 'integration at a higher level' – to describe these 'simpler societies'. His use of the term 'pre-state' to designate non-industrial societies is also evaluative in that it anticipates and reifies (as a societal inevitability) the complex historical process by which these societies continue to be forcibly integrated by colonial states. Elias talks of an 'unplanned social process' which 'urged tribes to combine in the wider integration unit of the state' (1991a, p. 213); such an analysis surely constitutes a highly naive and uncritical reading of the history of modern colonialism. Moreover, many anthropologists have argued that the idea of distinctive, pre-colonial 'tribes' was invented by colonists, providing settlers with a 'knowledge' through which complex groups of indigenous peoples could be understood and efficiently administered. Elsewhere, Elias prefers to use the term 'social habitus' to describe the deep cultural beliefs of these 'simpler societies'. Using a term like 'culture' would facilitate a more relativistic, less evaluative reading of America's pre-colonial inhabitants, for example, but it is clear that Elias favours a strictly rationalist, modernist reading of knowledge-systems. He dismisses the idea of 'different types of knowledge' that sit alongside one another, arguing instead that knowledge systems are 'connected with each other in the form of a clearly recognizable sequential order of ascent and descent' (1987, p. xl). He compares this 'sequential' model of knowledge to a staircase: you cannot reach the tenth floor without passing through the other floors.

For anthropologists or critical sociologists, this ethnocentric, rationalist model, with its assumptions regarding the backwardness of non-Western societies, is ripe for criticism. Anton Blok (in Mennell, 1992, p. 230), for example, describes some elements of Elias's thinking as 'racist'. In defence, Mennell posits that Elias is not an ethnocentric. However, the claim that process-sociologists exercise due care in comparing other societies across time and space, is rather vitiated when Mennell (ibid.) compares the apparently 'quaint and irrelevant' people of Western court society to those groups studied by anthropologists. Another Eliasian, Maguire (1999, p. 43), makes a similar, sweeping comparison across time and space, when describing the relations between Western and non-Western societies as 'equivalent' to those between the court society and other social classes in Medieval times. The impression thus remains that Elias and his followers are inclined to compare, according to a single Western development chart, the social relations, cultural beliefs and systems of knowledge that exist across starkly different cultures.

Third, the civilizing process has been strongly and persuasively criticized on empirical grounds. Cross-cultural criticisms identify Elias's lack of concern with both universal processes and historical particularities. Robertson (1992, p. 120) argues that Elias pays too little attention to questions of history, civilization and social theory that fall outside the scope of the West. Koenigsberger (1977, p. 300) notes Elias's unfortunate indifference to specific historical events that are really of 'intrinsic concern' to historians and the development of world affairs. From historical materialist or post-structuralist perspectives, the civilizing process fails to interrogate the power relations surrounding the body. Modern capitalism is most adept at socially constructing and interpolating new consumer 'needs' to its citizens. Elias describes our concern with bathrooms, bedrooms, toilet paper, soaps, shampoos, make-up and so on; but he fails to connect adequately this material culture to the production of surplus value. Correlatively, Foucauldians would point to Elias's work as describing some manifestations of 'bio-power' and 'governmentality', while failing to analyze sufficiently the role of professionals in shaping disciplinary power and knowledge over bodies, and omitting to explore the governing of subjectivities, the 'conducting of our conduct', within consumerism.

These arguments encourage us to be skeptical towards the civilizing process, on the grounds that it broadly constitutes an expression of faith in the civilizing qualities of modernity. Certainly, Elias was only too readily aware of the personal dangers of 'decivilizing spurts', but the notion of the civilizing process was conceived, elaborated and defended during the 1930s. Would Elias, in different circumstances, have originated and defended the civilizing process during the 1940s, or the 1980s? More substantively, we may view as sadistic or symbolically violent the way that dominant groups humiliate, oppress or frustrate the personal and social development of larger social groups across time and space.[5] Bourdieu and Passeron (1977), for example, have drawn particular attention to the symbolic violence that is endured by the lower social classes, notably in education. In more post-modernist vein, Mestrovic (1993, pp. 187–188) describes the civilizing process as 'quaint' in its presumption of oversocialized human beings. Drawing on Schopenhaueur, Durkheim and Freud, he argues that the contemporary mask of civilization merely disguises the transfer of human barbarism into other, psychic outlets. We may congratulate ourselves on the felicitous control of bodily emissions, while exercising our more incisive, 'civilized' skills in sarcasm, insult and calumny. Bauman (1989, p. 12) makes an analogous point at the societal level in his critique of the myth of modern civility with reference to the Holocaust. Indeed, late modernity is littered with the uncivilized consequences of finely calibrated, rationalized killing machines. As Armstrong (1998, p. 305) reports, 'the latter half of the twentieth century has seen 130 wars with 27 million dead, whilst the first eight decades of the century saw 99 million die in warfare – a figure twelve times greater than that for the previous century and twenty-two times that of the eighteenth century'. This excludes the continuing, systematic deployment of civilian rape, murder, starvation or forced migration as strategies of state terrorism within conflict zones. The rising toll is not satisfactorily explained by the description of people in late modern times as 'late barbarians' (Elias, 1991a, p. 147).

The civilizing process has also come under fire inside sport. Lewis (1996, p. 335) notes that the Eliasians were effectively employing football hooliganism merely to corroborate the civilizing process rather than explain a complex social phenomenon.[6] Elias (1986, p. 154) had hoped that sports studies would provide 'a comparatively manageable field' through which 'figurational' sociology could be demonstrated to work (rather than rigorously tested). Yet, there is clearly a lack of fit between evidence and theory. In England, Armstrong's (1998) extensive research into the Sheffield United hooligan group, and its social relations with other hooligan formations, draws consistent reference to the Eliasians' shortcomings. Moreover, the Eliasians' principal researcher, John Williams, decided after a decade that his data on football fans could not sustain the theory, and so parted company with the process-sociologists in acrimonious (uncivilized?) circumstances. In Scotland, the largest and most notorious hooligan formation during the 1980s hailed from Aberdeen, and its presence cannot be successfully explained according to the core precepts of the civilizing process. The habitus of the formation was upper working-class or even lower middle-class in terms of class background, consumption patterns and the relatively 'established' status of its suburban social cradles. Perhaps more problematically, Aberdeen and its surrounding regions were undergoing wider social developments that would otherwise underwrite rather than challenge the inculcation of a civilizing process: relatively strong economic growth and stability through the oil industry, and a more complex division of labour through an expanding service economy. There were no local challenges to state monopolies on violence and taxation, nor was there a militant pressure for greater democratization of local affairs and social rights. In short, for this research into violent fan behaviour, the civilizing process would offer little explanatory assistance (Giulianotti, 1999, pp. 44–47). Similar empirical criticism has been directed at the process-sociological portrait of folk football games and their apparent civilization within English public schools of the 19th century (Dunning & Sheard, 1979; Elias & Dunning, 1986). Harvey (1999, p. 114) argues that the distinction between traditional and modern sport has been exaggerated, and that 'civilized' modes of playing were not the result of public school influence. Additionally, Goulstone (1974, 2000, pp. 135–136) insists that, compared to public school games, folk football was more 'civilized' in terms of rule-following and restraint from violence.

To conclude, Elias's standpoint does at least promote the sociological imagination through its emphasis on social interdependencies, and point towards the greater dialogue between natural and social sciences. But, as we have seen, figurational sociology continues to carry within it some highly debilitating weaknesses in theoretical and empirical terms. The factual problems that the civilizing process currently encounters are such that, for his followers, it would be unwise to translate Elias's general claims into a more testable and theoretically sound framework. The application of the civilizing process to the sports context serves to dramatize these weaknesses, and to highlight the surrender of critical imagination by his followers when they seek to develop his work. Ironically, it may be that Elias's claim to stand alongside the other deceased social theorists in this book will not be persuasive until his work goes through the process of radical refinement and imaginative overhaul of arguments, as in the cases of Marx, Weber and Durkheim *inter alia*.

Notes

1. In one book index (Elias, 1978a, p. 187), the reader is advised simply, when consulting 'structure', to 'see figurations'.
2. Bourdieu gives the concept of 'habitus' more systematic, sociological development.
3. Several historians dispute the Eliasians' claims regarding levels of violence at football fixtures in the late nineteenth and early twentieth centuries (Tranter, 1998, pp. 47–48).
4. See, for example, Dunning & Van Krieken (1997).
5. Merton (1973, pp. 131–132) measures social sadism against the tendency of sociologists to employ euphemisms that ignore intense human experiences.
6. Stokvis (1992, pp. 126–127) indicates that Elias uses a poor array of sources on fox-hunting to confirm (rather than test) his theory of the civilizing process.

References

Armstrong, G. (1998) *Football Hooligans: Knowing the Score*, Oxford: Berg.

Bauman, Z. (1989) *Modernity and the Holocaust*, Cambridge: Polity.

Bourdieu, P. & Passeron, J.-C. (1977) *Reproduction in Education, Society and Culture*, London: Sage.

Dunning, E. (1977) 'Power and Authority in the Public Schools (1700–1850)', in P.R. Gleichmann, J. Goudsblom & Hermann Korte (eds) *Human Figurations*, Amsterdam: Amsterdam Sociologisch Tijdschrift.

Dunning, E., Murphy, P. & Waddington, I. (1991) 'Anthropological versus Sociological Approaches to the Study of Soccer Hooliganism: some critical notes', *Sociological Review*, 39(3): 459–478.

Dunning, E., Murphy, P. & Williams, J. (1988) *The Roots of Football Hooliganism*, London: Routledge.

Dunning, E. & Sheard, K. (1979) *Barbarians, Gentlemen and Players*, Oxford: Blackwell.

Dunning, E. & van Krieken (1997) 'Translators Introduction to Norbert Elias's "Towards a Theory of Social Processes"', *British Journal of Sociology* 48(3): 353–354.

Elias, N. (1969) *The Court Society*, Oxford: Blackwell.

Elias, N. (1978a) *What is Sociology?*, London: Hutchinson.

Elias, N. (1978b) *The Civilizing Process: the history of manners*, Oxford: Blackwell.

Elias, N. (1982) *The Civilizing Process: state formation and civilization*, Oxford: Blackwell.

Elias, N. (1985) *The Loneliness of the Dying*, Oxford: Basil Blackwell.

Elias, N. (1986) *The Germans*, Cambridge: Polity.

Elias, N. (1987) *Involvement and Detachment*, Oxford: Blackwell.

Elias, N. (1991a) *The Society of Individuals*, Oxford: Blackwell.

Elias, N. (1991b) *The Symbol Theory*, London: Sage.

Elias, N. (1992) *Time*, Oxford: Blackwell.

Elias, N. (1994a) *Mozart*, Cambridge: Polity.

Elias, N. (1994b) *Reflections on a Life*, Cambridge: Polity.

Elias, N. & Dunning, E. (1986) *Quest for Excitement*, Oxford: Blackwell.

Giddens, A. (1984) *The Constitution of Society*, Cambridge: Polity.

Giuliamotti, R. (1999) *Football: a sociology of the global game*, Cambridge: Polity.

Goody, J. (2001) 'Elias and the Anthropological Tradition', unpublished paper.

Goulstone, J. (1974) *Modern Sport*, Bexleyheath.

Goulstone, J. (2000) 'The Working-Class Origins of Modern Football', *International Journal of the History of Sport*, 17: 135–143.

Harvey, A. (1999) 'Football's Missing Link: the real story of the evolution of modern football', in J.A. Mangan (ed.) *Sport in Europe*, London: Frank Cass.

Lewis, R.W. (1996) 'Football Hooliganism in England before 1914: a critique of the Dunning thesis', *International Journal of the History of Sport*, 13(3): 310–339.

Koenigsberger, H.G. (1977) '*Dominium regale* or *dominium politicum et regale?* Monarchies and parliaments in early modern Europe', in P.R. Gleichmann, J. Goudsblom & Hermann Korte (eds) *Human Figurations*, Amsterdam: Amsterdam Sociologisch Tijdschrift.

Maguire, J. (1999) *Global Sport*, Cambridge: Polity.

Mennell, S. (1992) *Norbert Elias*, Oxford: Blackwell.

Merton, R.K. (1973) *The Sociology of Science*, Chicago: University of Chicago Press.

Mestrovic, S. (1993) *The Barbarian Temperament*, London: Routledge.

Robertson, R. (1992) *Globalization*, London: Sage.

Smelser, N. (1992) 'The Rational Choice Perspective', *Rationality and Society*, 4: 381–410.

Stokvis, R. (1992) 'Sport and Civilization', in E. Dunning & C. Rojek (eds) *Sport and Leisure in the Civilizing Process*, Toronto: University of Toronto Press.

Tranter, N. (1998) *Sport, Economy and Society in Britain 1750–1914*, Cambridge: Cambridge University Press.

Van Krieken, R. (1999) *Norbert Elias*, London: Routledge.

10

Pierre Bourdieu and the Sociological Study of Sport: Habitus, Capital and Field

Alan Tomlinson

Introduction

Pierre Bourdieu was one of the most influential social theorists of his generation, both in his home country France and throughout the international sociological community. For close to half a century he researched a range of anthropological and sociological topics and, as a consequence, has had an enormously influential impact across the academic world. His initial specialism was in anthropology, and his publications in the early 1960s addressed issues concerning gender relations and unemployment in peasant cultures in Algerian society, and were published in rural studies and sociology of work journals. His broadening interests reflected his commitment to a wide-ranging sociology of culture, in the realms of education, art, the media, sport and around the general theme of symbolic power. His initial piece on sport and social class (Bourdieu, 1978) was one of the first commentaries by a major social theorist, apart from the *oeuvre* of Norbert Elias and his collaborator Eric Dunning, to take sport as a serious sociological issue. In his major study of taste and consumption, *Distinction: A Social Critique of the Judgement of Taste* (Bourdieu, 1986), first published in 1979, sport is acknowledged as a major focus of sociological analysis, and his conceptualization of the sociological significance of sport – as both institution and practice – has since influenced many theoretical and empirical investigations into the social and cultural significance and representation of bodily practices, not solely in sport but also in education, arts, and the media.

Any cursory trawl of the more sociologically informed and critical sociological literature on sport, culture and society will reveal the range of influences and applications. John Hargreaves (1987, p. 154), in his exploratory essay on the body, sport and power relations, cited Bourdieu's comments on the aesthetically conceived and trained body of the *petite bourgeoisie*. Richard Gruneau (1993, p. 105) argued for the relevance of Bourdieu's work – above that of Foucault – for "the study [of] the politics of the body as part of the critique of sport in modernity". Jennifer Hargreaves (1994) lined up Bourdieu, alongside Althusser, as the major theorist within what she labels the structuralist Marxism tradition of reproduction theory (1994, pp. 18–21). Back, *et al.* (2001, p. 90) talk of a single football player as a form of embodiment of class values and cultural capital, and Robson (2000) has developed Bourdieu's notion of embodiment in his work on football. Stamm and Lamprecht (1995, p. 220) salute the seminal contribution of Bourdieu in their study of social stratification, lifestyle and leisure. Sage (1990, p. 210) cites Bourdieu in his discussion of sport as a site of social struggles, even around the very definition of the term. Bourdieu's key concepts have been applied to subcultures of female boxers (Mennesson, 2000) and black male boxers (Wacquant, 1995). There are literally hundreds of further evaluations and applications. It is not the purpose of this chapter to review the range of these sources, nor to provide any definitive bibliographic guide to Bourdieu's *oeuvre*. For the latter, Bourdieu and Wacquant (1992) is a good starting point, and they themselves recommend Delsaut (1988) and an appendix to one of Bourdieu's (1990) own works. My aim here is a modest one: to outline the central concepts that characterize Bourdieu's overall theoretical framework, and to consider how these continue to inform the sociological analysis of sport. The central concepts are habitus, capital and field. Prior to that, a consideration of *Distinction* provides a context for locating these concepts within Bourdieu's overall theoretical framework, and showing how sport is located within that general framework.

Distinction

Bourdieu calls *Distinction* "a sort of ethnography of France" (p. xi), informed by a comparative method, and forwarding a "model of the relationship between the universe of economic and social conditions and the universe of lifestyles" (p. xi). This involves an explicit response to the German sociologist Max Weber, in rethinking the Weberian "opposition between class and Stand (status)" (p. xii). In the lofty trad-ition of French thinkers, Bourdieu also declares his "perhaps immoderate ambition of giving a scientific answer to the old questions of Kant's critique of judgement, by seeking in the structure of the social classes the basis of the systems of classification which structure perception of the social world and designate the objects of aesthetic enjoyment" (pp. xiii–xiv). This is a heady mix of ambition and aspiration, and part of that ambition is also to avert misleading specialisms. His study therefore overtly connects what to others might be separate sociologies – of knowledge, of culture, of food, of sport – and argues for a more integrated analytical approach, overlapping the historical, the anthropological and the sociological in the cultural analysis of tastes and practices. This is imperative for Bourdieu, for one can "observe and understand everything that human practices reveal only when they are seen in their mutual relationships...as a totality" (p. xiv). The key implication here is that sport cannot be understood in isolation, as if it has no connection with other cultural practices and social influences.

The empirical analyses, the findings reported, in the study were based on a questionnaire survey carried out in 1963 and 1967–68 on a sample of 1217 people. The survey explored "how the cultivated disposition and cultural competence that are revealed in the nature of the cultural goods consumed, and in the way they are consumed, vary according to the category of agents and the area to which they are applied" (p. 13). The survey established that there is a very close link between cultural practices or the opinions embodied in those practices, and educational capital and social origin. Social class features centrally in the analysis, and is at the heart of the first substantial commentary on sport in the book. In typically dense prose in one drawn-out sentence, Bourdieu writes:

> to understand the class distribution of the various sports, one would have to take account of the representation which, in terms of their specific schemes of perception and appreciation, the different classes have of the costs (economic, cultural and 'physical') and benefits attached to the different sports – immediate or deferred 'physical' benefits (health, beauty, strength, whether visible through body-building or invisible through 'keep-fit' exercises), economic and social benefits (upward mobility etc.), immediate or deferred symbolic benefits linked to the distributional or positional value of each of the sports considered (i.e. all that each of them receives from its greater or lesser rarity, and its more or less clear association with a class, with boxing, football, rugby or body-building evoking the working classes, tennis and skiing the bourgeoisie and golf the upper bourgeoisie), gains in distinction accruing from the effects on the body itself (e.g., slimness, sun-tan, muscles obviously or discreetly visible etc.) or from

the access to highly selective groups which some of these sports give (golf, polo etc.).

(p. 20)

This passage is from the first chapter of the book, on the aristocracy of culture, concerned mostly with art, aesthetics, and discussion of cultural tastes in history. It provides nevertheless a comprehensive statement on the relationship between sport and social class in both historical and sociological contexts, also developed in a separate piece published almost at the same time (Bourdieu, 1978). The most sustained discussion of sport in the book is in the third chapter, entitled "the habitus and the space of life-styles", in a subsection on "the universes of stylistic possibles" (pp. 208–223). The "universe of sporting activities" presents itself to new entrants as a set of objectively constituted possibilities and values, with social significance and historical meanings. So sport cannot be comprehended as the free choice of individuals, and practitioners of the same sport may bestow different meanings on the sporting activity or practice. Abstract, formal typologies of sports are meaningless to Bourdieu. Rather, "only a methodical analysis of the variations in the function and meaning conferred on the different sporting activities will enable one...to construct the table of the sociologically pertinent features in terms of which the agents (consciously or unconsciously) choose their sports" (p. 211). To understand the meaning of a sporting practice it is necessary to look at when and how a sport was learnt, how it is played, in what context it is played and how often it is played, considerations that lead Bourdieu to note that much available statistical data are therefore very difficult to interpret. So in the case of tennis, new players will flaunt dress codes of traditional tennis players, and this reveals the complexity of the question of the meaning and social significance of the sport:

Tennis played in Bermuda shorts and a tee shirt, in a tracksuit or even swimming trunks, and Adidas running shoes, is indeed another tennis, both in the way it is played and the satisfactions it gives.

(p. 212).

In this section Bourdieu also argues that sport, as with other body-directed practices such as diet or beauty care, can be seen as class-based. Much of physical culture, and health-oriented activities such as jogging or walking, are dominated by the "culturally richest fractions of the middle-classes and the dominant class" (p. 215), whereas team sports are engaged in across the classes. But there are deep distinctions among different team sports:

> indeed, the most typically popular sports, football and rugby, and wrestling and boxing, ... combine all the features which repel the dominant class: not only the social composition of their public, which redoubles their commonness, but also the values and virtues demanded, strength, endurance violence, 'sacrifice', docility and submission to collective discipline – so contrary to bourgeois 'role distance' – and the exaltation of competition.
>
> (p. 214)

Class differences are also notable in spectatorship, the dominant class watching less sport, either live or on television, than the other classes, except for tennis, rugby and skiing. Particular sports are adopted by a social class too in terms of the class's relation to the body, and a world-view encompassing a "whole philosophy of the person and the body" (p. 218):

> the bourgeois treats his body as an end, makes his body a sign of its own ease. Style is thus foregrounded, and the most typically bourgeois deportment can be recognized by ... above all ... a restrained, measured, self-assured tempo. This slow pace, contrasting with working-class haste or petit-bourgeois eagerness, also characterizes bourgeois speech.
>
> (p. 218)

Connections, always connections. For Bourdieu, sociological analysis requires connections after connections, so that sport practices and their meanings are understood as part of the social and cultural totality. And contextualizing trends or broader social processes also frame the interpretation of the sporting practice. The sexual division of labour, and the "division of the work of domination" (p. 218) can be revealed by the analysis of the distribution of sporting practices. Exercise and diet within "the new morality of health" is replacing a more traditional ethical pedagogy in the shaping of minds and bodies (p. 219). New sports and new forms of classic sports provide the elements of a counter-culture, all demanding a "high investment of cultural capital in the activity itself, in preparing, maintaining and using the equipment, and especially, perhaps, in verbalizing the experiences" (p. 220).

For Bourdieu, sporting activities and entertainment constitute a system of practices on offer to potential participants or consumers. But these consumers will not make free and unconstrained choices. Such choices will be led by the system itself, which is "predisposed to express" sociologically pertinent differences, such as gender/sex differences, or oppositions between class fractions: "The agents only have to follow the leanings of their habitus in order to take over, unwittingly, the intention immanent in the corresponding practices, to find an activity which is entirely 'them' and, with it, kindred spirits" (p. 223). The predispositions determining such choices or "leanings" are generative of the "habitus", covered in more detail in the following section.

Put at its simplest, Bourdieu's analysis of sports practices in *Distinction* demonstrates the value of an integrated approach in which sport is not analyzed in isolation from the other practices that confer status and distinction upon social groups. It treats the legacies and resonances of history seriously, as a way of identifying major breaks in the formation and meaning of sports. It demonstrates the deeply entrenched relation between social class and sport, but without ossifying this dynamic. It blends minute empirical observation with sophisticated interpretation and theorization. In compiling this excerpt-based section I have chosen to allow Bourdieu's words to speak for themselves, and inevitably some of his key terms have been included in these citations – habitus, and cultural capital for instance. In the following sections the main terms and concepts characterizing Bourdieu's framework are outlined and discussed, in the context of both that overall framework, and other sociological concepts.

Habitus

The term habitus was first used by the French anthropologist Marcel Mauss in a 1935 essay on "body techniques" (MacAloon, 1988, p. 150). In *Distinction* one of most succinct single definitional statements on habitus is buried in a footnote. It is worth citing in full, as a basis for discussion and for the elaboration of complementary statements and more concrete examples from the study. Bourdieu states that the habitus is a system of dispositions:

> It expresses first the *result of an organizing action*, with a meaning close to that of words such as structure; it also designates a way of being, a habitual state (especially of the body) and, in particular, a *predisposition, tendency, propensity* or *inclination*.
>
> (p. 562, footnote 2)

The critical emphasis here is that within the one concept, structure and action are embraced as interrelated elements, without any one-sided determinism: "The habitus is not only a structuring structure, which organizes practices and the perception of practices, but also a structured structure" (p. 170). This is a theoretical principle underlying the whole of Bourdieu's framework, and empirical studies and empirical studies alone have the capacity to identify the balance between the structuring and the structured in any given case. "Life-styles are thus the systematic products of habitus, which...become sign systems that are socially qualified" (p. 173). A particular case is made with reference to a particular view of the world that underlies a distinctive conception of pedagogic commitment, or the vocation of the teacher:

> the theoretical space of habitus...the generative formulae (e.g. for teachers, aristocratic asceticism) which underlie each of the classes of practices and properties, that is, the transformation into a distinct and distinctive lifestyle of the necessities and facilities characteristic of a condition and a position.
>
> (1986, p. 126)

The concept of habitus captures the complexities of human agency as that agency repeatedly engages with forms of structure and influence. The example cited in the previous section talked of the "leanings" of the habitus being followed by agents, and the unwitting fashion in which this might be accomplished. There is therefore certainly a tendency to stress a determinist structuring process (Sugden & Tomlinson, 2001, p. 318), but this is not a simple emphasis within the concept. Habituses can of course change, lose position and influence, and this can only be, logically, a consequence of the interrelatedness of the practices of agents with the extant habitus. This allows the use of the recognition of the related concept of doxa, the challenging of orthodoxies and dominant values, as writings on women's activism in sport (von der Lippe, 2000) have demonstrated. Bourdieu has consistently pointed to the centrality of agents/agency in any process of reproduction: "agents are the product of this structure and continually make and remake this structure, which they may even radically transform under definite structural conditions" (Bourdieu & Wacquant, 1992, p. 140).

Habitus, then, points to the central dynamics and processes in the making and changing of societies, and the different cultural spheres and practices in those societies. It permits "the researcher to outflank the conceptual knots of individual and society, agency and structure and nature versus nurture" (Jarvie & Maguire, 1994, p. 190).

Capital

The conceptual category of capital is widely used in *Distinction*, but never systematically defined, more applied within the overall analysis. Very generally, for Bourdieu, capital is a form of power, the capacity individuals and groups might have to impact upon, change or control situations. The degree of capital available to the social agent will determine the extent of control he will have over himself and others. Bourdieu talks of economic capital, cultural capital, educational capital and symbolic capital. Economic capital refers to wealth and money, cultural to the consumption of cultural goods and the expression of taste, educational to the accumulation of qualifications, and symbolic to reputation and image. The challenge is not to take these one by one and analyse them separately, but to see how they interact in the case of specific practices and social classes. The forms of power, too, will be closely connected to habitus.

Field

The term field completes the conceptual trilogy around which much of Bourdieu's work is based:

> In analytic terms, a field may be defined as a network, or a configur-
> ation, of objective relations between positions. These positions are
> objectively defined, in their existence and in the determinations they
> impose upon their occupants, agents or institutions, by their present
> and potential situation (*situs*) in the structure of the distribution of
> species of power (or capital) whose possession commands access to
> the specific profits that are at stake in the field, as well as by their
> objective relation to other positions (domination, subordination,
> homology, etc.).
>
> (Bourdieu & Wacquant, 1992, p. 97)

Bourdieu cites as examples, the artistic, religious or economic fields. We cannot talk of any capital, either, without reference to a field. The field is the potential space where change is mooted or implemented: "As a space of potential and active forces, the field is also a *field of struggles* aimed at preserving or transforming the configuration of these forces" (ibid., p. 101). The emphasis of most concern in this chapter is of course the field of sport, though there is a conceptual elasticity to the concept. Madsen (2001, p. 16) mobilizes the concept in a consideration of "empirical studies of international arenas", which he claims enables him to dispute the primacy of an internationalist emphasis on the globalization process, and to champion a revitalized emphasis upon the "mode of pro-duction of the State" in the "building up of the international" (p. 17). Field refers to particular sets of relations between agents engaged in the same activity. Chinca and Young (2000) synopsize Bourdieu's writings on the literary field, pointing to three main properties: "its structure; its internal dynamic, characterized by competition between agents; its relative autonomy" (p. 29).

Sport cultures and the Bourdieu model

I have given some examples of Bourdieu's most integrated, and sustained, analyses of sporting practice, followed by an exegetical presentation of coherent definitional extracts of his three core organizing concepts. In this final section I will seek to stretch the logic of some of the examples cited in *Distinction* – smart clubs (*les clubs chics*), the health/exercise body-shaping sports and new sports – in general discussions drawing upon the core concepts. The examples are not rooted in any compre-hensive review of research, or revelatory new empirical material. They are literally heuristic constructions, emphasizing the sort of interpretation that the Bourdieu framework provides.

Smart clubs might organize around "some rare, selective activity" (p. 162) such as golf, polo, hunting, riding, pigeon-shooting or sailing, or the values of the "whole social person". Sponsors are needed for application for membership. Waiting-lists can be several years long. Some clubs will give you credit in your application if a father or an elder brother has been or is a member. Formal rules are often there to "protect the group against outsiders". Subscriptions will be very high. In some contexts, without doubt, shared schooling or alma mater would favour an applicant. Here we see – regardless of performance merit, playing potential or even economic means – different dimensions of the Bourdieu model at work. The sports/golf field has specific features, operating as a network around a set of positions. These smart clubs constitute an exclusive and privileged class habitus, in which particular combinations of capital (educational and cultural as well as economic) will determine your suitability to enter that habitus. Historically, in England, golf clubs might have stretched the boundaries of their exclusivity, but they have in many cases stayed remarkably exclusive by controlling membership and using recruitment practices that are really forms of person-profiling, whereby the individual's combination of economic, educational and cultural capital is assessed. This has ensured that the habitus remains class-based and patriarchal in such golf clubs, and in corresponding smart or elite and exclusive sport clubs. Historical, late nineteenth century forms of marginalization such as the Artisan's Club, offering limited access and membership rights to working-class members, may not have survived in any explicit form. But the remarkable continuity of exclusivity of sport clubs is testimony to the power of the habitus to reproduce itself through changing times, to adapt yet preserve its essential features. The elite nature of sport clubs and institutions such as the Marylebone Cricket Club (MCC) at the Lords cricket ground in London, with its long waiting lists and legendary snobbery, can be understood as a classic form of cultural reproduction in which all of the elements of capital are drawn upon to construct and create a particular dominant class and patriarchal habitus that has endured across generations and centuries.

The new morality of health, as Bourdieu dubbed the exercise and fitness boom, can be seen to be a social class-based phenomenon: "The health-oriented hedonism of doctors and modern executives who have the material and cultural means of access to the most prestigious activities, far from vulgar crowds, is expressed in yachting, open-sea swimming, cross-country skiing or underwater fishing..." (1986, p. 219). The different manifestations of this health industry have produced specific forms of provision, in health clubs, gyms, marinas, hotel spas, some generating vulgar crowds of their own on the running machines and techno-gadgetry of the contemporary fitness room. But everywhere you look in this health-driven fitness industry, you will be looking at the public articulation of forms of capital. New sports – forms of trekking, windsurfing, canoeing, cross-country skiing, archery, hang-gliding are mentioned by Bourdieu – with their stock-rooms of accompanying clothing and equipment (ibid., p. 220), are also reminders that sports practices are closely bound up with access to financial resources, to economic capital. Again, the boundaries of exclusivity might shift a little, and educational capital might have little influence on an individual's desire to participate in hang-gliding. But closer scrutiny of any sporting practice will reveal the pertinent combination of capital that has driven the participants to engage in the practice, to be drawn into and become in turn generative of that particular habitus.

Conclusion

Much criticism has been directed at Bourdieu. He has been accused of verbosity and obscurantism, to which he has vigorously responded. He justifies his long complex sentences, saying that they are "constructed as they are with a view to reconstituting the complexity of the social world in a language capable of holding together the most diverse things while setting them in rigorous perspective" (1986, p. xiii). His overall framework has been criticized as too closed, stressing reproduction rather than change, recognizing too little the place of opposition or resistance (Rojek, 1995, p. 69). He has been accused of underemphasizing gender relations and overemphasizing class as his major analytic category. But a close reading of his key work *Distinction* demonstrates his overall awareness of the range of sociological influences on culture. And his interest in the body that is manifest in that major study in particular always sensitized him to the nuances of gender and influence of male power in the construction and perpetuation of particular cultures and habituses. Rojek (2000, p. 88) acknowledges that, despite a range of criticisms, "Bourdieu does succeed in revealing the complexity of performative culture in contemporary society". The criticisms far from undermine the lasting impact of his main concepts, as continuing applications and explorations of his work, evidence in journals such as *Sociology of Sport Journal* and the *International Review for the Sociology of Sport* – Kay and Laberge (2002) on adventure sports and the new corporate habitus, Thrane (2001) on sport spectatorship in Scandinavia, Wilson (2002) on class and participation in the USA, von der Lippe (2000) on gender and struggle. Sport cultures do change, new sport cultures do emerge, and Bourdieu was always utterly clear that they can. But sport cultures and practices have continued to be shaped by human agents drawing on their various reserves of different types of capital, in the construction of class and gender-influenced habituses that have characterized the field of sporting practices. It would be churlish not to recognize Bourdieu's major contribution to the sociological study and understanding of sport, and the centrality of his major concepts to the continuing analysis of sport's place in contemporary culture.

References

Back, L., Crabbe, T. & Solomos, J. (2001) "Lions and Black Skins", in B. Carrington & I. McDonald (eds) *"Race", Sport and British Society*, London: Routledge.

Bourdieu, P. (1978) "Sport and Social Class", *Social Science Information* 17: 819–840.

Bourdieu, P. (1986) *Distinction*, London: Routledge & Kegan Paul.

Bourdieu, P. (1990) *In Other Words*, Cambridge: Polity Press.

Bourdieu, P. & Wacquant, L.J.D. (1992) *An Invitation to Reflexive Sociology*, Cambridge: Polity Press.

Chinca, M. & Young, C.J. (2000) Unpublished Paper on Bourdieu and the Library Field.

Delsaut, Y. (1988) *Bibliographie des Travaux de Pierre Bourdieu, 1958–1988*, Paris: Centre de Sociologie Europeenne du College de France.

Gruneau, R. (1993) "The Critique of Sport in Modernity", in E. Dunning, J. Maguire & R. Pearton (eds) *The Sports Process*, Champaign, Ill.: Human Kinetics.

Hargreaves, Jennifer (1994) *Sporting Females*, London: Routledge.

Hargreaves, John (1987) "The Body, Sport and Power Relations", in J. Horne, D. Jary & A. Tomlinson (eds) *Sport, Leisure and Social Relations*, London: Routledge & Kegan Paul.

Jarvie, G. & Maguire, J. (1994) *Sport and Leisure in Social Thought*, London: Routledge.

Kay, J. & Laberge, S. (2002) "The 'New' Corporate Habitus in Adventure Racing", *International Review for the Sociology of Sport* 37(1): 17–36.

MacAloon, J.J. (1988) "A Prefaratory Note to Pierre Bourdieu's 'Program for a Sociology of Sport'", *Sociology of Sport Journal* 5(2): 150–152.

Madsen, M.R. (2001) "Exploring International Fields with Bourdieu in the Suitcase", paper to the 5th Conference of the European Sociological Association, Helsinki, August.

Mennesson, C. (2000) "'Hard' Women and 'Soft' Women", *International Review for the Sociology of Sport*, 35(1): 21–33.

Robson, G. (2000) *No One Likes Us, We Don't Care*, Oxford: Berg.

Rojek, C. (1995) *Decentring Leisure*, London: Sage.

Rojek, C. (2000) *Leisure and Culture*, London: Macmillan.

Sage, G. (1990) *Power and Ideology in American Sport*, Champaign, Ill.: Human Kinetic Books.

Stamm, H. & Lamprecht, M. (1995) "Social Stratification, Lifestyle and Leisure Choice", in G. McFee, W. Murphy & G. Whannel (eds) *Leisure Cultures*, Eastbourne: Leisure Studies Association Publication Number 54.

Sugden, J. & Tomlinson, A. (2001) "Theorizing Sport, Class and Status", in J. Coakley & E. Dunning (eds) *Handbook of Sports Studies*, London: Sage Publications.

Thrane, C. (2001) "Sport Spectatorship in Scandinavia", *International Review for the Sociology of Sport* 36(2): 149–163.

Von der Lippe, G. (2000) "Heresy as a Victorious Political Practice", *International Review for the Sociology of Sport* 35(2): 181–198.

Wacquant, L.J.D. (1995) "Pugs at Work: Bodily Capital and Bodily Labour Among Professional Boxers", *Body & Society* 1(1): 65–93.

Wilson, T. (2002) "The Paradox of Social Class and Sports Involvement: The Role of Cultural and Economic Capital", *International Review for the Sociology of Sport* 37(1): 5–16.

11

Habermas on Sports: Social Theory from a Moral Perspective

William J. Morgan

Jürgen Habermas is, without question, one of the leading social theorists and cultural critics of our time. His large and impressive body of work has attracted the attention of scholars worldwide in such fields as sociology, philosophy, political theory, history, and cultural studies. This wide readership confirms his own far ranging intellectual interests and wide berth of learning. Habermas studied economics, philosophy, history, and psychology at the Universities of Göttingen, Zurich, and Bonn. The conspicuous absence of sociology here is not owed to any indifference on Habermas's part, but to the rather astonishing fact that it was not taught at any of these universities. This explains why he did not take up its study until he had completed his dissertation and was working as a freelance journalist. The sociology of labour was his first and main interest in this period, as can be gleaned from the title of one of his early publications, 'The Dialectics of Rationalization: Concerning Alienation in Production and Consumption', which was published in the German journal *Merkur* (Adorno, 1954). It was around this time that Habermas was introduced by a mutual friend to Theodor Adorno, one of the leading intellectuals of his time and a chief architect of the so-called Frankfurt School of critical theory, who had per chance read his essay in *Merkur*. Adorno subsequently invited him to the University of Frankfurt to become his research assistant. Thus began Habermas's long association with Adorno and his fellow Frankfurt School compatriots Max Horkheimer and Herbert Marcuse, and the long identification of his work with this critical school of thought – an identification not all to his liking.[1]

Despite his wide-ranging scholarship, however, Habermas hardly gave sports and other leisure fare a notice. The closest he came was in an essay published in 1958 entitled 'Sociological Notes on the Relationship Between Work and Leisure'.[2] Aside from this early effort, however, one will search in vain for any references to sport or leisure in his published writings. The English-language literature dealing with his work in the sociology of sport is similarly threadbare.[3] To be sure, social theorists of sport who contribute to this literature are certainly aware of his work, and frequently cite Habermas in their own works. But to my knowledge no one in this camp has ever published a major critical study of sport that takes its main inspiration from Habermas's ideas.[4]

So in trying to piece together how Habermas's work might be profitably brought to bear on sports, and thus how one might envisage Habermas as a social theorist of sport, one has little choice but to turn directly to his published writings for clues. Fortunately, there is much in them that, if carefully read and dissected, suggests how he might have critically approached sports. My plan here is to start where Habermas himself started, his previously mentioned 1958 essay on the relation between work and leisure, and on a certain critique of what he and others have famously called instrumental reason that he begins to articulate in this essay. What makes this essay and the critique it initiates so important is not just that it was to become a central theme in his later work, especially his two volume magnum opus *The Theory of Communicative Action* (Habermas 1984, 1987) but also because it explains his most recent effort to incorporate ethical and moral ideas into his social theory. Indeed, I will argue, not uncontroversially, that it is this later Habermasian emphasis on the ethical and moral dimensions of our social lives that especially warrants the attention of present day critical theorists and students of sports.

The rationalization of labour and sport and the critique of instrumental reason

As I noted above, my reason for starting with Habermas's essay on the relationship between work and leisure is not because it is an especially novel or noteworthy analysis, it is clearly neither, but because it lays out a social problem that was to occupy Habermas throughout his career and change how he conceived of critical social theory. That problem, at least as he first began to think about it in this essay, had to do with the institutionalization of labour as wage-labour in capitalist society, in which the purposive-rational character of labour was contoured to fit the dominant profit orientation of capitalist society. It was bad enough, argued Habermas, that labour was rationalized (institutionalized) to serve the interests of capitalism in this fashion, but what was even worse, he reasoned, was that our leisure was similarly rationalized to serve the interests of profit. That meant that leisure practices like sports largely replicated the rationality and norms of wage-labour, that is, were practiced, organized, and financed in much the same way as wage-labour was practised, organized, and financed. Far, then, from being an alternative to labour, sport turned out to be just another instance of it, a mere after-image of labour that prolonged, rather than brought up short, the work day.

As I said, there is nothing especially original or compelling about this analysis. Indeed, his mentor, Adorno, had a much more sophisticated, even if somewhat similar, conception of leisure and sports.[5] But we can already see here the outlines of a social dilemma that Habermas has devoted much of his career to understanding and remedying. That dilemma, as he later articulated it, had to do with 'overcoming the one-sidedness of the capitalist process of rationalization. One-sidedness, that is, in the sense of the rise to dominance of cognitive-instrumental aspects, which results in everything else being driven into the realm of apparent irrationality' (quoted in Dew, 1986, p. 91). What Habermas meant by this rather forbidding prose is that the triumph of capitalism in the modern world brought in its train a certain dominant way of thinking about our lives in which rational reflection on what means most effectively satisfy the ends we seek pretty much becomes the point of human life. Since ends on this view are mere preferences, subjective expressions of what we desire and value, and since no one preference can be said to be rationally superior to any other, they are said to be beyond rational scrutiny. But since the means we employ to reach our ends can be more or less efficient in achieving them, they do admit of rational calculation. I should say rational calculation of a certain sort; for the way in which we are to decide what to do on any given occasion is to weigh the costs and benefits of any action, and choose only those actions that maximize our chances of getting what we want. So the rational way to live one's life, at least in market-based societies, is to act in those ways that most effectively further our self-interests.

Someone might object at this point that it is hard to see what Habermas finds so troubling about societies of this ilk who socialize their members to look out for themselves and pursue their own interests. After all, another more flattering and equally valid way to describe such societies is to say that they place a premium on individual autonomy and freedom, in which individuals get to decide for themselves how they want to live free of the shackles that traditional societies, with their overarching world views and religious conceptions, typically impose on their members. Rather than decrying modern capitalist societies, the critic might argue further, we should welcome them for undermining older, traditional notions like the 'Great Chain of Being', which slotted people into their proper places along with angels, heavenly bodies, and other earthly creatures, and which justified the social hierarchies they created (hierarchies that privileged men over women, citizens over slaves, heathens over nonbelievers, and whites over blacks) by appeal to a supposed non-human standard binding on all beings. The displacement of traditional by modern capitalist societies thus meant that instead of having to ask whether what I want to do accords with what the Great Chain of Being or some other cosmic scheme demands of me, I am free to do whatever I want to do, to follow my own interests wherever they take me, provided no one else is harmed in the process.[6]

There is much to be said for this objection, if for no other reason than to romanticize these traditional societies and to mourn the fading of their cosmic moral visions would be to miss the very real advance in freedom and individual autonomy achieved by modern bourgeois societies. But there is also much to be said against this objection, since this very advance in individual freedom set the stage for a worrisome preoccupation with self, a certain, in Taylor's (1992, p. 4) words, 'narrowing and flattening' of our lives that leaves them 'poorer in meaning and less concerned with others'. This 'narrowing' and impoverishing of our lives is precisely what Habermas had in mind when he referred to the one-sided rationalization of capitalist societies, to their championing of instrumental reason. And nowhere was this more apparent, he argued, than in the decline of our moral regard for others. For when individuals lose whatever larger significance they held in older, traditional worldviews like the Great Chain of Being, they become mere resources (means) for one another's individual projects. This accounts for why in these societies the very same cost-benefit analysis we use to further our self-interests in everyday life is put to use to guide our moral dealings with others. By thus turning moral deliberation into a species of instrumental reason, argued Habermas, capitalist societies give their members license to exploit and manipulate others, to push their favoured agendas on one another.

Nowhere, perhaps, is this seepage of instrumental reasoning into moral reasoning, and the social/moral decline it sets in motion, more apparent than in the case of contemporary sports. The present win-at-all-costs ethos that drives most of the sports world today makes no secret of this fact, of its sanction of an unreconstructed and unapologetic pursuit of self-interest. Bredemeier and Shields (1986) have even gone so far as to describe this naked privileging of self-interest as the key to the 'game-reasoning' that goes on in sports, in which egocentric calculations of 'what's in it for me' trump all other considerations.

But the point can be made less abstract if we train our eyes on what has been happening in sports in the last few years. To say that this recent past has not been, morally speaking, a good one for sports is to say the obvious. In fact, examples of misconduct in sports nowadays are so widespread and well publicized, that it is hard to know where to start. The Tyson–Holyfield boxing ear-biting debacle and the Latrell Spreewell coach-choking incident in professional basketball come immediately to mind, as does the sickening spectacle of Boston Bruins hockey player Martey McSorely, who, with a mere three seconds left in the game, levelled a defenceless and unaware opponent with a stick to the head rendering him unconscious, twitching, and bleeding on the ice.[7] I am sure that my readers can readily supply their own examples of morally questionable behaviour in sports. All I want to say further on the subject is that the moral travails of sports are not confined to the playing fields or to athletes. Indeed, when we throw in the bad behaviour of fans, most notoriously football hooligans, and the bribery scandals currently swirling around the awarding of the Olympic Games to host nations, we can see just what a moral mess sports presently find themselves in.

A Habermasian take on sports

It follows from our sketch of Habermas's early critique of instrumental reason and its moral fallout, I want to argue, that if Habermas were to seriously take up the case of contemporary sports, he would most likely take them up on precisely these moral grounds. For it is this moral rot that explains for him not just the sorry state of social practices like sports, but the sorry state of most social practices (economics, politics, religion) in market societies – all of which seem to be infected by the instrumental reason virus and the narcissism it spreads. Before I try to spell out what such a Habermasian moral critique of sports might look like, however, I would first like to say something about why Habermas's effort to reserve an important place for moral considerations in his social theory warrants our attention in the first place.

What, then, is so novel and important about Habermas's morally angled social theory? The answer has to do with what Taylor (1992, pp. 19–21) somewhat polemically calls the 'normal fashion' of sociological explanation. What he means by this is the current tendency in social theory to downplay, if not reject altogether, the role moral ideals (notions of what constitute a 'better' or 'higher' life) play in social life and in explaining why people do what they do.[8] We can see this not only in crude Marxist models of social explanation that rely on supposedly 'harder' economic facts to explain the course of our social lives, but in supposedly more sophisticated approaches that, for example, appeal to notions of class bargaining (hegemony theory) or to considerations of power (Foucault) to account for social phenomena. According to these views, then, important social transformations, like the presently discussed rise to dominance of instrumental reason, are only or principally to be explained in the non-moral terms of the advantages they bestow on particular social groups and actors. What is left out of this picture, as noted, is that moral ideas and beliefs might have anything to do with these social shifts and with redirecting or countering them. If Taylor is right about this, and I think he largely is – though this would require a paper in its own right to defend adequately – then Habermas's attempt to give moral beliefs and ideals their due is not only unique and goes against the grain of much present social theorizing, but also edifying of our present plight. For what many of us still find so disagreeable about our current social predicament and the runaway individualism that lies behind it is morally rooted. That means that if we hope to turn things around, to honor Marx's dictum, which doubles as the dictum of critical theory itself, that the point is not just to understand the world but to change it, we can scarcely turn our backs on this moral dimension of our lives.

How, then, would Habermas pursue this moral line in sports? The answer, I believe, is along two fronts. On the first, the task of social theory as Habermas conceives it would be to make clear how what we earlier described as the seepage of instrumental reason into our moral reasoning about sports is pulled off, such that our moral connections and commitments to others in sports are not only weakened but seemingly eliminated. Here the point is to show how we explain away the morally retrograde actions of athletes like Tyson and McSorely, so that they no longer seem proper objects of moral inquiry at all – so that even shining a moral light on them appears deeply mistaken. On the second front, Habermas poses a critical and not just an explanatory task for social theory, whose aim is to show that social practices like sports are still capable of arousing our moral ire because they are still informed by moral ideals. Here the point is to find some way to give these admittedly suppressed moral ideals a hearing, to become more articulate about them not just to correct what may be errant views of them, but, more importantly, to goad people to live up to them 'in fuller and more integral ways' (Taylor, 1992, p. 22). In order to accomplish this critical aim, argues Habermas, sports must be subjected to what he calls a 'discourse ethics', a discourse which makes certain moral demands on the way we think and talk about sports. In the space that remains, I want to sketch out in greater detail how Habermas would likely have developed both of these lines of inquiry had he applied them to sports.

The disappearance of the moral dimension of sports

How, then, are we to account for this vanishing of the 'moral' in sports? Habermas's answer points us in two directions, the first at the level of action where sports are constituted as social practices of a certain type, and the second at the level of discourse where the point and purpose of sports is debated in public ways.

Let us begin, then, where Habermas begins, with the ensemble of actions that define sports and other practices as the particular social enterprises they are. The key to the social definition of these practices is bound up with what he famously calls communicative action, which includes both those forms of action oriented to reaching a consensus and those forms of action based on a prior consensus, and where the consensus reached or acted upon concerns how we are supposed to act and conduct ourselves in given situations. All such social agreements, Habermas argues, involve the raising of validity claims (explicitly when forming a consensus and implicitly when acting upon a prior consensus) regarding the truth of what parties to the agreement say to one another as well as the rightness of the way they treat one another. Obviously, one will not be able to reach a consensus with others unless they believe what you are saying is true and that the way you are treating them is right, just as one will not be able to act on an already accepted consensus unless you and your compatriots believe what has been agreed to is truthful and accords with appropriate norms of conduct.

The social construction of sports proves to be no different in this regard. For they too, Habermas would say, are the product of communicatively anchored agreements which set out what constitutes intelligible and acceptable conduct within them. That is to say, they shape the social and moral ethos of sports (what sorts of action and what norms of conduct are in keeping with their basic point and purpose), and the social and moral intuitions of their participants and devotees (what kinds of beliefs and actions are comprehensible to them, and what kinds of values and ideals should guide their actions).

Any effort to make this moral dimension of sports go away, therefore, would have to disrupt the consensus that underpins it. This is precisely what happened in our previously cited examples of athletic misconduct, in which acts were committed that contravened accepted standards of conduct in sports. So when Spreewell, Tyson, and McSorely acted as they did, they were understood to have crossed the line of what was regarded as appropriate behaviour in their respective sports. Of course, matters need not escalate beyond this point. For one quick and effective way to remedy such disruptions of the prevailing consensus is to petition that consensus directly, that is, to appeal to the intersubjective norms violated by these acts. If they still resonate, then the consensus will have been restored and the actions of the perpetrators in question properly censured. But appeals of this sort are not fated to succeed, especially if the violations they are supposed to check are part of a larger pattern of misconduct that challenge these norms. In such instances, what we are faced with is not a simple disturbance but a wholesale breakdown in the communicative practice of sports, one which nullifies the existing consensus and makes further interaction impossible.

Given what Habermas had to say about the one-sided rationalization of contemporary bourgeois societies, and what we know about the vulnerability of sports to such processes, it is safe to assume that Habermas would regard the frequent moral lapses of sports we are witnessing today as a fundamental breakdown in their communicative practice. And it is also safe to assume that he would single out the shift from communicative to purposive-strategic action, the target of his critique of instrumental reason, as the causal force responsible for this breakdown. That is because strategic action leaves no room for communicative action, since its egoistic calculus accords others 'only the status of means or limiting conditions for the realization of one's own individual plans of action' (Habermas, 1993, p. 3). And where there is no room for communicative action, argues Habermas, there is no room for moral consideration of others. So the reason why moral mischief is rife in contemporary sports is because strategic calculations of self-interest are rife in sports today. Further, the reason why so much of this sporting moral mischief goes unnoticed, or gets confused for something else (either as strategic miscalculations by players who press their quest for self-advantage too far or as strategic miscalculations by game authorities who assign costs for rule-breaking that do not outweigh its benefits), can also be traced to the dominance that strategic action currently enjoys in the world of sports.

At this first level of practice, then, the 'moral' turns out to be a casualty of the triumph of strategic action over communicative action. This fact cannot but affect our discourse about sports, since it means there will be less and less that goes on in sports that can reasonably be regarded as moral, and so, less and less to say about them that is amenable to moral scrutiny. But the disappearance of the moral in our discourse about sports is further attributable to a shift in the way we think about them that follows on the heels of the shift from communicative to strategic action just discussed. Evidence of such a discursive shift is apparent, Habermas thinks, in our increasing tendency to explain away morally troubling actions by trying to pass them off as less morally offensive than they are. This same tendency, I contend, is clearly evident in our public reckoning of sports as well, and so we shall look there first, mindful of Habermas's further warning that such excuse-mongering inexorably leads to the purging of the 'moral' altogether from our public discourse.

One way we try to soften the impact of athletic moral transgressions is to make them less egregious than they seem without undermining the competence of the perpetrator. So one might say that Spreewell had little choice but to attack his coach when provoked, given the authoritarian and hierarchical institutional setup of organized sports, which delegates practically all decision-making power to coaches and their minions and almost none to athletes themselves. Another way we minimize the moral failings of players and their surrogates is by attacking directly their competence. So one might say that McSorely did not intend in a self-conscious way to injure his opponent but simply got carried away by the intensity and passion of the moment.

Whereas the first excuse aims to throw a different light on the action, the second aims to throw a different light on the actor. But no matter where this different light is cast, what is most telling is the darkness that remains. And the answer, as previously hinted, is not just the moral gravity of the violations committed but as well the specifically moral character of these violations. What change in perspective in the way we think about sports is in force here that makes us, for all intents and purposes, oblivious to their moral features? Habermas offers as the likely culprit what he labels 'objectivistic' accounts of social practices like sports, accounts that put us at some remove from their communicative practice.

To understand what Habermas is driving at here we need only to recall that the intersubjective agreements regarding how we ought to act in sports are thrashed out in the communicative interactions that take place between their participants. The only way to access these agreements and their moral contents, therefore, is to adopt, at least reflectively, the 'performative' attitude of someone who participates in the communicative practice of sports, who takes up the communicative roles of the first and second person (the I and you) and engages in the dialogical give and take that constitute such practice. But if the adoption of a 'performative' attitude is the key to understanding the moral language of sports, then the adoption of the contrary, what Habermas calls 'objectivating' attitude (the attitude of the non-participant observer), is the key to understanding how this language is garbled and thus made incomprehensible. Moral inarticulacy, then, is the price we pay when we reach for 'objectivistic' accounts of sports, which renounce the communicative roles of the first and second person and reject the back and forth of dialogical interchange in favour of the monological perspective of the third person (the very perspective we entertained previously when we made excuses for Spreewell's and McSorely's actions). So if we want to explain the marginalization of moral talk in our public discourse about sports, we need look no further than the growing popularity of communicatively challenged, objectivistic accounts of sports for our answer.

Just how steep a moral price we pay when we forsake a 'performative' for an 'objectivist' take on sports is made clearer yet by Strawson. For when we privilege the latter over the former, he argues, we end up cutting ourselves off from 'the range of reactive feelings and attitudes which belong to involvement or participation with others in interpersonal human relationships . . . [in which others] feel reciprocally for one another' (quoted in Habermas, 1990, p. 46). It is hard to imagine what anyone would find compelling about a life shorn of all such attachments and associations, in or outside of sports, and harder still to imagine a life shorn of the capacity to think morally, again in or outside of sports, that would be the consequence of such detachment. For, as Strawson further notices, 'If your attitude toward someone else is wholly objective . . . you may talk to him, even negotiate with him, [but] you cannot reason with him' (Habermas, 1990, p. 49). Reasoning, in our specific case moral reasoning, is not an option here because there is no persuading someone that they ought to act in a certain way when the communicatively grounded norms that we draw such reasons from are no longer acknowledged, let alone recognized.

McSorely's own post-game effort to explain away his craven actions on the ice is instructive in this regard. For on his recounting of this tawdry episode we described earlier, he was merely trying to provoke a fight with his opponent, a rather common tactic in professional hockey, and his effort to do so just miscarried. Any hint that McSorely might have morally violated the person of his victim, or the intersubjective norms of the practice, is not to be found in his public explanation. It is not to be found precisely because McSorely's reaching for this objective, third-person account of his actions, rules out any true moral probing of his behaviour.

And so is it with any objective account of sports. We can count on such accounts being morally sanitized ones, since they provide no access to the communicative practice that underwrites sports as moral undertakings. No doubt, this explains why sports ruling bodies often view athletic violations like the ones we have been considering thus far not in moral terms but in public image terms, not as moral problems demanding genuine moral reform, but as public relations problems requiring better management of the image of sports. Of course, once moral problems in sports are effectively neutralized in this fashion, the work of turning things around, of redemption, falls to public relations experts rather than moral critics and reformers. It is no accident, therefore, that there are plenty of the former in sports but hardly any of the latter.

Sports, moral ideals, and moral discourse

In the remaining part of the chapter, I want to say briefly something about the second task Habermas's work poses for a social theory of sports, a critical task that aims to recover our moral voice in sporting matters by becoming more articulate about the moral ideals that, notwithstanding their present corruption, continue to inform their practice. The importance of this feature of Habermas's work should not be underestimated. For it is still a little appreciated fact in many circles of critical theory today, and, I believe, in the present circle of critical sport theory, that social criticism rises or falls on either uncovering existing moral ideals and breathing new life into them or inventing new ones that might resonate with present social actors. That is because without such ideals the social criticism of sports is reduced to little more than exposing their corruption, to mere debunking. And the reason why so much of what passes for social criticism of sports today falls into this ideal-less, muckraking genre is precisely because it is based on the presumption that sports and their kind are so far gone, so utterly co-opted, that there is no saving them. Specifically, I have in mind here critics like David Remnick (1999, p. 24) who, commenting on the Sprewell incident we discussed and on the positively revised estimate of his character generated by his winning play after this incident, concluded that 'Like it or not, goodness is a bonus, not a requirement, for playing ball'; or of commentators like Jason Zengerle (1999, p. 6), who, commenting on the Olympic bribery scandals we also noted, declared that the Games 'are so far gone there's only one surefire way to fix them: abolish them'.

For all of his talk of the rise to dominance of instrumental reason and the resultant breakdown in communicative action and critical public discourse in modern society, one will find no such hand-wringing in Habermas's work, no giving up on the liberal democratic societies he so meticulously analyzed. The reason is he never stopped looking for cracks in those social orders, for ideals that might not just counter but overturn the disturbing tendencies he turned up in his work. But where, it might reasonably be asked, might we find similar cracks in the present order of sports. A full answer would require a paper in its own right. But a partial one might start with the fact that the public response to all of the examples of athletic misconduct I cited was uniformly, even if only initially, one of moral outrage. This suggests that in most parts of the globe today sports, despite their present moral difficulties, are still held accountable to moral ideals, however poorly understood and articulated. As long as such ideals can be located, Habermas insists, the job of social criticism is not finished. It will be complete only when the critic is able to divine some way to articulate them so as to make their force more apparent to all concerned.

But how is the social critic supposed to carry out this task of critical articulation? Habermas provides two suggestions, the first of which I find compelling and the second of which I do not. The first suggestion follows up on Habermas's account of communicative action, and on the necessity of adopting the 'performative' attitude of a participant in such communicative action. This requires that sports become the object of a special moral discourse, in which the communicative practice of sports is continued in a reflexive attitude. By 'moralizing' our sporting discourse in this fashion, argues Habermas, we will be able to dispatch once and for all with the pragmatic question 'what do I want and how can I effectively get it?', and put in its stead the moral question 'what is equally good for all?'.

So far so good. The problem arises when Habermas insists that thinking morally, be it about sports or anything else, is synonymous with thinking universally, that moral discourse is necessarily universal discourse since only those norms that meet with the approval of all competent social actors, and not just those of particular practice communities, can be considered valid. What I find troubling about this universalist conception of moral discourse is that it subscribes to, as Habermas (1990, p. 210) himself acknowledges, a 'relatively narrow conception of morality that is uncompromisingly abstract.' My own view is that pitching our deliberations about sports at this extreme abstract level will only make it harder to articulate the moral ideals embedded in their practice precisely because it will make it harder to penetrate the communicative contexts in which such moral ideals are first shaped and reshaped. In short, thinking about sports at this abstract level is only likely to make us more not less morally obtuse about their inner, communicative workings.[9]

Notes

1. Habermas makes clear his dissatisfaction with the Frankfurt School tag in an interview (see Dew, 1986, p. 94).
2. This essay was first published in 1958 and later reprinted in Plessner *et al.* (1967, pp. 28–46). One of Habermas's colleagues and collaborators, Karl-Otto Apel, a noteworthy theorist in his own right, has written an important essay on sport (Apel, 1998).
3. A notable exception is Sigmund Loland (1998, pp. 79–103) whose work on fair play draws significantly from Habermas's writings, especially those dealing with discourse ethics.
4. The same cannot be said for the German sociology of sport literature, where Habermas's influence is impossible to miss. For a sampling, see Morgan (1994, p. 52).
5. Interestingly enough, Adorno conjectured that Habermas's earlier analysis of labour in *Merkur* was influenced by his reading of Horkheimer's and Adorno's *Dialectic of Enlightenment*, a point Habermas conceded was probably true (Dew 1986, p. 192). For an analysis of Adorno's nuanced account of sports see Morgan (1988).
6. For an especially robust defence of capitalist societies along this line, see Rorty (1999, pp. 262–277).
7. For those unfamiliar with my North American examples of sporting misconduct, I offer the following as background. In my first example, Tyson was disqualified in his heavyweight championship fight with Holyfield for biting off part of his ear during a clinch. In the second, Latrell Spreewell attacked and choked his coach in practice after heated words were exchanged between them. And in the third and last example, hockey player Martey McSorely, more known for his brawling than his hockey skills, retaliated against an opponent he had previously fought with by knocking him unconscious with his stick.
8. Taylor's target here is contemporary social theory, and not, therefore, social theorists like Weber, who, of course, were abundantly aware of the influence moral ideas exercise over our social lives.
9. A much revised and more detailed version of this paper was published earlier (Morgan, 2002).

References

Adorno, T. (1954) 'Die Dialektik der Rationalisierung: Von Pauperismus im Produktion und Konsum', *Merkur*, 8: 701–724.

Apel, K.-O. (1998) *Disjurs und Verantwortung – Das Problem des Omegabergangs zur Postkonventional Moral*, Frankfurt: Suhrkamp.

Bredemeier, B.J. & Shields, D.L. (1986) 'Game Reasoning and Interactional Morality', *The Journal of Genetic Psychology*, 147: 257–275.

Dew, P. (1986) *Habermas, Autonomy and Solidarity*, London: Verso.

Habermas, J. (1984) *The Theory of Communicative Action Volume One: reason and the rationalization of society*, Boston: Beacon Press.

Habermas, J. (1987) *The Theory of Communicative Action Volume Two: lifeworld and system*, Boston: Beacon Press.

Habermas, J. (1990) *Moral Consciousness and Communicative Action*, Cambridge, Mass: MIT Press.

Habermas, J. (1993) *Justification and Application*, Cambridge, Mass: MIT Press.

Loland, S. (1998) 'Fair Play', in M. MacNamee & J. Parry (eds) *Ethics and Sports*, New York: E & F Spon.

Morgan, W.J. (1988) 'Adorno on Sport: The Case of the Fractured Dialectic', *Theory and Society*, 17: 813–838.

Morgan, W.J. (1994) *Leftist Theories of Sport*, Urbana and Chicago:University of Illinois Press.

Morgan, W.J. (2002) 'Social Criticism as Moral Criticism: A Habermasian Take on Sports', *Journal of Sport and Social Issues*, 26: 281–299.

Plessner, H., Boch, H. & Grupe, O. (1967) *Sport und Leiberziehung*, Munich: Piper.

Remnick, D. (1999) 'Goodfellas, Badfellas', *The New Yorker*, 5 July: 24.

Rorty, R. (1999) *Philosophy and Social Hope*, New York: Penguin Books.

Taylor, C. (1992) *Ethics of Authenticity*, Cambridge, Mass: Harvard University Press.

Zengerle, J. (1999) 'Unspecial Olympics', *The New Republic*, 15 February: 6.

12
Querying Sport Feminism: Personal or Political?

Jennifer Hargreaves

Introduction

Sport feminism is hard to define. In reality, there has been no coherent, cohesive, authentic sport feminism, but many different manifestations, philosophies or *feminisms* which, it has been argued, have common characteristics with the many faces of mainstream feminism (Hargreaves, 1994; Hall, 1996; Birrell, 2000, pp. 25–41). Like the latter, sport feminisms have occurred both at the intellectual level, resulting from ideas, arguments, theories, or academic discourses and, secondly, as expressions of political action through membership of official bodies, sport organizations and related institutions. However, until postmodernism emerged, all the different forms of sport feminist activity have had a common kernel: to expose, challenge and eliminate gender-based dominant policies and practices. Sport feminisms have been linked historically to anti-discriminatory work regarding subordinated women (and relatively recently to the production of hegemonic and subordinated sporting masculinities – see, for example, Messner & Sabo, 1990) in particular to their sense and reality of dislocation, marginalization and disenfranchisement in sport.

The strong coupling of theory with practice has been consolidated by academic sport feminists who provide better understandings of gender discrimination in sport through research and analysis, and who strive towards improved opportunities and an end to oppression through their practical sport roles. This brief overview endeavours to demonstrate how sport feminist academics have made sense of the histories, philosophies and practical implications of the different sport feminist perspectives.

Characterizing sport feminisms

The emergence in the 1970s of liberal sport feminism – a feature of second wave feminism – was linked to the specific quest for equality of opportunities between men and women. This approach, using gender as a distributive category, is based on liberal-democratic ideologies and is linked to equal rights policy-making through government initiatives and the work of sport organizations. In contrast, radical sport feminism emphasizes the limitations of equal opportunity programmes, and spotlights the powerfully patriarchal character of, and the centrality of sexuality to, women's oppression in sport. Redistribution of power through separatism is the logical implication for radical feminists. Alternatively, Marxist feminism draws particular attention to class differences and the capitalist structures that prevent working-class women from participating in sport in equal numbers to their middle-class counterparts. Although the well-documented leisure patterns of working-class women confirm the significance of oppressive capitalist class relations, most sport feminists oppose the Marxist privileging of class over gender. A further, highly influential development in sport feminism has been cultural (or socialist) feminism (deriving from Marxism) because it addresses the reductionism in both radical and Marxist accounts that argue for patriarchal relations of power or capitalist relations of power respectively as the primary determinant of gender discrimination. For cultural studies (embodying cultural feminism), the concept of hegemony recognizes that women are active agents struggling creatively for better opportunities in sport; that male and other forms of domination are incomplete; and that agency (freedom) and determination (constraint) are dialectically interrelated.

Each feminist position tends to treat women as a homogeneous group and to generalize from the perspective of white, Anglo-Saxon, middle-class, heterosexual women, thereby overriding numerous other differences related to 'race', ethnicity, sexuality, and class, as well as ability, age, nationhood, and religion. The demands of marginalized groups have highlighted the heterogeneity of women, not only in the West, but also between Western nations and in particular between women from the developed and the developing worlds. Consequently, difference and identity have become significant conceptual strategies. In the West, lesbian feminists have always been centrally involved in the sport feminist movement – usually as radical sport feminists – and have been productive researchers in regard to questions of sport and sexuality.[1] Very few Aboriginal disabled, elderly or ethnic minority women (Black and Asian) have been attracted to the movement and their histories and experiences have been marginalized. (Most of the few accounts regarding these women have been written by non-organic 'outsiders' i.e. white 'mainstream' academics).[2] The issue of exclusion relates even more starkly to non-Western women who typically endure even greater gender inequalities in sport than women in the West. In many cases, gender discrimination is linked to colonialism, neo-colonialism, and politico-cultural, traditional, and religious influences. In addition, differences between Third World women based on, for instance, sexuality and disability, are linked to exceptionally harsh oppressions, hugely reducing opportunity on a far greater scale than occurs for lesbian and disabled women in the West. For women worldwide, access and attitudes to sport and exercise are significantly influenced by globalization processes.

Postmodern feminists have rejected specific feminist standpoints and have deconstructed the supposedly overarching systems of power related to capitalism, patriarchy, and 'race' – the 'grand narratives'. Attention is on the *intersections* between class, gender, ethnic differences, and other categories of difference that arguably result in complex differentiation, destabilizing of identities, ongoing uncertainties, and the fracturing of experience. Feminist postmodern analyses have focused particularly on the body, sexuality and identity, including Foucault's sense of ubiquitous power linked to the discourses of pleasure and discipline, surveillance techniques, and the production of 'docile bodies' (Cole & Hribar, 1995; Markula, 1995; Chapman, 1997; Cole, 1998). Characterized as mainstream feminists, Susan Bordo and Judith Butler have both appropriated Foucault's theories in their depictions of the female body (Bordo, 1989, 1993; Butler, 1993); their work has been used by sport feminists in analyses of radical representations of the female body in sport (e.g. Heywood & Dworkin, 2003). Particularly significant has been Butler's concept of 'performativity': the idea of actively and intimately 'doing', 'sensing' and 'living' gender which renders the notion of an innate or imposed gendered self inadequate. Gender, for Butler, is like sexuality, not 'naturally' ascribed, but a changing social construct, concretely expressed, but also fluid and changing through public performance. Butler (1993, p. 2) argues that discourse produces:

> the regulatory norms of 'sex' (that) work in performative fashion to constitute the materiality of bodies and, more specifically, to materialize the body's sex, to materialize sexual difference in the service of the consolidation of the heterosexual imperative.

Sport feminist academic discourses have become divergent and extremely complex. They have critiqued mainstream theories for silencing or marginalizing gender, women's histories and women's issues; and in eclectic fashion they have 'borrowed' from different conceptual frameworks to make sense of the experiences and cultures of oppressed women (and men). In developing and developed societies, single-issue gender politics in sport have been challenged and the emergence of multi-issue politics has linked gender to other categories of difference. The accompanying sport feminist struggles have been going on across differences linked to individual identities and to local, national, and global contexts. Thus, it becomes increasingly difficult to characterize all variants of sport feminism – the more varied and complex they become, the less discrete they become, and the more they overlap with, and lend from, each other. For example, the work of Sykes (1998) could be described as lesbian sport feminism (because of her investigation of lesbian sexualities and identities); corporeal feminism (her focus on bodies); and postmodern feminism (her use of postmodern and queer theories).

The complexities and intertwining of different sport feminisms reflect the absence of iconoclastic figures or doctrinal approaches. Sport feminist thinking has been pluralist in outlook and theoretical practice – for example, deploying mainstream male theorists, including Baudrillard, Bourdieu, Elias, Foucault, Freud, Giddens, Gramsci, Marx; and feminist theorists, including Bordo, Butler, Chodorow, Hill Collins, hooks, Lorber and Young. Thus, Birrell (2000, pp. 61–62) observes that feminist theorizing is dynamic, complex, and unsettling, as feminists move towards 'more truly interdisciplinary theoretical frameworks'. But there is an uncomfortable relationship between postmodern theorizing and feminism's original emancipatory politics. The recent outpouring of postmodern theorizing on gender, sexuality, and corporeality reflects its growing influence, and the observable loosening of links between theory and praxis. Stanley and Wise (2000, p. 263) claim that, 'feminist theory now contains considerably more of the latter (theory) and considerably less of the former (feminist)'. Postmodernism in sport stands the risk, therefore, of becoming an idea without value, associated with privileged academics in the West for whom it represents above all symbolic and career capital, reflected in the growing volume of analysis tied to the work of individual postmodern theorists. If so, this may threaten the original, interventionist distinctiveness of academic sport feminism.

The influence of postmodernism

Political, theoretical and epistemological questions have arisen over postmodernism's influence on sport feminist research. Postmodernism has embraced deconstructionism and its resistance to concretize empirically distinct and unequal relations of power and politics. Postmodernism challenges the essentialist grand narratives of modernism – the theories and structures of patriarchy, racism and capitalism – which, it is argued, because of diversity, have become incoherent and complex. Walby (1992, p. 2) uses the concept of 'post-modern' broadly to refer to 'changes which lead to fragmentation on a number of different levels, from substantive social reality to modes of social analysis'. Specifically, it challenges the modernist tendency of speaking in one unified voice about women.

Responding to previous, homogenizing representations of women, postmodern analyses of sport celebrate diversity and difference, breaking down women's experiences according to age, class, disability, 'race', and sexuality, or any other category of difference. Doing so results in very fractured, diverse, and disassociated understandings of women's sporting experiences and identities.

Questions of lifestyle and aesthetics made possible by the postmodern commodification of culture also feature increasingly in academic publications and analyses of sport and culture, seemingly displacing the 'morality' (the concern for equality and humanist values) inherent in first and second wave sport feminism. Cole (1998) explains how sport and exercise are linked to insatiable consumption, seducing individuals into an addictive pursuit of pleasure and the promise of a transformed self. The worked-on body as a metaphor for an improved life is always at the centre of this postmodern enterprise. Cole views the discourse of addiction as a technology of the body, but argues that, 'While the modern body and subject have become the objects of disciplinary strategies, they have necessarily become pathologized because the conceptualizations of the organic body and free will are no longer viable' (p. 266). The high visibility of body-centred hyper-consumption activities linked to subjectivity, excitement, style, and image keeps alive the 'youth' appeal of extreme sports that, in turn, attracts establishment attention, adding to the complexities of the subject-object-body nexus. For example, because of extreme sports' growing popularity with young people, the government sport agency, Sport England, is considering funding them out of its dwindling pile of lottery cash and, in turn, cutting funding to traditional 'modern' sports which are losing followers or considered obscure (*The Guardian*, 1 October 2003, p. 32).

The historical interest of sport feminists in embodiment has attracted some to the body-focus of postmodern analysis and others to its inherent 'alternative ontology, epistemology and methodology', its focus on difference, and its embrace of the voices of disparate women, including the marginalized and oppressed (Rail, 1998, p. xv). The female experience of self in postmodernism highlights the importance of agency and the 'unapologetic' approach that increasing numbers of women have about their sport involvement. For example, writing about lesbians in women's rugby, Broad (2001, p. 181) claims that the unapologetic is comprised of 'transgressing gender, destabilizing the heterosexual/homosexual binary, and "in your face" confrontations of stigma – all characteristics of queer resistance'. She cites Seidman's (1997, p. 192) characterization of 'queer' as, 'a style, at once personal and political marked by a certain brashness – a refusal to apologize or to account for homosexuality and a refusal to accept either intolerance or mere tolerance'. Broad's perspective reflects a shift away from viewing sexuality as a civil rights issue towards a critique of 'normative' heterosexuality.

In summary, postmodernism is to do with transgressing boundaries in sport – those between manhood and womanhood, homosexuality and heterosexuality, ability and disability, the 'natural' and the cyborg. And it is to do with widening bodily possibilities and vocabularies, and the emergence of radical images and meanings, body regimens, addictions, aesthetics, and lifestyles. Despite the climate of excess and extremes in postmodern society, Pronger (1998, pp. 291–293) argues that we have not yet gone far enough and should be looking 'for practices in physical culture that are "de-differentiating" in order to develop "new" postmodern physical activities' (p. 291). He seeks 'an ironic exploration of the body and its possibilities for pleasure in a highly modernized socio-cultural setting' and views erotic pleasure as an ideal de-differentiating postmodern strategy because, he says, 'Pleasure can be limitless' (ibid.). Pronger wants us to re-read the body and for it to 'stand out from the limits of its socio-cultural boundaries' and to let 'ecstasy position us as complicitous critics of the modern project' (p. 292). His desire is for us to escape from the regular socio-cultural readings of the body – the modern 'sport for health' paradigms – and into the 'postmodern pleasure paradigm' (p. 293). Pronger (ibid.) concludes:

This means that physical activity needs to play with the pleasure of chaos. This will be an innovative, educational form of erotic play whose anarchic, indeed wild tendencies are both socially/psychically dangerous and full of positive potential.

Not surprisingly, postmodernism has resonances in particular for young sport academics in the West. Their generation, in particular, recognizes that today's world is complex and changing, they appreciate the ironies of contemporary life, and they understand their own shifting identities and insecurities of self.

Critiques of postmodernism

Pronger's celebration of untrammelled erotic pleasure attracts uneasiness and censure; there is opposition, too, to the less 'outrageous' features of postmodern thinking and culture. Walby (1992, p. 32) argues that fragmentation has gone too far, arguably leading to a rift with political feminism; and because postmodernism does not look for values or solutions egalitarian feminists, in particular, are opposed to it (Cole, 1998, p. 273). The perceived poverty of soul and conscience in postmodernism has attracted considerable academic hostility (Callinicos, 1989; O'Neill, 1995). Postmodernism is castigated for being simply a theoretical construct, self-indulgent, disinterested in social justice, and failing to address questions about rationality, the nature of discrimination, the politics of minorities, differences based on structures of power, and the powerful character of knowledge. O'Neill (1995, p. 2) argues that in postmodern discourse, 'What matters . . . is what goes with what but not at all what is what.' O'Neill (1995, p. 116) points to the 'postmodern exorcism of ideology and class struggle essential to the culture industry of late capitalism', of which commodified and lifestyle-obsessed sport is an intrinsic feature.

Ironically, the acquisitive individualism and resultant unsatisfied desire of the supposed postmodern condition, as criticized by O'Neill, have become established as popular subjects for scholarship. A growing body of postmodern research focuses on the individual body, representation and consumption, technologies of self, and on the notion of empowerment through exercise (e.g. Bordo, 1990; Cole, 1993; Markula, 1995). Markula (2003, p. 104) asks how technologies of self might relate to the ethics of the use of power and how women's sport might act as a transgressive practice. Although Markula, like other feminists using postmodern ideas, points to the importance of cultural context in determining the 'liberating' or 'oppressive' status of sport, she does not herself engage with the wider parameters of the contemporary political, social world. The critical self-reflection that Markula argues for still remains insular so that the story may be only partial, or mask really important issues. The following (albeit extreme) example illustrates this point. Mandell (1971) argues that in Germany in the 1930s, during the National Socialist party's Neuremberg rallies, the highly disciplined rituals of young women's and men's bodies moving en masse, in unison, created not only a sense of empowerment through the body, but also strong identification with Nazi ideology. The argument here is that analysis of the process of self-reflection must have an ethical basis that is related to *specific* structures, relations of power, and 'ethics of the use of power'. But postmodern researchers resist engaging with questions of justice, values, or ideologies and so fail to address questions about the specific character of engagement, empowerment, liberation, oppression, or transgression.

Agency, and listening to young third wave feminists

The issue of agency is central to the development of sport feminism. McDonald and Birrell (2001) refute the suggestion that postmodernist thinking terminates the relevance of human agency. They consider how a new form of politics may replace the identity politics of the 1970s, 1980s and 1990s, to explore how institutional knowledges and social practices repress difference (Seidman, 1997, p. 93; cited in McDonald & Birrell). They query, and wish to move beyond, the agency/constraint, voluntarism/determinancy dichotomies and argue for the formation of new political alliances beyond the boundaries of identity. They describe a form of agency 'that works by providing tactics and strategies for asking new questions that open up new possibilities for new kinds of actions to emerge' (McDonald & Birrell, 2001, p. 5).

Young women are forging new possibilities for themselves in sport. The normalization of the body through various sport and exercise regimes and medico-scientific technologies is being challenged, so that different sporting femininities are being regularly and spontaneously produced, reproduced and changed. Different groups of women, through self-regulation, are defining for themselves ways in which the female body is used and celebrated – not in ways that are assimilated to the male-dominated system, or that are in opposition to male-defined practices, but *on their own terms*, 'for themselves'. There is a sense of authenticity about these developments – a recognition of agency and of self. Sportswomen are no longer necessarily 'in the shadow of men' or judge their performances 'in comparison with men', but participate in a range of activities *as women* and *on their own terms.*

The new generation of young Western sportswomen, proud of their well-honed bodies and achievements, assumes and expects more (Foudy, 2003, p. ix). They are changing public consciousness about women in sport, they are redefining gender roles and meanings, and they are strong, determined, perceptive, and inspirational. Heywood and Dworkin (2003) have articulated the new world of women in sport resulting from huge cultural shifts and political changes. These young women feel, in an intensely personal way, a physical sense of empowerment and control, strength and beauty in the female body. Messner (2002, p. 105) urges caution regarding Heywood and Dworkin's claims for female agency, because we are now witnessing a 'new iconography that redeems sexuality from objectification'. Furthermore, many other young women from lower-class backgrounds, or facing other forms of marginalization, do not feel good about their bodies, and are in destructive relations of power that prevent participation. Today's young female athletes represent idealized healthy and muscular images of womanhood which Heywood and Dworkin link to 1996 – 'The Year of the Women' – the time when there was widespread acceptance and encouragement of female athleticism which, they argue, coincided with the mass marketing of women's empowerment through sport. They show awareness of the complexities and ethics of this radical shift in perception, and go on to argue:

> Athleticism can be an activist tool for third wave feminists and can have important social consequences. Today, women nationwide are participating in classes like kickboxing, spinning, rock-climbing, and boxing, relegating to the dustbin mythologies of the 'weaker' sex and assumptions of female incompetence. Any day you can walk into your local gym and see the women seated alongside the men and walking in the same proud way, owning their bodies like never before.
>
> (p. 45)

There is a very marked link here between a strong sense of agency, of womanhood, and of physicality that is complex and difficult to understand. Although French and Italian feminisms have made little impact on sport feminist literature which has emanated mostly from Northern

Europe, North America, and the Antipodes, sexual difference thought – a feminist theory of social practice that stems from Italian feminism[3] – may be of some help. Sexual difference thought is being applied for the first time to women's experiences in sport (Martin, 2004). It is a theory predicated on notions of female freedom 'within a frame of reference no longer patriarchal or male-designed, but made up of perceptions, knowledges, attitudes, values, and modes of relating historically expressed by women for women' (De Lauretis, 1994, p. 23). The context is 'the common world of women' (Rich, 1979) in which relationships between women are the substance of a radical politics of womanhood and separatism, that recognizes 'sexual difference as constitutive of one's sense and possibilities of existence' (De Lauretis, 1994, p. 18) – that is, of 'being-woman' and 'being-man' as 'primary, originary forms' (p. 16). Women are self-affirming subjects, 'not altogether separate from male society, yet autonomous from male definition and dominance' (p. 25). Referring to Irigary's position that women should speak of desire in and for ourselves, Young (1990, p. 181) suggests 'a discovery, recovery, and invention of women's culture'. Sexual difference theory seems to have some potential for understanding female agency and social responsibility in both the practice and the politics of female sport. But if its proponents fail like other postmodern theorists to position the unique, intimate, and meaningful constructions of womanhood and female relationships within particular social, cultural, and political frameworks then their stories of female sport will remain only partial and inward-looking. Like other postmodern approaches, this theory may fail to position women's relationships *within* a social and cultural framework.

For sport feminism to progress, links and collaborations need to be forged with mainstream feminism (Hall, 1996, p. 50). Sport feminism has taken on board mainstream feminism's preoccupations – with theory and aspects of bodily welfare and imagery – but mainstream feminism has not taken account of sport. This is a substantial omission because not only is the body central to sport, but conventionally, women have been identified with the body, women's oppression has been tied to the body, and 'central to feminist theory . . . is criticism of masculinist control over and symbolization of female bodies' (Young, 1990, p. 11). Particularly because women are making greater inroads into sport than ever before, it behoves mainstream feminists to address the issues of sport and the female body. It is also important that men are pulled into feminist strategies, since more and more men – in common with women – are narcissistically concerned about their bodies.

The forgotten postcolonial 'others'

There is growing interest in sport for women throughout the developing world, and sport feminist movements – in practice if not in name – can be seen in Africa, Asia, and the Middle East (Hargreaves, 2000). However, there is an absolute dearth of sport feminist literature from outside the West.

Third world feminism has been used to characterize the work of women who have engaged with the political fights against colonial and neo-colonial oppression, class discrimination, racism, sexism, and monopoly capitalism (Mohanty *et al.*, 1991, p. 4; Elsdon, 1995, p. 266). Its contribution to postcolonial theory has been considerable: to challenge the dominance of male theorizing by investigating the gendered nature of colonial rule and its effect on contemporary postcolonial life; to challenge the dominance of white theorizing by focusing on global rather than Western Euroethnic influences; and to deconstruct the characterization of women from the developing world as 'Other' (Spivak, 1987; Said, 1993; Brooks, 1997). Ahmed (2000, p. 165) points out that 'Black and Third World feminists have provided powerful critiques for the way in which Western feminism has defined the universal in terms of the West.' Third world women have been characterized as a homogeneous group – 'ignorant, poor, uneducated, tradition-bound, domestic, family-oriented, victimized' – in contrast to the implicit assumptions about Western women as 'educated, as modern, as having control over their own bodies and sexualities, and the freedom to make their own decisions' (Mohanty *et al.*, 1991, pp. 56–57). Sweeping generalizations about 'third world women' ignore ethnic, class, religious and political differences, thereby ignoring human agency and some sense of the potential for change.

In sport feminism, specifically, there is a tendency to view sport development for Third World women as essentially beneficial and a way of addressing their underdevelopment and bringing them into the modern world. Women from the West and neo-colonial elites are characterized as benefactors arguing for sports resources on behalf of the dispossessed – a position that silences the voices and desires of women in poor communities who are struggling for autonomy in sport *on their own terms*. Spelman (1988, p. 13) is very clear about how misleading it is to generalize from the limited experiences of White women to those of women 'as a whole', pointing out that Black women cannot become 'White women with colour'; for this reason, the phrase 'as a woman' has been described as 'the Trojan horse of feminist ethnocentrism' (Spelman, 1988, p. 13).

There are different possible responses to feminist criticisms regarding the homogenization of women. One response is to revert to cultural relativism, remaining silent about 'Others' who are 'separate' and different', leaving traditional hegemonies intact (Ahmed, 2000, pp. 166–167). The other response is for privileged people to make alliances with the disadvantaged (hooks, 1984).

Postmodernism's persistent focus on historical heterogeneity tends to mask basic, structural causes of discrimination, reducing the effectiveness of Black oppositional voices. The complex interplay of class, 'race' and sex is easily understood in post-apartheid South Africa and, ironically, because of the symbolic effects of liberation, many Black women in sport suggest that patriarchy (not racism) is now their main enemy (Spelman, 1988; Hargreaves, 2000; p. 14). Others prioritize class because increasing numbers of Black people are reaping the benefits of the opening up of international capitalism and are becoming separated daily from the communities of their roots (Hargreaves, 2000, pp. 14–45). But there are important political reasons for South African women to speak in a single voice because gender inequalities occur in *all* ethnic communities at *all* levels of sport participation, and in the worlds of sport media, administration, and sponsorship.

Hill Collins (1990) tackles the relationship between causality and complexity in the lives of African-American women and this work could provide a template for sport feminist research of minority groups throughout the world. She uses 'diverse theoretical traditions such as Afrocentric philosophy, feminist theory, Marxist social thought, the sociology of knowledge, critical theory, and postmodernism' (p. xii). She places 'Black women's experiences and ideas at the centre of analysis' (ibid.) in order to privilege their ideas and to 'encourage white feminists, African-American men, and all others to investigate the similarities and differences among their own standpoints and those of African-American women' (p. xiii). She uses multiple voices of Afro-American women since demands for women's rights have come mainly from middle-class African women. Representation raises questions about whether sport is a culture of assimilation or resistance for women in postcolonial countries; and whether it is a powerful expression of these women's progress or a form of manipulation.

Conclusion: has sport feminism lost the plot?

The future of academic sport feminism is in the balance. There has been a shift in recent times away from a 'victimization to emancipation' stance, alongside the risk of the previously strong links between theorist (personal) and activist (political) being further loosened and a non-politicized postfeminist discourse being consolidated. Because post-modernism does not prioritize praxis and its new narrative research methods are increasingly popular, it is especially urgent that those of us who maintain a feminist position review our histories and re-create our diverse and separate engagements in ways that have meaning for all women in sport, particularly those who are dispossessed and those from the developing world. A significant and often overlooked feature of academic politics is that struggles come from ideas. Moreover, as Walby (2000, p. 189) points out, 'Differences of social location, such as those of class, "race", ethnicity, nation, religion, linguistic community, sexual orientation, age, generation and ablebodiedness, as well as those based on gender, are important and need to be included in feminist theory.' Walby also argues against partial and situated knowledges and for a wider solution involving the 'practical recognition of difference within the project of equality'. Walby (p. 203) goes on:

> It involves argument over the standards which should be used to constitute equality and justice. Feminist theory can be more ambitious in its claims than story-telling. A future-oriented transformatory politics requires argumentation and not confinement to historic locations.

It would be a radical move forwards if sport feminists were to explore systematically the links between difference and inequality, and the precise nature of inequality, to ensure that sport feminism does not lose its democratizing potential. More research is needed to help us understand the realities of injustice and discrimination in sport, the lived social experiences of oppressed groups. This is not an argument to throw away all narrative methods, but to remind ourselves that stories *can* be used as an aid for change, stories *can* persuade others of beliefs and notions of value, they *can* act as arguments, and they *can* influence public opinion. But to nurture such a potential we should also link personal, individual, 'different' accounts to wider social circumstances.

The significant continuities, convergences and overlaps at the level of theory should be more systematically explored *in the research process*. The 'linguistic turn' in cultural studies coincided with the early development of postmodernism with the clear implication that their relationship could be productive. Both are transdisciplinary and both engage with language and meaning. Postmodernism opened aspects of 'private' life to analysis (Green, 1998, p. 173), but an investigation of the relation between the private and the public (social, political, economic, global) is needed to make better sense of individual experiences. In postmodernism and cultural studies there is sensitivity to difference, recognition of the complexities and lack of coherence of contemporary life, awareness of structural shifts. But postmodernism distances itself from political activity whereas cultural studies is intrinsically interventionist.

Hall (1996, p. 34) argues for combining feminism with cultural studies, ensuring historically grounded accounts that are sensitive to difference, centered on the body, including studies of masculinity, and relating feminist cultural politics to sport. This approach recognizes the liberative *and* controlling features of sport. McDonald and Birrell (1999) recommend a particular 'new form of critical sport analysis' which they associate with 'critical cultural studies', critical theories (including feminism, Marxism, and racial-relations theories), qualitative methods, and 'the ontological and epistemological (re)groundings suggested by poststructuralist thought' (p. 283). Their preference is for reading non-literary cultural forms as texts, providing critical analyses of the narratives surrounding sports events and sport personalities which, they argue, 'offer unique points of access to the constitutive meanings and power relations of the larger world we inhabit' (p. 283). They are concerned with the fluid character of power relations and they point as well to the vital importance of investigating the intersection of several axes of power – ability, age, class, gender, nationality, 'race', and sexuality – avoiding the tendency to privilege one power relation only. Sykes (1998) has addressed the potential drift away from political feminism by combining queer and feminist theories of sexuality. She cites the work of Cahn (1994) 'who documented historical changes in lesbian and heterosexual femininities within the racialized context of U.S. women's sport', and Pat Griffin (1992) and Helen Lenskyj (1991) who investigated 'the negative impacts of homophobic lesbian stereotypes on straight women in physical education' as being queer yet distinctly feminist in orientation (Sykes, 1998, p. 156).

Heywood and Drake (1997, p. 1) are two of a new generation of young feminist activists who have noted the slippage from 'Third Wave Feminism' to 'Postfeminism'. They criticize 'conservative post-feminism' and its spokespersons (who have argued against feminist critiques of rape, sexual harrassment, and abortion) who, they argue, rely 'on an opposition between "victim feminism" (second wave) and "power feminism" (third wave)' (pp. 1–2). In contrast, they define feminism's third wave as:

a movement that contains elements of second wave critique of beauty culture, sexual abuse, and power structures while it also acknowledges and makes use of the pleasure, danger, and defining power of those structures.

(p. 3)

Heywood and Drake (1997, p. 3) argue for learning from, and building on, the histories of past feminisms in order to develop:

> modes of thinking that can come to terms with the multiple, constantly shifting bases of oppression in relation to the multiple, interpenetrating axes of identity, and the creation of a coalition politics based on these understandings – understandings that acknowledge the existence of oppression, even though it is not fashionable to say so.

They argue for continuity between feminist generations and suggest that 'by embracing the second wave critique as a central definitional thread', the focus on cultural production, sexual politics and the search for desire and pleasure (postmodern) can – subject to critique – 'be used to rethink and enliven activist work' (p. 7). They add that, 'The female athlete's positive imagery needs to take its place alongside broader struggles for social justice that can help make illusions of possibilities real' (p. 165) – an approach which if adopted by sport feminists, could turn the division between political feminists and postfeminists into a productive liaison.

Sport feminists need to address the nature of activist work. Sport feminists are products of their circumstances as well as producers of their circumstances. Much academic research relates to the lives of the privileged. There is very little research on the underprivileged, marginalized, forgotten women in sport whose voices and ideas have been suppressed. Making the invisible visible by allowing more and more women to talk about their oppressions is an important first step in understanding the structured relations of inequality in sport. As Messner (2002) points out regarding the US, advances for women in sport – in participation rates, resources, media representation – have not resulted in anything like equality between the sexes, and in many instances there have been setbacks and reactionary trends. If sport feminists opened themselves more systematically to the alternative interpretations of 'Other' women, it would provide the initial rationale for tackling widespread and continuing discrimination and would show more concern for, and be more representative of, those who need most help.

However, we should not forget those women and men whose work in sport is politically engaged. 'Sport and Human Rights' was the topic of the North American Society for the Sociology of Sport (NASSS) Annual Conference in 2003, symbolizing academic interest in humanist issues, and there is political activity in different contexts and among different groups and individuals. Messner (2002, p. xii) has alerted us about the efforts of individuals and organizations in the US 'to bring about equity and fairness and to confront core issues of violence, misogyny, and homophobia in sports'. The focus is on discrimination and inequalities within the nation state; some liaisons have been made between researchers in different countries; but there has been very little attention by the academic community to local-global connections or to the anti-consumerist and anti-elite roots of feminism.

Many beneficiaries of First and Second Wave feminism have lost the sense that women any longer have a political cause, believing that feminist activity and legislation have transformed the lives of women as a whole. For example, Cole and Hribar's (1995) description of a specifically 'postfeminist' body implies an end to feminism altogether. But Scraton (1994, p. 251) points out that there is a 'void between theorizing and the real world that most of us inhabit' in which so many women lack the resources to play sport, take part in exercise regimes, or take up lifestyle activities. Chapman (1997, p. 221) argues further that, 'At the same time that sport offers women discursive tools to oppose oppressive power relations, it also further enmeshes them in normalizing discourses that limit their vision of who and what they can be.'

Sport feminism is manifestly muddled, complex, and full of contradictions, but certainly not dead! The quest is to nurture sustainable forms of sport feminism which can tackle the needs of *our times*. The importance of being sensitive to the lived realities of those in the developing world as well as those in the developed world is undeniable, so, too, is the significance of developing analyses and ways of working that negotiate between the local and the global – a sort of transnational feminism. If the direction of postmodern sport analysis is towards moral nihilism, text, simulation, the hyperreal, and the rupturing of affiliation, then sport feminism should reclaim the moral high ground and reappropriate the social values of equality, justice, humanism, and scientific reason. This would require creating and sustaining collaborations, carrying out research in local communities, in institutions, and in organizations with 'ordinary women' from all backgrounds at the centre of the story. bell hooks (1990) suggests a model of coalition-based feminist politics and urges that we examine three levels – the personal, the politics of society, and global revolutionary politics. This approach could be replicated in sport feminist research. The most important single issue is to reconfirm, by whatever means, the humanism and moral base of sport feminism.

Notes

1. See, for example, Cahn (1994), Griffin (1992, 1993), Lenskyj (1986, 2003), Nelson (1991, 1994).
2. The following examples are representative of both insider and outsider researchers: Hargreaves (2000), Paraschak (1997), Smith (1992), Wearing (1995).
3. This refers to the specific feminism that arose out of meetings of the Women's Group held at the Milan Women's Bookstore between 1966 and 1986.

References

Ahmed, S. (2000) *Strange Encounters*, London: Routledge.

Birrell, S. (2000) 'Feminist Theories for Sport', in J. Coakley & E. Dunning (eds) *Handbook of Sports* Studies, London: Sage Publications.

Bordo, S. (1989) 'The Body and the Reproduction of Femininity', in A. Jagger & S. Bordo (eds) *Gender/Body/Knowledge*, New Brunswick, NJ: Rutgers University Press.

Bordo, S. (1990) 'Reading the Slender Body', in M. Jacobus, E. Fox Keller & S. Shuttleworth (eds) *Body/Politics*, New York: Routledge.

Bordo, S. (1993) *Unbearable Weight*, Berkeley, C.A: University of California Press.

Broad, K. (2001) 'The Gendered Unapologetic', *Sociology of Sport Journal*, 18: 181–204.

Brooks, A. (1997) *Postfeminisms*, London: Routledge.

Butler, J. (1993) *Bodies That Matter*, New York: Routledge.

Cahn, S. (1994) *Coming on Strong*, New York: Free Press.

Callinicos, A. (1989) *Against Postmodernism*, Cambridge and Oxford: Polity Press.

Chapman, G. (1997) 'Making Weight', *Sociology of Sport Journal*, 14(3): 205–223.

Cole, C. (1993) 'Resisting the Canon', *Journal of Sport and Social Issues*, 17: 77–97.

Cole, C. (1998) 'Addiction, Exercise, and Cyborgs', in G. Rail (ed.) *Sport and Postmodern Times*, New York: State University of New York Press.

Cole, C. & Hribar, A. (1995) 'Celebrity Feminism *Nike* Style', *Sociology of Sport Journal*, 12(4): 347–369.

De Lauretis, T. (1994) 'The Essence of the Triangle or, Taking the Risk of Essentialism Seriously', in N. Schor & E. Weed (eds) *The Essential Difference*, Bloomington: Indiana University Press.

Elsdon, D. (ed) (2nd edition, 1995) *Male Bias in the Development Process*, Manchester: Manchester: Manchester University Press.

Foudy, J. (2003) 'Foreword', in L. Heywood & J. Drake (1997) (eds) *Third Wave Agenda*, Minneapolis: University of Minneapolis Press.

Green, E. (1998) 'Women Doing Friendship', *Leisure Studies*, 17(3): 171–205.

Griffin, P. (1992) 'Changing the Game', *Quest*, 44: 251–265.

Griffin, P. (1993) 'Homophobia in Women's Sports', in G.L. Cohen (ed.) *Women in Sport*, Newbury Park, CA: Sage.

Hall, M.A. (1996) *Feminism and Sporting Bodies*, Champaign IL: Human Kinetics.

Hargreaves, J. (1994) *Sporting Females*, London: Routledge.

Hargreaves, J. (2000) *Heroines of Sport*, London: Routledge.

Heywood, L. & Drake, J. (1997) 'Introduction', in L. Heywood & J. Drake (eds) *Third Wave Agenda*, Minneapolis: University of Minneapolis Press.

Heywood, L. & Dworkin, S. (2003) *Built to Win*, Minneapolis: University of Minnesota Press.

Hill Collins, P. (1990) *Black Feminist Thought*, London: Unwin Hyman.

hooks, b. (1984) *Feminist Theory*, Boston: South End.

hooks, b. (1990) 'Postmodern Blackness', in b. hooks (ed.) *Yearning: Race, Gender and Cultural Politics*, Boston: South End Publishers.

Lenskyj, H. (1986) *Out of Bounds*, Toronto: Women's Press.

Lenskyj, H. (1991) 'Combating Homophobia in Sport and Physical Education', *Sociology of Sport Journal*, 8: 61–69.

Lenskyj, H. (2003) *Out on the Field*, Toronto: Women's Press.

Mandell, R. (1971) *The Nazi Olympics*, New York: Macmillan.

Markula, P. (1995) 'Firm but shapely, fit but sexy, strong but thin', *Sociology of Sport Journal*, 12(4): 424–453.

Markula, P. (2003) 'Technologies of the Self', *Sociology of Sport Journal*, 20: 87–107.

Martin, M. (2004) *Women's Relationships in Rugby Union*, Unpublished PhD thesis, Department of Sport Sciences, Brunel University, West London, England.

McDonald, M. & Birrell, S. (1999) 'Reading Sport Critically', *Sociology of Sport Journal*, 16: 283–300.

McDonald, M. & Birrell, S. (2001) 'Rethinking Agency in Postmodern Times', unpublished conference paper given at the NASSS Annual Conference.

Messner, M. (2002) *Taking the Field*, Minneapolis: University of Minnesota Press.

Messner, M. & Sabo, D. (eds) (1990) *Sport, Men, and the Gender Order*, Champaign, IL: Human Kinetics.

Mohanty, C., Russo, A. and Lourdes, T. (eds) (1991) Third World Women and the Politics of Feminism, Bloomington, IN: Indiana University Press.

Nelson, M.B. (1991) *Are We Winning Yet?*, New York: Random House.

Nelson, M.B. (1994) *The Stronger Women Get, the More Men Love Football*, New York: Harcourt Brace.

O'Neill, J. (1995) *The Poverty of Postmodernism*, London: Routledge.

Paraschak, V. (1997) 'Variations in Race Relations', *Sociology of Sport Journal*, 14(1): 1–21.

Pronger, B. (1998) 'Post-sport', in G. Rail (ed.) *Sport and Postmodern Times*, Albany, NY: State University of New York Press.

Rail, G. (1998) 'Introduction', in G. Rail (ed.) *Sport and Postmodern Times*, Albany, NY: State University of New York Press.

Rich, A. (1979) *On Lies, Secrets, and Silence*, New York: Norton.

Said, E. (1993) *Culture and Imperialism*, London: Chatto & Windus.

Scraton, S. (1994) 'The Changing World of Women and Leisure', *Leisure Studies*, 13: 249–261.

Seidman, S. (1997) *Difference Troubles*, Cambridge UK: Cambridge University Press.

Smith, Y. (1992) 'Women of Color in Society and Sport', *Quest*, 44: 228–250.

Spelman, E. (1988) *Inessential Woman*, London: Women's Press.

Spivak, G. (1987) *In Other Worlds*, London: Routledge.

Stanley, L. & Wise, S. (2000) 'But the Empress has no Clothes!', *Feminist Theory*, 1(3): 261–288.

Sykes, H. (1998) 'Turning the Closets Inside/Out', *Sociology of Sport Journal*, 15(2): 154–173.

Walby, S. (2000) 'Beyond the Politics of Location', *Feminist Theory*, 1(2): 189–206.

Wearing, B. (1995) 'Leisure and Resistance in an Ageing Society', *Leisure Studies*, 14: 263–279.

Young, M. (1990) *Throwing Like a Girl and Other Essays in Feminist Philosophy and Social Theory*, Bloomington and Indianapolis: Indiana University Press.

13
Michel Foucault: Studies of Power and Sport

C.L. Cole, Michael D. Giardina and David L. Andrews

> If power were never anything by repressive, if it never did anything but say no, do you really think one would be brought to obey it? What makes power so good, what makes it accepted, is simply the fact that it doesn't weigh on us as a force that says no, but that it produces and traverses things, it induces pleasure, forms of knowledge, produces discourses. It needs to be considered as a productive network which runs through the whole social body, much more than a negative instance whose focus is repression.
>
> (Foucault, 1980, p. 119)

As a historian of the present, Michel Foucault sought to undermine modern vernaculars by disrupting the certainties that govern contemporary ways of thinking. Foucault's interventions encourage us to detach from established knowledge, ask fresh questions, make new connections, and understand why it is important to do so. Given Foucault's generative role in intellectual thought – evidenced most especially by extensive citation and frequent discussion of his work – serious scholars of sport cannot avoid Foucault's formulations. Indeed, an increasing number of academics studying sport have turned to Foucault to "think through" sport's relevance on the one hand, and for rethinking what is relevant to their work on the other. Correlatively, scholars who once imagined sport to be distinct and distant from their domain of study are, because of Foucauldian styles of thinking, now sensitive to sport's significance to their own work.

Two essays have expressly considered Foucault's influence with respect to sport studies. In "Desperately seeking Michel: Foucault's genealogy, the body, and critical sport sociology", David Andrews (1993) introduces

Foucault's understanding of "the body" by highlighting its relation to the epistemological and methodological underpinnings of Foucault's more general focus on modern power. He then conscientiously reviews the then relatively small number of Foucauldian works within sport studies. Genevieve Rail and Jean Harvey's (1995) essay "Body at work: Michel Foucault and the sociology of sport" reviews and classifies Foucauldian-inspired sport scholarship into four categories: calls for Foucauldian-informed research; archeological approaches; *Discipline and Punish*-inspired analyses; and "technology of the self" studies. Rail and Harvey's essay is particularly useful because it foregrounds numerous Francophone studies typically overlooked by Anglo-oriented sport scholars.

We imagine our essay to be engaged in a neighbourly conversation with those written by Andrews and Rail and Harvey. We aim to provide readers who are unfamiliar with Foucault with an explanation of what is arguably his single most important – but also most controversial and misunderstood – contribution, his conceptualization of power. Ironically, critics of Foucault's characterization of modern power typically rely on and reproduce the very assumptions about power that Foucault sought to undermine. We agree with Foucault, who sees his critics' appeal to long established understandings of power as manifestations of the steadfast desire to give power definitive form, the difficulty in imagining power's characteristics in new ways, and the effect of modern power itself.

Biographer James Miller (1993) claims that at the time of his death, Foucault was "perhaps the single most famous intellectual in the world" (p. 13). Indeed, his work has crossed over and influenced the disciplines of communications, history, literary criticism, political science, sociology, and a large subset of interdisciplinary studies. Given Foucault's intellectual project and his incalculable influence, our aim is quite modest. After providing a brief introduction to Foucault, we begin the work of drawing together Foucault's theoretical contributions and sport scholarship, offering through sport-related examples a discussion of Foucault's conceptualization of modern power. More specifically, we have organized the sections around the key terms that help explain the operations of modern power: panopticism/discipline (liberalism, liberal individual, surveillance, micro-physics of power, subjection, technology, automatic docility, docile bodies, normalization, dividing practices, self/other, corporeal identities, visible/invisible, violences, prison, soul) and bio-power/ governmentality (repressive hypothesis, truth, bio-politics, power over life, sexuality, racism, population, biological self-betterment, incitement to discourse, conduct of conduct, neo-liberalism, citizenship). We conclude with a brief summary and suggestions for future Foucauldian sport-studies.

Situating Foucault

> My objective...has been to create a history of the different modes
> by which, in our culture, human beings are made subjects.
>
> (Foucault, 1982, p. 208)

Paul-Michel Foucault was born in Poiters in 1926. Although he endured early periods of academic failure and disappointed his father by not following in the family's professional footsteps – his father and both of his grandfathers were surgeons – the young Paul-Michel ultimately excelled at school, placing fourth in the nationwide university entrance exam for the prestigious École Normale Supérieure in Paris. Once at university, Foucault suffered bouts of depression, which prompted his father to arrange for him to visit a psychiatrist. As a result of these visits, Foucault became skeptical of psychiatry, and was motivated to study psychology. To this end, he received his Licence de Philosophie and Licence de Psychologie from the Sorbonne in 1948 and 1950, respectively. In 1952 he was awarded his Diplôme de Psycho-Pathologie from the Université de Paris. Between 1951 and 1955 Foucault lectured at the École Normale Supérieure, until taking up a brief appointment lecturing in French at the University of Uppsala in Sweden. While at Uppsala, he took advantage of the University's extensive medical history library and carried out research for his first two major works examining madness (Foucault, 1973a) and the clinic (Foucault, 1975).

After teaching in Sweden, Poland, and Germany, Foucault returned to France in 1960 to direct the Institut de Philosophie at the Faculté des Lettres in Clermont Ferrand. In this position, Foucault finalized his archaeological approach (Foucault, 1973b, 1974) to the history of ideas which "attempts to identify the conditions of possibility of knowledge, the determining rules of formation of discursive rationality that operate beneath the level of intention or thematic content" (Best & Kellner, 1991, p. 40). Foucault's academic superstardom was confirmed by his election to the chair of History of Systems of Thought at the Collége de France in 1970. The publication of *Discipline and Punish* (1975) marked Foucault's shift to a more genealogical approach focused on "the mutual relations between systems of truth and modalities of power, the way in which there is a 'political regime' of the production of truth" (Davidson, 1986, p. 224). Foucault's next project was envisioned as a six-volume genealogy of modern sexuality. The project was interrupted by Foucault's AIDS-related death in 1984, by which time only the first volume had been published (Foucault, 1988a). Volumes Two (*The Uses of*

Pleasure) and Three (*The Care of the Self*) were posthumously released (Foucault, 1988b,c). Most recently a three-volume collection of Foucault's essays and a collection of his lectures on race at the Collége de France have been published.

Foucault, discipline and sport

> What's going on just now? What's happening to us? What is this world, this period, this precise moment in which we are living?
>
> (Foucault, 1982, p. 216)

Discipline and Punish: The Birth of a Prison (1977) marks Foucault's entrée into discussions of power by disturbing conventional understandings of modernity. Through an account that moves from a description of a horrific public torture enacted on behalf of Louis XV during the 18th century to the modern prison timetable, Foucault calls on his readers to recognize the familiar Enlightenment narrative of superiority, civilization, and humaneness that such a transformation typically signals. Immediately, he asks his readers to question this apparently self-evident Enlightenment narrative by suggesting that our fundamental challenge lies in understanding the comparative punishments not as evidence of our evolved humaneness but as inventions of different historical logics, new systems of truth, reconceptualizations of the criminal, and innovative operations of power. Indeed, the depth of Foucault's account is evidenced by his multifaceted discussion of history, power, and ways of thinking and being.

Foucault facilitates our understanding of modern power by explicating how it differs from sovereign theories of power. To explain sovereign power or traditional conceptualizations of power, Foucault recounts the king's power. Spectacles of torture, such as those discussed above, were successful, according to Foucault, to the extent that they made visible the king's power to the criminal and, more importantly, to the ritual's spectators. In so doing, the spectacles restored (or, at the least, reinforced) the king's power. Foucault, again drawing on the symbolism of the king's body, states that "we moderns" have yet to cut off the head of the king. By this, he means that we are still preoccupied with imagining power as if it were concentrated in one space or as if it were personified or possessed by a specific individual. Moreover, he contends that administrative operations of power have evolved: modern power is more efficient, productive, and cooperative than its predecessor through its very dispersal from a central "possessor". Unlike the power associated with the king, modern power operates invisibly but is visible in its effects. While modern power has evolved, our ways of thinking about power have not. Foucault maintains that if we base our political interventions on outmoded characterizations of power as visible and solely repressive, then our actions will – in the end, and despite our attempt to do otherwise – reinforce modern power's operations and effects.

Panopticism

To illustrate how modern power functioned, Foucault invoked Jeremy Bentham's Panopticon. Bentham's model prison was based on an architectural trick: a guard tower placed in the center of a cellular, circular prison structure led inmates to believe (and thus behave) as if they were under constant surveillance. As Foucault (1977, p. 201) summarizes it, the Panopticon functioned:

> to induce in the inmate a state of consciousness and permanent visibility that assures the automatic functioning of power. So to arrange things that the surveillance is permanent in its effect, even if it is discontinuous in its actions; that the perfection of power should render its actual exercise unnecessary; that this architectural apparatus should be a machine for creating and sustaining a power relation independent of the person who exercises it.

Foucault claimed that these effects of power were not exclusive to prisons; rather, he used the Panopticon to provide an idealized illustration of power's everyday techniques and effects. Everyone, not just inmates, is power's subject and instrument: everyone is "caught up in a power situation of which they are themselves the bearers" (p. 201). As Foucault describes it, power is realized in its reach "into the very grain of individuals…their actions and attitudes, their discourses, learning processes and everyday life" (1980, p. 39). In sum, the individuals who make up and circulate through the social body are made by and are the primary vehicles of modern power (Orlie, 1997, p. 28).

The sporting panopticon

Several sport scholars have drawn on the Panopticon, emphasizing the micro-physics of power, to underscore the principles of modern sport. Robert E. Rinehart (1998) shows how the combination of the spatial organization of the swimming pool and the coach constitute a panoptic space. According to Rinehart, the possibility of the coach's gaze turns the swimmers into agents who exercise power on themselves. As he writes, "panopticism is built into the coach- (or teacher-) centered team (class) concept; it is reinforced in the hierarchical structure of lane (lesson) assignments; and it is recollected in the lane-timing squad, whose decision supercedes the experience of the individual swimmers" (p. 43). In so doing coach, student, teacher, and teammate are cogs in the wheel of power that produces docile bodies, a category we discuss more fully below.

John Bale (1994) similarly draws compelling parallels between the development of modern geographies of punishment and sport and their concurrent relocation from the corporal/public to carceral/private. More specifically, Bale uses Foucault's discussion of panopticism to explain the contemporary sport stadium. Highlighting the seemingly indispensable technologies and geographies of rationalized order and surveillance (e.g. CCTV, security personnel, assigned entrances and seating, and directed spectator traffic flow), Bale argues that the collective experience of sport spectators has increasingly become one of "segmented and panopticized confinement" (p. 84).

Docile bodies

Foucault used the Panopticon specifically to illustrate how power ideally functions, not to argue, as his skeptics imply, that modern power functions flawlessly. Foucault used the category of discipline (discussed most fully in the final third of *Discipline and Punish*) to extend our perception of how modern power operates. Established accounts imagine power to be external to an individual (liberalism's self-possessed individual) in whose name claims to rights are made. In contrast, Foucault's category of discipline refers to a technology (defined in terms of technique as well as knowledge) that "carefully" fabricates – or creates – individuals. Discipline shapes and produces individuals through techniques of surveillance that reverberate through the social and individual bodies. Disciplinary matrices create "docile bodies": controlled, healthy, and regulated bodies, bodies whose training extends their capacity and usefulness.

According to Foucault, three key disciplinary mechanisms facilitate the production of docile bodies: hierarchical judgment, spatial organization, and examination. That is, bodies are never simply trained but are subjected to normative judgments (which include an ethical dimension), or what Foucault called dividing practices. At the very least, dividing practices are forces of "normalization" that produce and exclude through reference to a norm. Techniques of normalization distinguish the normal from the pathological, or the normal from the threatening. Again, Foucault calls into question liberalism's foundations – in this case, authentic identity and boundaries of the self – by implicating in the production of modern identity and the modern self's border the social process of producing, policing, and making visible the other. Modern identities, then, are: mutually dependent and parasitic; made visible through the body; and the effects and instruments of modern power.

Sport and technologies of normalization

In his essay, "Sport, Body, and Power", John Hargreaves (1987) applies Foucault's notion of discipline to modern sport. By emphasizing the relationship between the body and power, Hargreaves challenges the natural body and considers the body's social and cultural production. With an outline that historicizes the body and illuminates the naturalizing effects of scientific, common sense, and sporting discourses, Hargreaves considers sport's implication in naturalizing inequalities through the body. More specifically, Hargreaves brings into relief the sporting body in the transformation from repressive power – which he associates with early industrial capitalism – to consumer culture's "expansive system of discipline and surveillance based on stimulation and satisfaction of desires" (p. 141).

During the mid-19th century in Britain, sport became linked with the public school system's new regimen of the body, that is, health, diet, appearance, work and rest, and sexuality. However, as Hargreaves explains, this emphasis on bodily discipline was never "simply" about the cultivation of proper values, gait and posture. Instead, it was caught up in the regulatory production of identity and the cultivation of a bourgeois body. Hargreaves' depiction of the knowledge that delineated and rationalized hierarchies of privilege is worth quoting at length:

> Under this Spartan regimen the many hours per week devoted to the sporting ritual and physical exercise taught pupils the need for sustained effort and spirited determination in the face of adversity, for self-denial and control over one's egoistic impulses, the acceptance of authority, how to fit in with one's peers, how to take decisions and lead subordinates, and to accept responsibility. Gentlemen were constituted irrationally in the sense that such ritual activity engaged individuals in their bodies and their emotions; it appealed to their sense of good form rather than intellectual faculties. Shrouded in mystique, the social relations constructed in athleticist ritual were virtually impenetrable to rational appraisal.

(p. 143)

Thus, team sports, preferred by the public school, were vital to a ruling class, English self and all that such a figuration entailed: the bodies produced were positioned as naturally superior to internal subordinates such as working class men and women of any class, as well as to continental foreigners and the externally colonized in the context of empire. Hargreaves asserts that, "It would scarcely be an exaggeration to say that athleticism and the cult of the amateur which lay at its heart, in the main, provided the meaning for life of 'gentlemen' destined to rule the nation and empire... Athleticist principles followed the flag as part of this 'civilizing' mission (imperialism) and cricket and other sport accordingly accompanied the gun, trade, and Christianity" (pp. 144, 145).

In contrast to team sports, the history of power and subjection of the working class was bound up in individual exercise and fitness activities, practices associated with improvement and normalization. Moreover, during the century's final decades, a more "dangerous" working class emerged that "raised the question of national efficiency" (p. 145) and necessitated a regulated disciplinary program for the working class as established by the state and philanthropic organizations. Even in this context, certain working class sectors refused rationalized athletics, favoring quasi-disreputable recreational forms. Yet these resistances (and even what Hargreaves depicts as failed disciplinary programs) were limited and did not interrupt the power network as a whole. Divisions between the respectable and lower working class, sporting community rivalry, and a working class masculinity that excluded women, reproduced the interests of industrial capitalism.

At the core of his essay, Hargreaves is most intrigued by the reorientation of power associated with body-dominated, post-First World War consumer culture. Sport's strong appeal, states Hargreaves, "resides in its ability to harness and channel personal needs and desires – for health, longevity, sexual fulfillment, sociability, and so on". The conflation of these normalizing categories and sport, particularly their "vivid, dramatic, aesthetically-pleasing and emotionally-gratifying expression" (p. 158) through sport, makes sport particularly appealing. Because sport carries an authoritative promise of self-improvement, it is a good example, Hargreaves suggests, how power operates without coercive forces: individuals who recognize the necessity of their own discipline freely submit to governing techniques. Foucault used the term 'automatic docility' to refer to this dynamic in which governing norms become one's own.

Hargreaves' emphasis on the normalizing dimensions of the sport/consumer-culture relationship underscores the place of sport in individualization, a dynamic that refers to the reduction of the social to the individual, and to the production of corporeal identities surrounded by moral assumptions (what Foucault called the "soul"). Although Hargreaves makes only passing reference to the soul, his essay helps clarify Foucault's project in *Discipline and Punish*, which Foucault describes as "a correlative history of the modern soul and a new power to judge" (p. 23). Foucault does not depict the soul through the terms of Christian theology but sees the soul as a product of discipline, "the prison of the body" and "the effect and instrument of a political anatomy" (p. 30). The prison, the corporeal soul, and the invisible powers that render objects visible are central elements of the next essay we discuss.

To the extent that Hargreaves emphasized the historicity of the body, C.L. Cole's (1996) "American Jordan: P.L.A.Y., Consensus, and Punishment" emphasizes the corporeality of history. "American Jordan", it should be noted, is the term Cole uses to refer to former NBA superstar Michael Jordan's as a "representative character" of America's political culture and an affective figure in the national symbolic. Her essay's shared affinities with Foucault are underscored by its disruption of a familiar truth governing the American imagination (1986–1994). During this period, sport was posited as a bodily discipline vital to crime control. Accruing momentum through Reagan's war on drugs, this discourse linked sporting practices to family values, social order and utopic possibilities (appearing most vividly in the image of Michael Jordan) and non-sporting activities (appearing most vividly in the figure of the criminal youth gang) to the breakdown of law and order. That is, as a technology of normalization, sport produced and legitimated racially codified images of dangerous others. The moral panic implicated in the narrative suggested that in the struggle over the souls of African American youth, gangs were winning. The inner city, sport, the police, and "America" were losing.

Drawing on Foucault's insights, Cole seeks to demonstrate how the truth of the narrative relies on displacing historical forces, tensions, and inequalities. That is, Cole sets out to show how these corporeal identities (the spectacular and commodified bodies of black men) actively render invisible – even unrepresentable – the violence of the U.S. government's defunding of the welfare state and post-industrial economic reorganization. She argues that Michael Jordan's iconic status and the power network that commodified his body and aggressively inscribed the NBA in American culture are embedded in the violence of an America that refuses to recognize its practices' racialization and the violence of an American-dominated global economy. Yet, she argues, America's valorization of

Jordan, a production of both violent practices, contributes to America's imagination of itself as innocent.

As in *Discipline and Punish*, the prison (in this case, the rise of the prison-industrial complex) and punishment (calls for revenge) are central to Cole's argument. She argues that the erasure of the economic conditions and public policies that created urban poverty makes criminal gang activity unthinkable. In fact, this inexplicably motivates thoughtless desires for harsher punishment and revenge. Thus, while America imagines the fate of young African American men to be tied to forces competing for their souls and their imagined corporeal competencies, Cole argues the body politic is imprisoned by the fundamental categories associated with America and liberalism.

Bio-power and governmentality

In *Discipline and Punish*, Foucault highlighted "the body" as a key target and mechanism of modern power. In *History of Sexuality, Volume 1*, Foucault both expands on technologies of the body and introduces a second, interdependent target of modern power – the population. Thus, in order to understand Foucault's exposition of modern power, *Discipline and Punish* and *History of Sexuality* must be read together. In typical Foucault style, *History of Sexuality* begins by asking readers to recognize and then question the apparent truths of sexuality. Our fundamental challenge is to confront familiar (essentialist) views of sexuality as a natural property of the body and expression of the core self. He asks us to rethink the "repressive hypothesis" (Freud's classic claim that sexuality is natural but repressed) – as it applies to sexuality and liberation politics. Here again, Foucault repeats his challenge to habitual conceptions of power. More to the point, he asks us to think about the complex ways in which power produces – and functions through – sexuality. Foucault shows how the time-honoured idea of repressed sexuality is implicated not in sexuality's suppression, but in a "veritable explosion" of talk about sex. Using the Roman Catholic Church's institution of confession Foucault shows how sexuality incited discourse, became a problem of truth, and produced a detailed examination of the self. By Foucault's view, sexuality is neither opposed to nor transcendent of modern power; instead, it is an apparatus of power associated with subjectivity, morality, and techniques directed at regulating the body and the population.

Foucault uses the term bio-power to describe modern power's regulation of individual bodies and the population. As Foucault (pp. 140–141) depicts it, "this bio-power was without question an indispensable element in the development of capitalism; the latter would not have been possible with the controlled insertion of bodies into the machinery of production and the phenomenon of population to economic processes". For modern cultures, the population is a political and economic problem, linked not to "death" (the preoccupation of previous regimes), but to processes that "brought life and its mechanisms into the realm of the explicit calculations and made knowledge/power an agent of trans-formation of human life" (p. 141). Foucault makes the case that the technology of power concerned with improving the health of the population also produced and inscribed new forms of racism. Although obscured in virtually every scholarly discussion of *History of Sexuality*, racism, as suggested by Foucault's multiple references to the category throughout the text, was deeply implicated in his interest with biopolitics. In fact, he had planned to write the final volume of his six-volume genealogy of sexuality as a study on race and population.

Sport, bio-politics and race

Foucault's studies of discipline and sexuality play a crucial role in Lee Grieveson's (1998) "Fighting Films: Race, Morality, and the Governing of Cinema, 1912–1915". In "Fighting Films", Grieveson draws together insights from *Discipline and Punish* and *History of Sexuality* to explicitly locate America's response to black boxer Jack Johnson within a broad set of questions related to identity, value, policy, surveillance, and population regulation. By interrogating public attempts to discipline both Johnson's movements as well as cinematic representations of his body, Grieveson shows how racial exclusion and sexual politics shaped the institutions of boxing and cinema. To this end, Grieveson concentrates on regulatory spaces and practices, "including measures directed at the economic sphere – particularly the control of the flow of commerce and large corporations – and other measures directed at, for example, the control of sexual morality, of the 'traffic' in 'white slaves', of structures of white supremacy, of the dissemination of 'immoral' representations, and so on" (p. 42).

Among the concerns discussed by Grieveson are America's responses to Johnson's boxing victories over white contenders, his sexuality, and filmic representations of his body – three aspects of his life that repeatedly challenged the colour line. Johnson's boxing victories between 1908 and 1915 presented literal challenges to white supremacy whose authority relied upon the suppression and regulation of that which destabilized a white-dominated racial binarism. That a number of Johnson's boxing victories were delivered on Independence Day only enhanced their status as threats to the enormous power wielded in his symbolic threat to white supremacy. Whites, primarily in the South, rioted in response to the subversion of racial hierarchy symbolized by his victory over Jim Jeffries on 4 July 1910. For blacks, Johnson's victories were a prominent and strategic symbol around which to organize.

In a context defined by the mythic black male as rapist and racialized panics about the nation's fitness, purity, and immigrant-sponsored "white slavery", Johnson's regular relationships with white women were routinely policed and culminated in his legal prosecution as a white slaver under the "Mann Act" ("the transportation of a white woman across state lines for 'immoral purposes'" [p. 40]). In Johnson's case, his movements across state lines were placed under retroactive surveillance and, based on what was dubious evidence at best, resulted in his conviction under the White Slave Traffic Act (Mann Act). Grieveson asks readers to understand that conviction not simply as about the regulation of an individual, but the embodiment of a "considerably broader terrain – the aggregation and governing of populations so central to the proliferating ideologies of nationalism" (p. 52). Drawing on Foucault, Grieveson sees this practice of racism as "a concrete effect of the play of modern technologies on the life of the individual bodies...the level of populations and the way they reproduce" (p. 52).

The filming of Johnson's 1908 victory was the basis for attempts to extend disciplinary regimens from Johnson's body to the films of Johnson's fights. Proponents of censorship such as The United Society for Christian Endeavor and the Women's Christian Temperance Movement, fearing that the films would heighten rioting among whites and blacks, made claims about the social and moral depravity of the films. The governance of the film, however, relied on establishing the film's social function and its definition as commerce. Indeed, the Sims Act in 1912, which restricted the interstate movement of films, was passed in response to Johnson's 1912 victory over the so-called "Great White Hope", Jim Flynn. The legislation did not suppress the exhibition of fight films, but prohibited their transportation across state lines. By explicitly policing the fictions of white dominance, the Sims Act can be seen, by Grieveson's view, as a "literalization of a broader 'edgy, constant, patrolling' of whiteness, that, in its intensity, may, speak also to what Eric Lott has termed 'the necessary centrality and suppression of *blackness* in the making of American whiteness'" (p. 45). Taken together, the policing of Johnson's body and its filmic representations enable Grieveson to produce a remarkable genealogy of regulatory projects that pivot on racism, sexuality, and national identity.

Governmentality and neo-liberalism

Today, numerous scholars analyzing political power are building and expanding upon Foucault's concept of governmentality. Responding to long-standing charges that his early emphasis on the "microphysics of power" led to an insufficient account of the commingling of state and civil society, Foucault advanced an analysis – governmentality – that unequivocally linked micro-techniques and the state. Most famously defined as the "conduct of conduct" (Burchell *et al.*, 1991, p. 48), Foucault used the term governmentality to emphasize the critical role of *mentality* in governing populations.

Wendy Brown (2003) suggests that governmentality, unlike sovereign and state-centered political power, includes all of the activities of institutions concerned with the state formation (not control through repression and punishment) of subjects. Similarly, Nikolas Rose (1999) characterizes governmentality as encompassing all of those "fields upon which one might locate all investigations of power/knowledge" (p. 22). Moreover, Rose contends that Foucault's analysis of discipline and normalization in *Discipline and Punish* and bio-politics in *History of Sexuality* prefigured his analytics of governmentality. Recounting the technologies of discipline and sexuality from the perspective of governmentality, Rose suggests:

> Discipline seeks to reshape the ways in which each individual, at some future point, will conduct him or her self in a space of regulated freedom. Discipline is bound to the emergence and transformation of new knowledges of the human soul. And discipline is constitutively linked to new ways of thinking about the tasks of political rule in terms of the government of the conduct of the population...Bio-politics and the biologized state...are strategies which recognize and act upon the positivity of the domains to be governed – the factors affecting the rates of reproduction and populations growth, the genetic make-up of the race and the like. They seek, with some notable exceptions, to act upon these domains by reshaping the conduct of those who inhabit them without interdicting their formal freedom to conduct their lives as they see fit.
>
> (pp. 22–23)

We want to emphasize, in an effort to underscore Rose's point, that the essays we opted to discuss within the discipline and bio-politics sections of our essay are written from the perspective of governmentality. That is, they explicitly linked micro-techniques and the state.

The recent expansion of work on governmentality, it is worth noting, coincides with the set of complex questions raised by globalization, neo-liberalism, and democracy. Drawing on Thomas Lemke's (2001) translation of Foucault's still untranscribed lectures on neo-liberalism, Brown (2003) argues that the translation of all dimensions of human life through economic rationality is neo-liberalism's defining feature. Her depiction of neo-liberalism is worth quoting at length:

> [Neo-liberalism] entails submitting every action and policy to con-siderations of profitability... [and] all human and institutional action [to] entrepreneurial action, conducted according to a calculus of utility, benefit, or satisfaction against a micro-economic grid of scarcity, supply and demand, and moral value-neutrality. Neo-liberalism... develops institutional practices and rewards for enacting this vision... Neo-liberalism normatively constructs and interpellates individuals as entrepreneurial actors in every sphere of life. Moral autonomy is measured by their capacity for self-care [and] carries responsibilities for the self to new heights.... A fully realized neo-liberal citizenry would be the opposite of public-minded, indeed, it would barely exist as a public. The body politic ceases to be a body but is, rather, a group of individual entrepreneurs and consumers. (pp. 3–5)

Sport, governmentality and neo-liberalism

In "Doing good by running well: Breast cancer, the race for the cure, and new technologies of ethical citizenship", Samantha King (2003), using Foucault's conceptualization of governance, provides a concrete analysis of the National Race for the Cure. Race for the Cure, sponsored by the Susan G. Komen Breast Cancer Foundation, is the name of the largest and most popular series of 5K fund-raising runs in the United States. The National Race is an annual mass participation event (the world's largest 5K) based in Washington D.C. that garners a great deal of celebrity, govern-ment, corporate, and media attention. The race, promoted as an "authen-tic, mass participation, grassroots social movement to bring about change", represents, according to King, "a potent site through which to examine relations between and among generosity, citizenship, consumption, and political action" (p. 296). More specifically, the race – which King defines as a fund-raising venture, a marketing enterprise, a practice and site of consumption, a physical activity, a collective experience, a mass movement, and a pedagogical tool – provides an opportunity to illustrate "the ways in which government, or the conduct of conduct, has in the past two decades become centrally concerned with the production of civically active, self-responsible citizens" (p. 297).

Participants take their cues from a festive, prideful, patriotic, consumerist environment. The scene King depicts (she conducted her fieldwork during 1999 at the Tenth Annual National Race, which was co-chaired by Al and Tipper Gore) is most notably marked by signs of the nation and multinational capitalism, triumphalist speeches (delivered by representatives of the Komen Foundation and CEOs of pharmaceutical companies), and events inciting "survivors" to celebrate themselves and imagined future scientific cures. As King explains, although one of the Race's founders invoked Martin Luther King's name from the stage (and then misquoted him), it was an already sanitized MLK invocation appropriated to give authority to a discourse that erased dissent and linked proper activism with volunteerism. In her analysis, the Race is implicated in neo-liberal doctrines and a "war of position over what constitutes 'the problem of breast cancer' in the present moment" and legitimate actions and identities for social change.

She takes her analysis that Race for the Cure is "an ideal technology for the production of proper American citizens" one step further by contextualizing it in terms of the logic of biological self-betterment popularized under Reagan. King argues that a post-Reagan ideal of citizenship "demonstrates commitment to the nation-state by embracing bourgeois, humanistic values such as the need to perform organized, charitable works" (p. 297). However, this commitment is not solely about economic privatization in terms of charity, but the "capacity to solidify the contemporary articulation of physical health to moral and civic fitness" (p. 298). King's second point of orientation allows her to show how the ideal neo-liberal citizen is not just one committed to hard-work and philanthropy but is one committed to biological self-betterment – that is, self-responsibility for one's health, well-being, quality of life, and bodily maintenance.

Conclusion: toward a revitalization of sport studies

For the most part, power is a "certainty" that is thoughtlessly presumed by many scholars. In many studies, power, not its conceptualization, is the imagined object of struggle. Our aim in introducing Foucault's way of thinking about power has been to clarify the problems with and limits of its typical assumption. Indeed, our essay, based on Foucault's insights, can be understood as a critique of scholarship governed by conventional ways of thinking about power and the political and an attempt to make its conceptualization the site of struggle. Moreover, to demonstrate the promises of Foucault's studies, we have reviewed a number of analyses that, based on Foucault's challenge (represented clearly by our essay's opening epigraph), advance new understanding about how "we" and "sport" are implicated in power.

In the wake of neo-liberalism and globalization, we imagine that Foucauldian work will become even more useful for scholars interested in studying sport and our present conditions. For readers who intend to pursue these topics we highly recommend: Nikolas Rose's (1999) *Power of Freedom*, Mitchell Dean's (1999) *Governmentality*, Thomas Lemke's (2001) "The Birth of Bio-politics," and Wendy Brown's (2003) "Neo-liberalism and the End of Liberal Democracy." Although these scholars work from different and even colliding interpretations of Foucault, we think that read together, they, will facilitate ways of thinking that help us ask new questions and make new connections. Foucault has made clear why it is important to do so.

References

Andrews, D. (1993) "Desperately Seeking Michel", *Sociology of Sport Journal*, 10(2): 148–167.

Bale, J. (1994) *Landscapes of Modern Sport*, London: Leicester University Press.

Best, S. & Kellner, D. (1991) *Postmodern Theory*, New York: Guilford Press.

Brown, W. (2003) "Neo-liberalism and the End of Liberal Democracy", *Theory & Event*, 7(1): 4–25.

Burchell, G., Gordon, C. & Miller, P. (1991) *The Foucault Effect*, Chicago, IL: University of Chicago Press.

Cole, C.L. (1996) "American Jordan: P.L.A.Y., Consensus, and Punishment", *Sociology of Sport Journal*, 13(4): 366–397.

Davidson, A.I. (1986) "Archaeology, Genealogy, Ethics", in D.C. Hoy (ed.) *Foucault: A Critical Reader*, Oxford: Basil Blackwell.

Deans, M. (1999) Governmentality, London: Sage.

Foucault, M. (1973a) *Madness and Civilization*, New York: Vintage Books.

Foucault, M. (1973b) *The Order of Things*, New York: Vintage Books.

Foucault, M. (1974) *The Archaeology of Knowledge*, London: Tavistock.

Foucault, M. (1975) *The Birth of the Clinic*, New York: Vintage Books.

Foucault, M. (1977) *Discipline and Punish*, New York: Pantheon Books.

Foucault, M. (1980) *Power/knowledge*, New York: Pantheon Books.

Foucault, M. (1982) "The Subject and Power", in H. Dreyfus & P. Rabinow (eds) *Michel Foucault: beyond structuralism and hermeneutics*, Chicago: University of Chicago Press.

Foucault, M. (1988a) *The History of Sexuality, Volume 1: an introduction*, New York: Vintage Books.

Foucault, M. (1988b) *The History of Sexuality, Volume 2: the use of pleasure*, New York: Vintage Books.

Foucault, M. (1988c) *The History of Sexuality, Volume 3*, New York: Vintage Books.

Grieveson, L. (1998) "Fighting Films", *Cinema Journal*, 38(1): 40–72.

Hargreaves, J. (1987) "Sport, Body and Power Relations", in J. Horne, D. Jery & A. Tomlinson (eds) *Sport, Leisure and Social Relations*, London: Routledge & Kegan Paul.

King, S.J. (2003) "Doing Good by Running Well", in J.Z. Bratich, J. Packer & C. McCarthy (eds) *Foucault, Cultural Studies, and Governmentality*, Albany, NY: State University of New York Press.

Lemke, T. (2001) "The Birth of Bio-Politics", *Economy and Society*, 30(2): 190–207.

Miller, J. (1993) *The Passion of Michel Foucault*, New York: Simon & Schuster.

Orlie, M. (1997) *Living Ethically/Acting Politically*, Ithaca: Cornell University Press.

Rail, G. & Harvey, J. (1995) "Body at Work", *Sociology of Sport Journal*, 12(2): 164–179.

Rinehart, R. (1998) "Born-again Sport", in G. Rail (ed.) *Sport and Postmodern Times*, New York: State University of New York Press.

Rose, N. (1999) *Powers of Freedom*, Cambridge: Cambridge University Press.

14
The Fate of Hyperreality: Jean Baudrillard and the Sociology of Sport

Richard Giulianotti

Jean Baudrillard has been probably the most provocative and controversial social theorist of the last twenty years. His theories of the masses, fatal strategies, symbolic exchange and hyperreality have courted widespread critical comment across the social sciences. More general public controversy has surrounded his sensationalist claims that the Gulf War 'did not happen' and that women should be offered up as sacrifices in the American desert (1991, 1986, p. 132).

Baudrillard's notoriety is reflected immediately in the uncertain categorization of his social theory. Critics routinely situate him within the postmodern intellectual turn, typically allowing them to strike dual targets in a single blow.[1] Though his later work employs the terms intermittently,[2] Baudrillard does dismiss 'postmodernism' as 'a word which people use but which explains nothing' (Gane, 1993, p. 21) while the 'post-modern' is 'world-wide verbal fornication' (cf. Gane, 1991, p. 57). Sociological old hands like Turner (1991) and Chaney (1994, p. 188) play down Baudrillard's iconoclasm, describing him respectively as 'anti-modernist' and an 'old fashioned mass culture theorist'. Docker (1994, p. 105) even suggests that Baudrillard offers 'a classic modernist narrative' and 'a linear, unidirectional story of decline'. Levin (1996, p. 15) argues more persuasively that Baudrillard's work is 'a study in cultural metaphysics', in two general senses. First, the metaphysical (like Baudrillard) baldly announces its lack of firm foundations for theoretical play. Secondly, cultural metaphysics is a 'public theatre' for discourse on the 'pre-societal body', and on themes such as 'life and death, presence and absence, me and not me, beauty and the beast, projection, incorporation, awe, angst and passion'. This argument implies that Baudrillard is postmodern in two general senses: first, in shadowing the postmodern

225

themes of thinkers like Bataille, McLuhan, Deleuze and Nietzsche; second, in his very reluctance to accept a fixed disciplinary identity.

Baudrillard was born in Reims, France in 1929. His parents were lower middle class civil servants, his grandparents were peasants, and this peripheral social background extended into his intellectual career. Baudrillard undertook his tertiary education in Paris, culminating in a doctoral thesis completed under Henri Lefebvre at Nanterre in 1966. His early, major theoretical statements blended Marx, Barthes and Sartre to examine the emerging consumer society in 1960s France (1968, 1970). By the early 1970s, Baudrillard's use of Marx had evolved into a rigorous critique of the materialist conceptions of needs, use and exchange values, moving instead towards a theorization of symbolic exchange (Poster, 1988, p. 116).

Baudrillard's marginality to French intellectual life was confirmed with his publication of *Forget Foucault* in 1976. Since the mid-1980s his work has become increasingly epigrammatic and fragmentary in presentation, a transition signaled most obviously by his cultural travelogue, *America*. Baudrillard (1992/94) borrows Alfred Jarry's term 'pataphysics' – 'a science of imaginary solutions rising above physics and metaphysics' – to describe his preoccupation with the particular, the accidental, the supra-metaphysical (1992/94, p. 18). Baudrillard's fragmentary style reflects his distrust of orthodox sociological meta-narratives and antici-pates the form of 'postmodern social theory': knowledge is presented in sound-bites and musings rather than long narratives that, in a media-centred age, cannot be easily digested. Baudrillard retired from teaching in 1987 and continues to live in Paris, but has traveled extensively on his 'permanent sabbatical' (Butler, 1990, p. 8).

Sociologists of sport and leisure have made relatively limited usage of Baudrillard's *oeuvre*. Andrews (1996, 1998, 2001) has engaged Baudrillard's work most substantively, particularly to analyze the contemporary con-sumerism surrounding North American sport. Bale (1998), on fandom and space, and Redhead (1999), on the World Cup finals, have utilized Baudrillard to examine football (soccer). Baudrillard's theories have been deployed elsewhere to examine cultural identities among football players and spectators within the context of consumerism and intensive media simulation (Giulianotti, 1991, 1999; Giulianotti & Gerrard, 2001).

My concern here is to explore how Baudrillard's regular *aperçus* on sport and leisure help to elucidate the key elements of his imaginary. To that end, I identify three categories of sports-related analysis in his work. First, Baudrillard's assessment of the relations between sport spectators and authorities illuminates his 'fatal theory' with particular regard to 'the masses'; this has strong affinities to his readings of the body within the contemporary exercise and fitness culture. Second, Baudrillard's conception of symbolic exchange combines closely with discussions of gambling and Caillois's classification of games. Third, Baudrillard's analyses of 'hyperreality' and the mass media help to explain the nature, experience and sense of lack within contemporary sports events. I conclude by assessing how Baudrillard addresses questions of political agency.

The masses, the body and fatal theory

Baudrillard's analyses of spectator-authority relations, especially those within football, are the most explicit of his sports discussions. These discussions help to bring out his 'fatal theory' of the 'masses', and to show how power relations fall into reverse. Baudrillard argues that contemporary societies are constituted not by the 'social realm' but by 'the masses', the 'silent majorities'. He (1983a, p. 94–95) rejects the Marxist theory of false consciousness: the masses are not an 'object of oppression and manipulation', nor do they require liberation. The masses have no specific tastes or convictions, but 'drift somewhere between passivity and wild spontaneity' (1983a, p. 2). The masses are not a social aggregate of subjects; they are instead 'a cunning object' whose power comes from silence and apparent inertia (1997, p. 40). Various 'subjects' – such as opinion pollsters, publicity workers, political pundits, social scientists – try to understand the masses, to capture their desires, values, and structures. But the masses employ 'fatal strategies' – of ruse, artifice and ambiguity – to toy with these subjects and remain a step ahead (Poster, 1988, pp. 216–217; Baudrillard, 1990b, p. 169). Publicity people and the like are seduced into the impression that the masses do have true tastes or ambitions, when in truth the masses of our contemporary consumer society have none of these qualities. Thus Baudrillard's fatal theory stands the tradition of critical theory on its head: 'The political scenario is reversed: it's no longer power that pulls the masses in its wake, it's the masses that drag power down to its fall' (1983a, p. 95). The old elites of modern times may believe that they possess social power and influence, but this, for Baudrillard, is a 'hallucination' (1990c, p. 27). Supreme power comes not from leading people to modern liberation, but from the fatal strategy of keeping other people in eternal suspense (1977, pp. 51, 116–118).

By way of illustration, Baudrillard turns to the political extradition of a German barrister from France (protested against by several hundred activists) which coincided with an international football match (watched by twenty million viewers). A 'melodrama of indignation' enveloped France's intelligentsia who castigated 'the manipulation of the masses by power, their mystification by football'. Baudrillard (1978, p. 12–14) replies that 'the masses are neither mislead nor mystified' through the 'good faith and glee' in their preference for football over 'the recommended ideals, however enlightened'. A decade later, Baudrillard embellishes his arguments on the masses through discussion of football hooliganism and its attempted control. In a regularly cited essay (1990b), he describes hooliganism as a 'mirror of terrorism': it captures the public imagination, seems to threaten state monopolies on violence, and dares to subvert the (rather boring) play on the pitch by producing compelling spectacles of violence in the stands. Like contemporary terrorists, the hooligans' 'fatal strategy' seduces the state into unveiling its hidden power resources. Elsewhere, I have employed Baudrillard's theory to describe how football hooligans employ some fatal strategies – ranging from the symbolic threat of violence to sudden disappearance and reappearance – to stay a step ahead of those subjects (police, courts, media and many social scientists) that seek to know this object's essence (Giulianotti, 1994). Over more than thirty years, UK football grounds have become laboratories of social control, employing fencing, police 'spotters', undercover officers, and surveillance cameras to contain and analyse the energies of these masses. Yet, the extent to which real risks of violence may actually exist is a matter for conjecture (Armstrong & Giulianotti, 1998). The greater danger may reside instead with the apparatus of security itself. Baudrillard (1990c, p. 38) recognizes the 'tragic irony of safety' at the Hillsborough football stadium disaster in 1989: ninety-six supporters were fatally injured by crowd crushing inside a 'secure' fenced part of the stadium, after the police, fearing a disorderly pitch invasion, had denied fans the chance to escape. As Baudrillard suggests, all systems of such 'hyperprotection' have a propensity to lose their defences and slip into 'malignant reversibility' (1990b, p. 62).

Power's reversibility is further explored in Baudrillard's discussions of sports terrorism and hostage-taking. Certainly, sport itself can be held hostage by terrorist power, as at the 1972 Munich Olympics when Arab paramilitaries seized and killed several Israeli athletes. But states themselves can be seen as hostage-takers of sport, such as in the 1980s Olympic boycotts by the USA and USSR (1990a, p. 175). Sport's world governing bodies also hold their member nations hostage through the injunction: 'If you do not behave, we will hold tournaments somewhere else' (ibid.).

Baudrillard's fatal theory is further elaborated within his reading of the cultural mentalité surrounding bodily exercise. During the 1960s and 1970s, he argues, the obsession with fitness had been 'functional': it related mainly to the body's productivity. Now, exercise is performance-orientated, with a machine-like body asking to be turned on (1990b, p. 48). The body is a kind of satellite, waiting to be thrown into orbit; its muscles, nerves, neutrons and cells allocated an operational role. In jogging, the body is hypnotized, programmed to run 'like a somnambulent and celibate machine' (ibid., p. 47). Systematic doping merely extends the operational logic that governs contemporary sport and its supporting sciences. Sports heroes have subsequently mutated: the old heroes of bourgeois individualism reflected subjectivity and liberation; the new heroes of 'neo-individualism' are performance-centred, entrepreneurial, efficient and self-enslaving, pushing themselves to the limit (1992, pp. 105–106, 1990c, p. 27). Even disabled athletes engage in self-mutilation, removing more body parts, to improve performance (1997, p. 48).

Baudrillard is struck by America's 'omnipresent cult of the body'. An 'object of frantic concern', the body is something that individuals are 'into', like a scenario or new technological console (1986, p. 35). Fitness, exercise and jogging are part of a new asceticism wherein personal deprivation is culturally recycled. California is home to the fitness boom, the triathlon and extreme sports, each of which idealizes the savage, punished, sacrificed body. Thus, 'the jogger commits suicide by running up and down the beach'; the jogging body prefigures self-annihilation, like anorexics, 'vomiting energy' to 'attain the ecstasy of fatigue' (1986, pp. 38–39). In the New York Marathon, 'they are all seeking death' while running 'simply in order to feel alive' (1986, p. 20).

Baudrillard (1976) scoffs at 'naive specialists' who contend that physical exercise can counter listlessness. In any case, sport is full of such fatigue: at the extreme end, we may point to those body-builders whose startling outer image masks an exhausted body, driven to a kind of somatic, suicidal protest. Baudrillard extends this point to identify a fatal strategy of resistance in the fatigued conformity of post-industrial citizens. Tired workers, bureaucrats, voters, athletes, spectators go about their business with a resignation and indifference that betray a 'latent, endemic revolt, unconscious of itself' (1970, p. 183). In discussing the leisure of holidays or other non-work recreation, Baudrillard (1987a, p. 70) writes: 'No one is interested in overcoming alienation; the point is to plunge into it to the point of ecstasy... And getting a suntan serves as a supernatural proof of this acceptance of the conditions of normal life.' This fatalism is equivalent to the boredom of 'super-banality': 'no matter how boring, the important thing is to increase boredom; such an increase is salvation, it is ecstasy' (ibid.).

Baudrillard is clearly at odds with modernist narratives (e.g. Marxism, Freudian theory, most strands of feminism) that talk of empowerment, liberation and progress. Instead, the masses' listlessness in politics is transmuted into consumer culture; boredom and alienation, rather than pluralism and liberation, prevail. To extend Baudrillard's thinking, some sports celebrities and their fans appear to embrace this hyperconformity of consumption in self-parodic fashion. Particular stars like Dennis Rodman (basketball) and Paul Gascoigne (football) show a fatigued zeal and curious hyperconformity in stretching their public notoriety as 'bad boys' to new limits (Giulianotti & Gerrard, 2001, pp. 134–136). The masses that follow these celebrities devour the ancillary endorsed products and ventures: from sportswear to cosmetics, CDs, videos, cars and computers, the trashier the better.

Games, gambling and symbolic exchange

For Baudrillard, one way out of this rather depressing cultural diagnosis is through the anthropological reading of alternative systems of exchange. Baudrillard draws on the work of Mauss, Bataille and Caillois to argue that we should move to modes of symbolic exchange found in non-industrial societies. For Mauss, one aspect of symbolic exchange involved gift-giving, often through 'potlatch' ceremonies that could consume vast (indeed, suicidal) amounts of local resources. Thus, symbolic exchange (including gift exchange) is non-productive exchange; it may appear as a transgression of productive relations through consumption (as excess) of objects and energies. For Bataille, gift exchanges help to dissipate the excess energies of a society which, if unreleased, would otherwise consume it. Gift-giving is therefore double-edged. The gift appears as an act of altruism, but it becomes 'an accursed share' to its recipients who must reciprocate (and more), otherwise they will be consumed by its smouldering energy. Baudrillard (1997, p. 26) disparages 'vulgar interpretations' of potlatch, but one of his earlier analyses of leisure does combine Bataille with Veblen's critique of conspicuous consumption in a rather simple way (1970, p. 157). Leisure, on this reading, is productively enjoyed because it is 'wasted time' (ibid.).

Baudrillard's empathy for the apparent waste in symbolic exchange emerges in his discussions of games and gambling. He employs Caillois's (1962) taxonomy of games which distinguishes *agôn* (competition e.g. team sports), *alea* (chance e.g. lotteries), *mimicry* (imitation e.g. role-playing), and *ilinx* (vertigo e.g. bungee jumping). Baudrillard (1990c, p. 58) identifies a classificatory totality in Caillois's theory: every object must fit somewhere within his categories. Caillois (1962, p. 159) was particularly struck by the 'tenacious seduction of chance' in all societies, including Stalin's Soviet Union. Baudrillard concurs, arguing that we are abandoning meaningful, expressive and competitive pastimes, for 'ecstatic, solitary and narcissistic games . . . the aleatory and psychotropic pleasure of pure fascination . . . of chance and vertigo' (1983a, p. 9, 1990a, p. 196). In gambling, for example, the aleatory supersedes the instrumentality of profit; the idea of a 'neutral universe' or 'objective chance' with mathematically calculated outcomes is also dismissed (1983a, p. 144). Gambling represents 'the locus of both the ecstasy and the disappearance of value . . . money is neither produced nor destroyed, but re-emerges as appearance' (1990a, p. 184).[3] Hence, 'the idea of winning or losing is relatively unimportant compared to the seductive sequence of events' (Gane, 1993, p. 107). Baudrillard identifies a supreme congruity with gambling and the desert landscapes surrounding its most spectacular home, Las Vegas: 'Gambling itself is a desert form, inhuman, uncultured, initiatory, a challenge to the natural economy of value' (1986, pp. 127–128). Too bad if you lose: 'Afterward, you commit suicide' (Gane, 1993, p. 107).

Alongside this theorization of symbolic exchange, the *alea*, and gambling, Baudrillard argues for the resurrection of illusion. He marks out the battle-lines anthropologically: non-Western cultures contain the radical illusions of seduction, while Western cultures promote a cool and obscene 'hyperreality' (discussed in the next section) (1990b, p. 145). For example, for Baudrillard, the 'real Brazil' is a spectacle of 'monetary and temporal instability . . . football, the samba, the cults, the *jogo de bicho*'. Brazil's financial chaos should therefore be seen as a 'collective game', 'a gamble' on survival by a society lacking rational structure (1990c, p. 76). In contrast, the simulated Brazil is a Western techno-democratic model that is unconvincingly imposed upon a country that is committed to the joyous and cannibalistic sacrificing of its own wealth (1990c, p. 74).

In discussing the political history of relations between the West and these non-Western societies, Baudrillard employs the relatively conventional, post-colonial themes of difference and otherness. He plays upon the irreconcilable nature of cultures, the 'radical exoticism' of their foreignness to each other. Non-Western cultures acknowledge that their destinies are opposed to those of the West; they play upon the West's fascination with the exotic by deploying even greater mystification and more radical, unintelligible expressions of seductive difference. In turn, the West unleashes various policies of extermination and annihilation towards these others. The indigenous peoples of South America exposed the violent religiosity of the invading Spanish, and so were slaughtered in Christendom's name (1990b, pp. 133–134). The contemporary ethics of multiculturalism or human rights are seen to be just as destructive, since they obliterate the seductive elements of other cultures by forcing them to confess their 'difference' in Western terms.

In 'consuming' contemporary objects, or 'other' cultures, Westerners find themselves in a paradox. Consumption, Baudrillard (1968) maintains, has no limits, but is 'irrepressible'. Consumption is ultimately 'founded upon a lack', on the 'ever-disappointing' quality of objects (or, indeed, 'others') (1968, pp. 204–205). At the point of consuming this difference (whether such difference is an object or alien culture), disappointment settles in since radical difference has been negated and reduced to the codes of the contemporary world.

While Baudrillard's arguments on seduction, chance, illusion and symbolic exchange are presented in fragments, there is a theoretical consistency to their usage that reflects his 'anti-modernist' and culturally regressive impulses. For critics, Baudrillard forwards a crude, 'embarrassing' anthropology of cultural difference, a study in racism and sexism (Kellner, 1989, pp. 181–185; Docker, 1994, pp. 106–107). His description of Brazil, for example, borders on the Orientalist wherein Baudrillard regurgitates, rather than critically dissects, Western myths surrounding the magical, irrational, chaotic and sensuous nature of non-Western peoples (cf. Said, 1995). In turn, Baudrillard's loose language is also Occidentalist, in exaggerating the rational, scientific, bureaucratic culture of the West. Yet, notwithstanding his controversial metaphors and adjectives concerning symbolic exchange, Baudrillard's work does have fruitful potential when applied to sport and leisure.

Most simply, the continuing presence and allure of sports and games do reflect the tenacious presence of the *alea*. Sport's fascination depends upon uncertainty of outcome, the possibility that unlikely results are predestined rather than scientifically impossible. The ecstatic *alea* is at play in gambling, that self-consuming play with the forces of destiny. Rather aptly, Baudrillard's discussion of gift-giving and gambling might be best applied historically to pre-modern sporting pastimes (like racing or cricket carnivals) that drew the upper and lower classes, while challenging bourgeois emphasis on personal and financial restraint.

Baudrillard's analysis does point to the consciousness that Western sporting culture is permeated by predictability and performance, the dominance of the sports illustrated over the sports illusion, and thus by the West's profound sense of lack surrounding the absence of difference, the removal of the radically exotic. The role of British and American imperialism in imposing and inculcating Western sporting disciplines within non-Western nations is a matter of historical record. But what is particularly noteworthy, from a Baudrillardian viewpoint, is the Western perception that non-Western players routinely defeat their First World opponents, at Western games, by employing radical illusions. By a curious irony, it seems, these non-Western cultures appear to consume Western sports, along with the body techniques and practices that underpin these Western games; and, in return, they defeat the West through arcane bodily techniques, seductive forms of play that mystify the West. In cricket, for example, the 'sorcerers' that play on the Asian sub-continent have long been the custodians of the lost art of leg-spin, and introduced the new bowling technique of 'reverse swing' to bamboozle further the Western batsman. In football, the juggling, darting, fantastic Maradona from Argentina was a technical illusionist, an 'evil genie', capable of seducing and confusing the most scientific and instrumental defences.[4] Western professional sports clubs have attempted to capture and consume the powers of this radical difference, creating world labour markets of non-Western athletes, but this strategy is really doomed to failure since it serves to annihilate difference. Brazilian footballers are signed by top Italian sides, and instructed to perform their deceptions on a regular basis. English cricket clubs recruit non-Western players, putting them into the daily grind of a league championship system in a bid to lure in crowds. And so radical otherness becomes a scarce commodity on sport's stock exchange (1990b, p. 124). As difference is exterminated through encounter, we are still none the wiser, still unable to understand or mirror this exoticism in our own sporting culture, save through a crude simulation: we teach young football players the textbook tricks and deceptions that South Americans use; or we use televised images of the ecstatic non-Western sports crowds to market the atmospheric potential of our over-rationalized sporting occasions.

Hyperreality, sports mediation and the demise of artifice

For Baudrillard, Western cultures have entered the 'hyperreal'. As the neologism suggests, 'hyperreality' involves an intensification of reality. The hyperreal is the world as simulacrum, in the sense that it is both simulated and 'realer than real', characterised by the obscene attention to excessive detail. For example, in music, the essence of melody disappears at the point where hi-fi technical obsession enters to develop a simulated stereophonics, 'clinical, sterile, expurgated of all noise', the hyperreality of high definition sound (1995a, p. 29, 1995b, p. 104). Similarly, Baudrillard (1979, pp. 31–36) refers to pornography – the quadrophonics of sex – which simulates sex into a form far more graphic than ordinary sexual encounters. Spatially, Disneyworld simulates an idealized vision of Americana for its visitors (1983b, pp. 25–26). Thus, hyperreal constructs now determine how music, sexuality and the consumer environment are represented to us, and how they should be evaluated (Ritzer, 1995, p. 96). Perhaps the most disturbing representation of the hyperreal is the bubble-boy whose immunity system collapses and who thus must live in a faultless, sterile environment (Baudrillard, 1985).

In hyperreality, the confusion of the real and models of the real reflect the sense of historical suspense; we live through a 'post-history' that is in 'a state of simulation' (Gane, 1993, pp. 95, 99). The age of simulation belongs to the post-industrial, telematic age, to the era of digitality and operationality, where the real is already reproduced in simulated form before it can materialise (Bogart, 1996, p. 72); 'as against cause-and-effect logic, the event is there first' (1997, pp. 47–48).

The media are integral to hyperreality's confusion of reality and simulation. As noted, Baudrillard dismisses the idea that the 'social' survives; instead, only the cool technology of television can 'warm the dead body of the social' (1991, p. 50). Baudrillard (1987b) forwards a premonition of our disappearance inside the screen, such that we become our own screens as the differentiation of man and machine collapses. The most notorious illustration of the hyperreal emerges from Baudrillard's claim that the 'gulf war did not take place'; instead, it was a hyperreal event, a television moment, a virtual, mediated conflict. War deaths were 'immaterial'; more germane was the technological, simulated format of the conflict, submerged within a media culture saturated by such events (Gane, 1993, p. 185; Baudrillard, 1997, p. 17). The conflict's escalation was understood according to the telematic principles of virtual war games, and the clipboard managerialism of modern sport-speak (troops 'stayed focused' with 'game-plans' and 'teamwork').

Baudrillard's model of hyperreality has a deep resonance within contemporary sports, most obviously with the role of media and virtual technologies in reformulating our sporting experiences. Baudrillard (1990b, pp. 79–80) anticipates the day when football matches will be played before empty stadiums, save for banks of television cameras while all spectators watch at home. Televised sport provides superfluous streams of useless information transmitted in pornographic detail: the multiple camera angles (including from inside goal-nets or cricket stumps), the reams of physiological data on players, the seamless and confusing blend of live and recorded events. Technology promises the masses a directorial control over their favoured camera angles. Body suits will soon afford a virtual in-ground experience as we become our own sporting screens. 'Virtual tours' of distant sports stadiums can be undertaken, like those offered within Far East shopping malls by the English football club, Manchester United. In practicing sport, we exchange the interpersonal, corporeal turf encounters of modernity for the virtual exercise of simulated golf, cricket, baseball or football on video games consoles. Even for those groups that continue to inhabit sport stadiums, the experience is increasingly hyperreal. Sports stadium facilities come to be judged according to the armchair model of home, and so they must seek to provide match highlights and advertisements on giant screens, along with a larder of ground snacks and personal chairs for individual viewers. At major sports events, television units cruise around the passive stands of passionless sports events, invoking the masses to sing, chant and celebrate, to simulate a social occasion. New forms of hyperreal spectator culture emerge to simulate 'atmosphere' or the social cultures of past sports crowds. The favoured songs of these spectator groups are taken from media commercials; banners and flags are constructed, not to affect the sports event, but to transmit messages to viewers at home. Where greater passivity reigns among the spectators, the ground controllers and television directors pipe in 'crowd noise' to simulate atmosphere.

Baudrillard (1992, p. 6) observes that, 'We shall never again know what anything was before disappearing into the fulfilment of its model.' In the hyperreality of media sports, events do not 'take place' unless they are transmitted in the 'real time' of live television or radio (1995b, p. 98). Sporting action is organized around commercials or television deadlines, while media cities are constructed to billet reporters. Tournament organizers pass over discrediting images, transmitting adverts or pictures of happy fans to the virtual masses at home, while in the ground the actual event may witness the odd outbreak of crowd disorder, streaking, or the booing of officials and athletes. The competitions are less about the gladiatorial clash of athletes – that is left to the hooligans in the stands. Instead, we have the surgical execution of pre-programmed, simulated 'game' strategies. A loss for your team constitutes the operational failure of a computerized, tactical model, and not the temporary, playful defeat of your community representatives. During the sporting performances, we now have a hyperreal modeling of 'sportsmanship', the 'Olympian spirit' and 'fair play' when, of course, such values were never that central to the popular culture of sports.

Baudrillard's reading of the hyperreal gains its fullest articulation through his analysis of America, a country divided from Europe by an 'unbridgeable rift' (1986, p. 73). America possesses the 'zero degree of unculture'; it is 'the primitive society of modernity' because of its proximity to its origins, and its absence of history relative to Europe (1986, p. 73, 1993, p. 244). In the United States, especially in California, European cultural artefacts are constructed in simulated, hologrammatic form. Sports tournaments, with all their allusions to Antiquity, are no exception, notably those staged in the pastiche amphitheatre of the Los Angeles's Olympic stadium (venue of the 1984 Games). Baudrillard anticipates a hyperreal outcome for the modern Olympics, envisaging its permanent transplantation to Los Angeles, to become 'Totally sponsored, totally euphoric, totally clean, a 100 per cent advertising event' (1986, p. 57). If we think of the modern Olympics as a 'hyperreal' simulation of the Olympic festivals held in Ancient Greece, then now we contemplate a simulation of the 'second order', in which the over-perfect copy is itself copied. The cultural equivalent would be for the Disneyworld theme park – that simulation of American life in fantasy form – to itself be remodeled within a grander theme park (1996).

Sport and political agency: spaces of resistance

Baudrillard's vision may be fragmentary, dystopian and aristocratic. But, as I have sought to indicate here, when drawn upon selectively, it is a valuable and compelling heuristic, enabling a substantive reading of specific realms of social life. When adopted by the sociology of sport, Baudrillard captures the disenchanting instrumentality of contemporary sports. He provides a radical interpretation of embodiment within cultures of physical recreation. He helps to elucidate the complex politics of the masses *qua* sports consumers, as they flit between the ecstasy of consumption, the shadows of a seductive silence, and the sacrificial and even suicidal spectacles of revolt. The body is the most obviously self-destructive token in the symbolic exchange within sport and physical culture. It is exercised beyond health to the point of meltdown, in a kind of fatigued homage to the banality of 'the look'. We retreat into the aleatory games of gambling and chance, and search in vain for the illusions and artifice of the sporting other which, at its apparent moment of discovery, has surrendered already to the codes of performance. Baudrillard further provides us with a dissection of hyperreality; a mediated, sterile and dizzying reality defined by simulation.

At first encounter, Baudrillard appears skeptical about whether direct, political militancy can subvert hyperreality, and this has clear implications for sport. He argues that subversive impulses never get 'on air', but are negated in the act of their transmission. Public opinion becomes hopelessly simulated through street interviews, radio phone-ins and television chat shows. Rather romantically, the early Baudrillard (1973, pp. 176–177) finds a more radical form of communication in the symbolic exchanges of the street. For example, in sport, a definite array of delirious situationist practices is employed by spectators at everyday 'street level' to express moods of subversive opposition: impromptu demonstrations are held against club officials; players are booed or cheered in turn; some supporter groups aim critical shouts and songs against prominent media figures or politicians; graffiti around the stadium provides a direct or symbolic assault on the powerful. Yet, just as radical difference is destroyed when its otherness is 'discovered' and formally acknowledged, so too do these street discourses atrophy inside the codes of the media when they 'go public' and begin to use the 'proper channels' of communication.

Nevertheless, as we have seen, Baudrillard's later work does point towards at least three, alternative forms of political agency that reflect how resistance can be articulated. First, the masses may exercise their objective power in remaining a step ahead of powerful 'subjects'. Particular practices here would include disappearance, or toying with their public construction by opinion pollsters, or more generally plunging ecstatically into the desiderata of contemporary consumer culture. All of these fatal strategies contain an implicit mocking of those who would 'know' the masses, those who erroneously assume that the masses must wish to exercise choice or to determine their own destiny. Second, strategies of symbolic exchange, or extreme gift-giving, represent a kind of suicidal resistance towards power relations. Gambling, for example, is viewed as radically resistant: it wastes the dominant value of money while trusting in destiny and the *alea*. A third, more radical, profane response is rather more violent: the unleashing of the riotous energy of the dispossessed upon the system; to engage in what Merrin (1999, pp. 136–137) terms the 'communion of the excommunicated'. These three cultural spaces of resistance – ecstatic consumption, gambling with self-immolation, and disenfranchised destruction – are realized in sport through practices such as the fatigued consuming of endorsed products and media discourses; gambling on the predestination of results, and losing oneself in the *alea* of full immersion; or violent fan subcultures or death-driven athletes who create their own spectacular incidents. As cultural impulses, many may well drift between all three categories.

My concluding point is that Baudrillard's insights on the *alea* need to be taken up more fully within the sociology of sport (and other fields of leisure and popular culture). Sociologists elucidate the embodied, disciplinary and objectively alienating dimensions of contemporary sports practices, but rarely provide empathetic explorations of sport's aesthetics (Giulianotti, 1999). Baudrillard's social imaginary, fragmentary though it obviously is, implores us to think otherwise, even if sport's culturally seductive aspects have been fatally struck by the loss of radical exoticism.

Notes

1. For example, Kellner (1989, pp. 153–154) argues that Baudrillard's work 'terminates in a postmodern metaphysics'.
2. See Baudrillard (1990b, p. 97, 1990c, p. 36, 1992, pp. 34–35, 73).
3. Similarly, Caillois (1962, p. 157) argues that chance contains 'a mockery of work, of patient and persevering labor, of saving, of willingly sacrificing for the future – in sum, a mockery of all the virtues needed in a world dedicated to the accumulation of wealth'.
4. Elsewhere, in a paper co-authored with Michael Gerrard, we discuss the analogous case of Paul Gascoigne, an exceptionally gifted footballer of lower working class background from the poor northeast of England. We argue that Gascoigne's extra-ordinary public identity has strong congruity with Baudrillard's conception of the 'masses', and we interpret the player's self-destructive tendencies on and off the football field as extreme forms of symbolic exchange (see Giulianotti & Gerrard, 2001).

References

Andrews, D.L. (1996) 'The Facts of Michael Jordan's Blackness', *Sociology of Sport Journal*, 13(2): 126–153.

Andrews, D.L. (1998) 'Feminizing Olympic Reality: preliminary dispatches from Baudrillard's Atlanta', *International Review for the Sociology of Sport*, 33(1): 5–18.

Andrews, D.L. (2001) 'Between and Beyond the Post[s]', in J. Coakley & E. Dunning (eds) *The Handbook of the Sociology of Sport*, London: Sage.

Armstrong, G and R. Giulianotti (1998) 'From Another Angle: police surveillance and Football supporters', in C. Norris, G. Armstrong & J. Moran (eds) *Surveillance, CCTV & Social Control*, Aldershot: Gower/Ashgate.

Bale, J. (1998) 'Virtual Fandoms: futurescapes of football', in A. Brown (ed.) *Fanatics!*, London: Routledge.

Baudrillard, J. (1968/96) *The System of Objects*, London: Verso.

Baudrillard, J. (1970/98) *The Consumer Society*, London: Sage.

Baudrillard, J. (1973/75) *The Mirror of Production*, St Louis: Telos.

Baudrillard, J. (1976/93) *Symbolic Exchange and Death*, London: Sage.

Baudrillard, J. (1977/87) *Forget Foucault*, New York: Semiotext(e).
Baudrillard, J. (1978/83) *In the Shadow of the Silent Majorities*, John Johnston and Paul Patton, NewYork: Semiotext(e).
Baudrillard, J. (1979/90) *Seduction*, Basingstoke: Macmillan.
Baudrillard, J. (1983a/90) *Fatal Strategies*, New York: Semiotext(e).
Baudrillard, J. (1983b) *Simulations*, New York: Semiotext(e).
Baudrillard, J. (1985) 'The Child in the Bubble', *Impulse*, 11(4): 35.
Baudrillard, J. (1986/89) *America*, London: Verso.
Baudrillard, J. (1987a/90) *Cool Memories*, London: Verso.
Baudrillard, J. (1987b/88) *Xerox and Infinity*, London: Touchepas.
Baudrillard, J. (1990a) *Revenge of the Crystal*, London: Pluto.
Baudrillard, J. (1990b/93) *The Transparency of Evil*, London: Verso.
Baudrillard, J. (1990c/96) *Cool Memories II*, Cambridge: Polity.
Baudrillard, J. (1991/94) *The Gulf War Did Not Take Place*, Sydney: Power Institute.
Baudrillard, J. (1992/94) *The Illusion of the End*, Cambridge: Polity.
Baudrillard, J. (1993) 'Hyperreal America', *Economy and Society*, 22(2): 243–252.
Baudrillard, J. (1995a/96) *The Perfect Crime*, London: Verso.
Baudrillard, J. (1995b) 'The Virtual Illusion', *Theory, Culture & Society*, 12: 97–107.
Baudrillard, J. (1996) 'Disneyworld Company', *Liberation*, 4 March.
Baudrillard, J. (1997/98) *Paroxysm*, London: Verso.
Bogart, W. (1996) *The Simulation of Surveillance*, Cambridge: Cambridge University Press.
Butler, R. (1990) *Jean Baudrillard*, London: Sage.
Caillois, R. (1962) *Man, Play and Games*, London: Thames and Hudson.
Chaney, D. (1994) *The Cultural Turn*, London: Routledge.
Docker, J. (1994) *Postmodernism and Popular Culture*, Cambridge: Cambridge University Press.
Gane, M. (1991) *Baudrillard*, London: Routledge.
Gane, M. (ed.) (1993) *Baudrillard Live*, London: Routledge.
Giulianotti, R. (1991) 'Scotland's Tartan Army in Italy', *Sociological Review*, 39(3): 503–527.
Giulianotti, R. (1994) 'Taking Liberties', in R. Giulianotti, N. Bonney & M. Hepworth (eds) *Football Violence and Social Identity*, London: Routledge.
Giulianotti, R. (1999) *Football*, Cambridge: Polity.
Giulianotti, R. & Gerrard, M. (2001) 'Evil Genie or Pure Genius? The (Im)moral Football and Public Career of Paul "Gazza" Gascoigne', in D.L. Andrews & S.J. Jackson (eds) *Sports Stars*, London: Routledge.
Kellner, D. (1989) *Jean Baudrillard*, Cambridge: Polity.
Levin, C. (1996) *Jean Baudrillard*, Hemel Hempstead: Prentice Hall.
Merrin, W. (1999) 'Television is Killing the Art of Symbolic Exchange', *Theory, Culture & Society*, 16(3): 119–140.
Poster, M. (ed.) (1988) *Jean Baudrillard*, Cambridge: Polity.
Redhead, S. (1999) 'Baudrillard, "Amérique", and the Hyperreal World Cup', in G. Rail (ed.) *Sport and Postmodern Times*, New York: SUNY Press.
Ritzer, G. (1995) *Postmodern Social Theory*, New York: McGraw-Hill.
Said, E. (1995) *Orientalism*, Harmondsworth: Penguin.
Turner, B.S. (ed.) (1991) *Theories of Modernity and Postmodernity*, London: Sage.

Index

academic sociology, 68
Adorno, T.W., 5, 24, 82, 84–6,
     88–9, 91–2, 173
  approach towards sporting
     matters, 84
  as a critic of sport, 84–6
  characteristics of, 89
  contemporary language, 88
  denunciations of, 89
  domination according to, 86
  domination of positivism, 88
  and his times, 82–4
  in his youth, 87
  intellectual tradition, 87
  ironic rhetoric, 93
  language and dystopia, 87–91
  sport and disenchantment, 84–7
  sport and utopia, 91–4
  sports according to, 85–6
  theory of sports, 84
  utopian analysis and potential, 93
  vs Gramsci, 5–6
  writings on modern world, 84
  writings on sports, 88–9, 94
agency
  listening to young third wave
     feminists, 194–6
  and structure, 131
agonal games, 16
  see also competitive games; games
Ahmed, S., 197–8
Alexander, J., 45n16
Alford, R., 78n3
alienation, 19
American Journal of Sociology, 34
American Sociological Review, 34
Andrews, D.L., 58, 84, 207, 226
Angell, R., 125
Anglophone sport studies, 2
Apel, K.-O., 185n2
Archer, M., 45n6

Armstrong, G., 157, 228
Arond, H., 54
assembly line production, 13
Asylums, 50, 56
athletes
  African-American, 39
  as role models, 28
  see also black athletes

Back, L., 162
Bale, J., 134, 212, 226
Ball, D., 54
Ballard, H.B., 67
Bassano, B., 115
Baudrillard, J., 8, 26, 226–30, 232
  birth of, 226
  changes within sports culture, 8
  exercise and obsession to fitness,
     228–9
  French intellectual life, 226
  games, gambling and symbolic
     exchange, 230–3
  hyperreality, sports mediation and
     demise of artifice, 233–6
  notoriety of, 225–6
  sports and political agency,
     236–8
  sports-related works, 226–7
  the masses, the body and fatal
     theory, 227–30
Bauman, Z., 157
Beck, U., 135–6
Becker, H., 78n3
Beckles, H., 126n9
Bennett, T., 107
Berger, P., 15, 22, 68–9
Bernard, T., 43
Best, S., 209
Beyond a Boundary, 112–13, 117
  impact of, 123–5
Bhaskar, R., 70

bio-power and governmentality,
    216–17
  governmentality and neo-liberalism,
    219–20
  sport, bio-politics and race, 217–19
  sport, governmentality and
    neo-liberalism, 220–21
Birbalsingh, F., 119
Bird Whistall Ray, 50
Birrell, S., 54–6, 58, 61–2n3, 187,
    190, 194, 200
black athletes, 41
  over-representation of, 41–2
  positive advantage, 41
  UCLA, 41
Black Jacobins, The, 114
blacks
  over-representation in particular
    playing positions, 40
  proportional representation in
    North American sports, 39–40
Blalock, H., 38, 41–2, 45n7
  occupational discrimination, 38–9
Blau, P.M., 45n5
Bogart, W., 234
Booth, D., 33, 35
Bordo, S., 189, 193
Bosworth, R.J.B., 116
Boudon, R., 37
Bourdieu, P., 6, 7, 132, 157, 159n2,
    161–2, 164, 167–8
  American individualism vs French
    solidarism, 7
  concept of habitus, 132, 166–8
  conceptual category of capital, 168
  distinction according to, 162–6
  exercise and fitness boom, 170
  field according to, 168–9
  initial specialism in anthropology,
    161
  sociological analysis, 165
  sport according to, 164–5
  sports cultures and Bourdieu model,
    169–70
  views on sporting activities and
    entertainment, 165–6
Bredemeier, B.J., 176
Brickley, P., 34
Broad, K., 192

Brohm, J.M., 25, 90, 101
Brooks, A., 197
Brotz, H., 68
Brown, W., 219–20, 222
Brownell, S., 5, 77
Brundage, 21
Bryant, C., 129, 131–2, 141
Buck-Morss, S., 87
Budd, A., 108
Buhle, P., 111, 124
Burchell, G., 219
bureaucracy, 20, 21
Butler, J., 51, 61, 189
Butler, R., 226
Byzantinism, 98

Cahn, S., 200, 203n1
Caillois, R., 61–2n3, 230–1, 238n3
Callinicos, A., 193
Cantelon, H., 18, 105
capitalism, 13
  fundamental values of, 28
  instrumented rationality, 19–20
  unemployment, 14
capitalist society
  sport in a, 101
  valorization of sport, 14
capitalist modernity
  sports in, 90, 91
Cardus, N.,112
Caribbean cricket, *see under* West
    Indies
Carroll, R.,58
Cashman, R., 115
Castells, M., 137
Chaney, D., 137–8, 225
Chapman, G.,189, 202
character, 54
  motifs of, 54
Church from a Marxian
    interpretation, 25–6
Citius, Altius, Fortius, 22
civil society, 26
civilizing process, 149–54
Civilizing Process, The, 145, 146, 149
claims, 53
Clark, J., 34, 44n1, 45n7
Clark, P.P., 45n6
Clark, T.N., 45n6, 103, 105

Clarke, J., 103, 105, 132
Class, Sports, and Social Development,
    75, 105
Coakley, J., 54, 57, 99
Cohen, I., 131
Cole, C., 189, 191, 193, 202, 215
Coming Crisis of Western Sociology,
    The, 67
competitive games, 16
complex societies, 148
composure, 58–9
Constitution of Society, The, 130
Coser, L., 44n1
courage, 58
Court Society, The, 146
credentialing, 53–4
cricket
    an establishment game, 112
    Australian, 115
    changes in, 121–2
    contributions from C.L.R. James, 6
    James' love for, 111–12
    success of West Indies, 114
    the Other in, 114
    West Indian, 116–17
Critcher, C., 103, 105, 132
Crothers, C., 36–7, 44n1
Crouch, D., 138
cultural form, persistence of, 16
cultural relativity, 70
cultural studies, 105, 133
    combining feminism and, 200
    concept of hegemony, 104
Culture Industries, 5, 84, 92
    sportification of culture, 86
Curry, T., 54

Davidson, A.I., 107
Davidson, J., 209
De Lauretis, T., 196
Delsaut, Y., 162
Dew, P., 5, 175, 185n1
Dialectic of Enlightenment, 83, 85, 87
Discipline and Punish: The Birth of a
    Prison, 209, 210
Distinction: A Social Critique of the
    Judgement of Taste, 7, 161
Ditton, J., 55–6
docile bodies, 212–13

Docker, J., 225, 232
Domhoff, G.W., 67
dominant ideology, 101
Donnelly, P., 30n2, 54, 56, 61–2n3, 75
Drake, J., 200–1
dramaturgical model, 51, 60
Duncan, M.C., 59
Dunn, R.G., 108–9n5
Dunning, E., 16, 84, 108n1, 137, 150,
    153–4, 158, 159n4
    figurational theory, 7
    theory of civilizing process, 7
Durkheim
    analysis of religion, 25–6
    belief according to, 26
    legitimizing function of rituals, 24–8
    notion of collective effervescence,
        26
    ritual according to, 26
    serialized civic rituals, 27
Dworkin, S., 189, 195
dystopic modernity, 85

Early, G., 40, 42, 54, 56
Eitzen, D.S., 40
Eldridge, J., 65, 67, 78n1
Elias, N., 6, 16, 108n1, 137, 146–8,
    149–53, 157–8, 159n1, n6
    as a student, 145–6
    as an influential sociologist, 145
    birth of, 145
    civilizing process, 149–54
    conception of 'established-outsider'
        relations, 152
    criticisms on, 154–8
    explaining British football-related
        violence, 153–4
    figurations, process sociology and
        game models, 147–9
    sociological approach, 145
    'we–I' balance, 150–1
    works of, 146
Elsdon, D., 197
Established and the Outsiders, The, 146
estrangement, *see* alienation
Etzioni, A., 68
expropriation, 20
extreme 'postmodernism' theorist,
    see under Baudrillard, J.

face-work, 51
Farred, G., 113
Feagin, J.R., 68
feminism
  effects of postmodernism, 8
figuration, 147
figurational sociology, 148–9
figurational theory, 7
Fine, G., 54
Fiske, J., 81
Fordism, 13–14
Forms of talk, 58
Foucault, M., 108n5, 207, 209–11, 226
  bio-power and governmentality,
      216–21
  birth of, 209
  Bodily 'knowledge' to forms of
      racialization, 8
  career of, 209
  death of, 209
  discipline and sport, 210–16
  docile bodies, 212–13
  knowledge, 8
  Panopticism, 211
  panopticon, sporting, 211–12
  power, 8
  sport and technologies of
      normalization, 213–16
  works of, 207, 209–10
Foudy, J., 195
Frame Analysis, 58
Frank, A., 133
Frankfurt school, 82
  approach to cultural analysis, 86
  individual members of, 82–3
Frey, J., 54
Friedman, T.L., 125
Friedrichs, R.W., 67
functional analyst of sport, limitations
    of, 100
functional democratization, 150
functionalism, 131
  according to Merton, 35
  anthropological forms of, 35
  vs conflict theory, 99–100

gameness, 58
games, 15–16
  according to Marx, 17
  autonomy/heteronomy dualism, 23

exogenous factors, 16
habituation, 15
level of sociability, 16
Marx vs Freud/Marcuse vs Weber, 23
reciprocal typification, 15
rules in, 15
US sports, 16, 17
viability, 16
vs sports and play, 17, 18
see also competitive games
Gane, M., 225, 231, 234
gender, 61
Gender advertisements, 58, 59
Gerrard, M., 226, 230, 238n4
Giddens, A., 36, 44, 45n6,
      68–71, 99–100, 108n2,
      129–33, 135–8, 155
  application of views in theories of
      sport and leisure, 133–5
  as a global sociologist, 129–31
  as a public intellectual, 129, 130
  birth of, 129
  criticisms of, 141–2
  duality of structure, 132
  educational achievements, 129
  focus on globalization, 130
  globalization of sports and leisure,
      139–40
  key concepts in Giddens' sociology,
      135–7
  lifestyle and the ludic, 138–9
  lifestyle, life politics and leisure,
      140–1
  power according to, 133–4
  Reith Lectures, 129
  structuration theory, 6, 131–2
  view of society as utopian realism,
      130
  vs Nobert Elias, 7
Giese, R., 59
Gimenez, M.E., 45
Giulianotti, R., 158, 226, 228, 230,
      238, 238n4
global society, problems of, 130
globalization, 137
Goffman, E., 49, 51–4, 58, 61–2n3
  as a micro-sociologist, 55
  as a student, 49–50
  as a theorist, 50–3
  birth, 49

Goffman, E. – *continued*
  concept of demeanor, 54
  concept of stigma, 54
  concept of 'total institution', 57–8
  and critical theory, 57
  criticisms on his ideological
    position, 56
  criticisms on methodologies,
    55–61
  focus on everyday routine, 51
  indirect influence in the studies of
    sports, 54
  intellectual influences, 50
  interactions, 52
  justification of sociology, 49
  Lay's appreciation of, 61–2n3
  modern societies according to, 4
  motifs of character, 54, 58
  strategic interaction model, 51–3
  symbolic interactionism, 4
  *The Presentation of Self in Everyday
    Life*, 4
  and the sociology of sport, 53–5
Goffman's methodology
  different views, 55–61
  early criticisms, 55
Goldsen, R., 74
Gonos, G., 56
Goody, J., 155
Gouldner, A.W., 55–6
Goulstone, J., 158
governmentality
  and bio-power, 216–17
  and neo-liberalism, 219–20
  sport and neo-liberalism, 220–21
Gramscianism, 107
Gramsci, A., 14, 98, 101–4, 108n1
  application to sport, 102–7
  base (economics), 104
  birth of, 97
  concept of hegemony, 102–3, 104
  concept of 'national popular',
    101–2
  family details, 98
  football according to, 5
  hegemony according to, 24
  humanism, 12
  ideas in social analysis of sport, 97
  ideological superstructure (culture),
    104

  influence on sociology of culture,
    103–4
  intellectuals according to, 102
  lack of interest in sports, 104–5
  leaders of dominant class, 103
  rise of cultural studies, 6
  role in the Italian Communist
    Party, 97
  and social theory, 99–102
  vs Adorno, 5–6
  works of, 98–9
grand theory, limitations of, 67
Green, E., 199
Grieveson, L., 217
Griffin, P., 200, 203n1,
Gruneau, R., 11, 14, 61–2n3, 75–6,
  103, 105–6, 130, 132, 134, 162
  analysis of sport, 134
  arguments on the relevance of
    Bourdieu's work, 162
Guha, R., 114, 126n6
Guttmann, A.., 97

Habermas, J., 174, 180, 182, 184,
  185n1–5
  critique of instrumental reason,
    176–7
  disappearance of moral dimension
    of sports, 179–83
  Habermasian on sports, 177–9
  instrumental rationality, 7
  principles of modernity, 7
  rationalization of labour and sport,
    174–6
  sports, moral ideals and moral
    discourse, 183–5
  works concerned with sports and
    leisure, 173–4
habitus, 166–8
Halbert, C., 54
Hall, M.A., 187, 200, 204
Hall, S., 108n3, 125
Hargens, L.L., 68
Hargreaves, J.A., 5, 8, 75, 77,
  103–6, 108n5, 134, 161–2,
  197–8, 203n2, 213
  power according to, 134
  views on postmodern social
    theory, 8
  views on sport, 106–7

Harris, D., 107
Hart, M.M., 54, 59
Harvey, A., 158
Harvey, J., 139, 208
hegemony, 24–5, 102–3
Held, D., 137
Hetherington, K., 139
Heydebrand, W.V., 45n6
Heywood, L., 189, 195, 200–1
Hill Collins, P., 190, 198
*Histories in Cultural
    Systems*, 126n2
Hoberman, J.M., 22, 87, 89
Hochschild, A., 59
Hooks, B., 190, 198, 202
Horne, J., 6, 132–4
Horowitz, I.L., 65, 66–8, 73, 78n1
Hribar, A., 189, 202
Huber, J., 68
Hughes, R., 20, 54, 57
Human Variety, The, 70
Hunt, M., 34, 44n1
Huntington, S.P., 125

ideologies
    dominant, 24
    oppositional/critical, 24
impression management, 51
Ingham, A.G., 14, 16, 27–8, 56,
    61–2n3, 75, 105
    analysis of occupational subcultures
        of athletes, 56–7
    essay of, 57
Inglis, David, 5
*Insiders vs. Outsiders: A Chapter in the
    Sociology of Knowledge*, 36
Institute for Social Research, 82
institutionalization, 12
    as a process, 12
    positive and negative, 12, 18, 23
institutions, 12
instrumental rationality, 19–20, 83
    see also traditional rationality
instrumental reason, 176–7
integrity, 58–9
International Cricket Council (ICC),
    120
International Olympic Committee
    (IOC), 21, 120

*International Review for the Sociology of
    Sport*, 33, 106
ironic language, 88–9
irony, 88
Isis, 34

Jackson, S., 58
Jagose, A, 61
James, A., 114, 116, 126n1
James, C.L.R., 78n4, 140, 208
    approach to cricket/sport, 111–12
    birth of, 111
    cricket, 6, 111
    events witnessed by, 111
    influence in politics, 119–21
    see also cricket; *Beyond a Boundary*;
        West Indies
Jarvie, G., 130, 134, 168
Jarvis, S., 92
Jary, D., 56, 67, 129, 130–4, 140–1
Jary, J., 56, 67, 131–2, 134, 141
Jenkins, 21
Jennings, A., 21, 120
Jiobu, R., 54
Johnson, R., 108n3
Journal of Sport & Social Issues, 107

Kay, J., 58, 105–6, 109n6, 171
Kellner, D., 209, 232, 238n1
Kerckhoff, A., 18
King, S.J., 220
Koenigsberger, H.G., 156
Kohut, H., 14
Krich, J., 126n4

Laberge, S., 171
Lamprecht, M., 162
Lash, S., 138–9
last modernist, *see* Giddens, A.
Lawrence, G., 100, 126n5
Lemert, C., 129
Lemke, T., 220, 222
Lenskyj, H., 200, 203n1
Leonard, W., 30n3
Levin, C., 225
Levine, E., 122
Lewis, R.W., 157
linguistic theory, 51
Livingstone, S., 138

local and cosmopolitan influentials, 44
Loland, S., 185n3
London School of Economics (LSE), 130
Loy, J.W., 16, 21, 27, 30, 35, 40, 45n3, 53, 61–2n3, 84, 105,
Lunt, P., 138
Lüschen, G., 45n3
Lyman, 49

MacAloon, J.J., 108n4, 166
McDonald, M., 58, 194, 200
Macdonnell, A.G., 114
McElvogue, J.F., 40
McKay, J., 58, 105–6, 109n6
McPherson, B., 40
Madsen, M.R., 169
Maffesoli, M., 138
Maguire, J., 130
Malinowski, B., 35
Mandel. E., 13
Mandell, R., 194
manifest functions, 36
   dysfunctional consequences, 42–3
   and intended consequences, 41
Manly, M., 119
manual labour, 22–3
Marcuse, H., 12
Markula, P., 189, 193
Marquesee, M., 125
Marshall, G., 55
Martin, M., 196
Marx, K., 14, 18
   concept of valorization, 13
   games according to, 17
   philosophical sociology of 'modern' man, 20
   play according to, 16–17
   rationalization and sportification, 19–24
   religion according to, 25
   and the sportification process, 13–19
Marylebone Cricket Club (MCC), 170
masses, the body and fatal theory, the, 227–30
match-fixing scandals, 122
Mead, G., 14

means of production, 13, 17–18
Mennell, S., 146, 156
Mennesson, C., 162
Merrin, W., 237
Merton, R.K., 4, 35–7, 44–5n2–7, 159n5
   achievements of, 44–5n2
   birth of, 33–4
   bureaucratic structure and personality, 44
   career of, 34
   form of functionalism, 35
   functional analysis, 35–6
   graduation of, 34
   intellectual influences, 34
   manifest functions according to, 36
   'Social Structure and Anomie', 34
   structural analysis, 36
   structural-functionalism, 33
   theoretical and empirical contributions, 35
   theories of middle range, 36–7
   theory of anomie, 36, 45n3
   see also functionalism
Messner, M., 60, 107, 134, 187, 195, 201–2
Mestrovic, S., 130, 157
middle range theory vs general theory, 4, 36–7
Miliband, R., 65
Miller, J., 208
Miller, T., 105
Mills, C.W., 3, 5, 37, 50, 68–73, 78n1
   analysis of the 'power elite', 5
   as a student, 65–6
   birth of, 65
   colleagues of, 66–7
   conception of sociological imagination, 5, 68–9; *see also* sociological imagination
   crisis of sociology, 67–8
   criticism of sociological language, 72–3
   during college, 66
   filing system, 73–4
   opposition to empirical work, 72
   relevance for the sociology of sport, 75–8
   social analyst according, 68

in the words of Horowitz, 65
work on sociology
mimetic activities, 151
modern Prolympic sports, 26–7
modern sports, 5
  emergence of, 152
  Thorstein Veblen's assessment of, 85
Mohanty, C., 197
moral, 26
Morgan, W.J., 5, 90–1, 185n4
Mouzelis, N., 43–4, 45n6, 141
Muir, D., 53

Nandy, A.,122, 125, 126n8
National Basketball Association
    (NBA), 39
National Football League (NLF), 39
negative dialectical approach, aim of,
    88, 92–3
Nelson, M.B., 203n1
New Men of Power, The, 65
Nixon, H., 53
Notestein, R., 75

occupational discrimination, 38–9
Olympics, 21
O'Neill, J., 193
Orlie, M. ,211
Osiris, 34
Other, The, 114–16

Paget, H., 124
pankration, 153
Panopticism, 211
panopticon, sporting, 211–12
Paraschak, V., 203n2
Parker, J., 114
Passeron, J.-C., 157
passivity, 22
Petersen, R., 41
Piaget, J., 27, 45n6, 61–2n3
play, 14, 23, 93
  a child in, 14–15
  according to Marx, 16–17
  forms of, 15
  Marx vs Freud/Marcuse vs Weber, 23
  object of, 23
  vs sports and games, 17, 18
pleasure, 24

Plessner, H., 185n2
Polsky, N., 54
positivism, language of, 88
Poster, M., 226–7
postmodern social theory, 8
  effects on feminist thinking, 8
  extreme theorist, 8; *see also*
      Baudrillard, J.
  potential, 17
power, 12
  according to Baudrillard, 228
  according to Elias, 147
  according to Giddens, 133–4
  according to Gruneau, 134
  modern, according to Foucault,
      210–11
Power Elite, The, 65
predictability, 15
*Presentation of Self in Everyday Life,
    The*, 4
Prison Notebooks, 98
Production, forces of, 13
Prolympic, 18
Pronger, B., 192
*Protestant Ethic and The Spirit of
    Capitalism*, 28

Quarterly Journal of Economies, 34
Quest for Excitement, 146, 153
Quota system, 42

Rabow, J., 68
racial integration, 42
Radcliffe-Brown, A.R., 35
radical sociology, father of,
    see Mills, C.W.
radicalized modernity, 135
Rail, G., 192, 208
rational-legal, *see* societal
rationalization, 19, 20
  of our athletic selves, 22
  in the ludic domain, 22–3
  and valorization, 20
  see also instrumental rationality
reciprocal typification, 15
Redhead, S.,226
reflexivity, 135–6
religion, according to Marx, 25
Remnick, D., 183

Reynolds, J.M., 67
Reynolds, L.T., 67
Rich, A., 196
Richards, V., 123
Riganer, Biro, 90–1
Rinehart, R.,60, 211
risk society, 136–7
Ritzer, G., 234
Roberts, M.,116
Robertson, R., 156
Robson, G., 162
Rogers, M., 56
Rojek, C.,171
role distance, 51
Rorty, R., 185n6
Rose, G.,84, 87
Rose, N., 219, 222
Rowe, D., 1, 100, 103–4, 106, 126n5
rules, 23
Rustin, M.,141

Sabo, D., 187
sacred vs profane, 27–8
Sage, G., 39, 42, 106, 162
Said, E., 6, 197, 232
Sandiford, K., 125
Schegloff, E., 61—
Schmitt, R.,58
Schneider, J.J., 40
scholasticism, *see* Byzantinism
Scimecca, J.A., 65–6
Scott, M., 50, 54
Scraton, S., 202
Seidman, S., 192, 194
self-identity and lifestyle, 137
Shankly, Bill, 27
Sheard, K., 158
Shields, D.L., 176
Shiwcharan, C., 119
Shogan, D.,107
Simmel, G., 16
Simson, V.,21
Slowikowski, C., 27
smart clubs, 169
Smelser, N.J., 68, 154
Smith C.W., 45n6
Smith, G., 49, 55
Smith, P., 58
Smith, R., 115

Smith, Y., 203n2
smooth interaction, *see* supportive
    interaction
Snyder, E., 40, 54
social analyst, 68
social development, 28–9
    theory by Marx, 29
social domination, 12
social structures
    division by Gothers, 37
    Merton's approach through
        functional analysis, 35–6
    Merton's approach through
        structural analysis, 36
    structural determinants of variations
        in patterns of choice, 38–9
social theory, prose style of, 87
societal, 26
    characterised by total domination,
        88
    classical functionalist view of, 99
    unequal distribution of power in,
        100
sociological imagination, 68
    sociology as a form of commitment,
        74–5
    sociology as a form of
        consciousness, 69–71
    sociology as a form of craft, 71–4
Sociological Imagination, The, 67, 68,
    69, 70, 71, 75, 78
sociology
    as a form of commitment, 74–5
    different views of crisis of, 67–8
    of sociology, the, 67
    of sport, 51–5
    structure/agency split, 104
    twin evils of, 37
sociology as a form of consciousness,
    69
    corporeal sensibility, 71
    critical sensibility, 70–1
    cultural sensibility, 69–70
    historical sensibility, 69
    structural sensibility, 70
sociology as a form of craft, 71–2
    tactics, 73
    techniques, 73–4
    tools, 72–3

Sociology of Sport Journal, 33, 106
Solomon, M., 98
Spelman, E., 197–8
Spivak, G.C., 114, 197
sport feminism, 187
  agency and third wave feminists,
    194–6
  characterizing, 188–90
  critiques of postmodernism, 193–4
  forgotten postcolonial 'others',
    197–8
  influence of postmodernism,
    191–3
  victimization to emancipation,
    198–9
sport sociology
  structural-functionalism in, 33
sport(s)
  according to Brohm, 25
  according to Hargreaves, 106
  in capitalist modernity, 91
  character building qualities, 58
  counter-hegemony movement,
    30–1n5
  cultures and Bourdieu model,
    169–70
  disappearance of moral dimension
    of, 179–83
  and disenchantment, 84–6
  domination and resistance, 105
  emergence of, 99
  equal to Durkheim's positive rites,
    27
  essence of, 91
  feeder system, 17–18
  from a conflict perspective, 100
  from a functional perspective,
    99–100
  functionalist perspective of,
    99–100
  globalization of leisure and, 139
  Gramscian perspective towards, 102
  hostile approach to, 100–1
  Marx vs Freud/Marcuse vs Weber, 23
  men vs women, 58–9
  moral ideals and moral discourse,
    183–5
  over-representation of blacks in
    particular playing positions, 40

  and political agency, 236–8
  politics, 119–21
  presentation and style of sport
    theory, 87
  proportional representation of
    blacks in north American,
    39–40
  remarks by Adorno, 85
  role of technological innovations,
    20–1
  rule-making process in, 23
  social theories of, 108n1
  strategic interaction model, 51–3
  and technologies of normalization,
    213–16
  tension management, 99–101
  in the late capitalism, 85
  theorizing, 107–8
  today, 90
  valorization in, 14
  voluntary association vs compulsory
    organization, 21
  vs games, 16
  vs play and games, 17, 18
  Whannel's analysis of television,
    104, 105
  within Gramscian
    framework, 104
  women in, 59, 60
Sport, Power and Culture, 76–7, 106
sportization process, 132
Spreitzer, E., 40
stacking, 4
Stamm, H., 162
Stanley, L., 190
Stevenson, C., 54
Stigma, 52, 56, 59
stigma, 54
stigmatization, analysis of, 52
Stinchcombe, A., 37–8, 43–4
Stoddart, B., 111–12, 118, 125
Stokvis, R., 159n6
Stone, G., 16, 53–4, 61n2
Stones, R., 142
strategic interaction,
    model of, 51–3
  games as central metaphor, 51
structural analyst vs. functional
    analyst, 45n4

structural-functionalism
dominant perspective in sociology
(1930s and 1960s), 33
Robert K. Merton, 33
Talcott Parsons, 33
Structuration Theory, 6, 131–2
according to Jarvie and Maguire,
130
three syntheses provided by, 132–3
structure, 131
Sturrock, J., 45n6
Sugden, J., 134, 167
supportive interaction, 52
surveillance, role of systems of, 8
Sykes, H., 190, 200
Sztompka, P., 37, 44n1, 45n4

Taylor, C., 30, 176–8, 185n8
Telemaque, 114–58
tension management, 99–100
The Elementary Forms, 25
Theory of civilizing process, 7
*Theory of Communicative Action,
The*, 174
Third Way, The, 129
Thrane, C., 171
Tomlinson, A., 7, 105, 134, 138,
140, 167
total domination, 88
Touraine, A., 68
traditional rationality, 20, 30n4
see also instrumental rationality
Training the Body for China, 77–8
Tranter, N., 159n3
Tucker, K., 138
Turner, B.S., 225
Turner, G., 103
Turner, J.H., 68
Turner, S.P., 68
Turner, V., 26
Turowetz, A., 54
Tyson, Mike, 185n7

unemployment, 14
Unità, 98
University of California, Los Angeles
(UCLA), 41
Urry, J.,138
Uses of History, 70

valencies, positive and negative, 24
valorization
linking to instrumental rationality
and rationalization, 20
and rationalization, 20–1
value-rational, *see* moral
van den Berghe, P., 45n8
Van Krieken, R.,146, 159n4
voluntary association vs compulsory
organization, *see under* sports
Von der Lippe, G., 167, 171
Voy, R., 22

Wacquant, L.J.D., 57, 162, 167–8
Walby, S., 193, 199
Wallace, W.L., 45n6
'wanting to'/ 'having to' relationship,
11
Wearing, B., 203n2
Weber, M., 21, 30n4, 150, 185n8
alienation according to, 19
bureaucracy, 20
iron cage of estrangement, 22
philosophical sociology of 'modern'
man, 20
Weeks, J., 30n1
'we–I' balance, 150–1
Weinberg, S., 54
Welsh, S.L., 113
West Indian Cricket Board of
Control, 116
West Indies
cricket and politics, 119–21
history of cricket in, 116–17
importance of cricket, 113
Whannel, G., 104–5
What is Sociology?, 146
White Collar, 65, 71
White, P., 58, 65
Whiting, R., 126n4
Whitson, D., 103, 106
Wiggershaus, R., 82, 87
Willer, D., 37
Williams, R., 25, 105
model of co-existent cultural
forms, 105
Willis, E., 69–71, 74
Wilson, T., 171
Winkin, Y., 55, 61n1

Wise, S., 190
Wollen, P., 126n8
Women's sports, 59
Worcester, K., 111
Wrong, D., 12, 20

Young, K., 54, 58, 169
Young, M., 196

Zengerle, J., 183
Zucker, L.G., 68

Dat